This Unbearable Boredom of Being

This Unbearable Boredom of Being

A Crisis of Meaning in America

Genrich L. Krasko

iUniverse, Inc.

New York Lincoln Shanghai

This Unbearable Boredom of Being
A Crisis of Meaning in America

iUniverse, Inc.

For information address:
iUniverse, Inc.
2021 Pine Lake Road, Suite 100
Lincoln, NE 68512
www.iuniverse.com

ISBN: 0-595-31309-4

Printed in the United States of America

To
Viktor E. Frankl,
the Prophet of Meaning
and to my dearest granddaughter
Rachel
who makes my aspirations meaningful…

"There is but one problem—the only one in the world—to restore to men a spiritual content, spiritual concerns."

—Antoine de Saint Exupery

"What threatens contemporary man is the alleged meaninglessness of his life, or as I call it, the existential vacuum within him. And when does this vacuum open up, when does this so often latent vacuum become manifest? In the state of boredom."

—Viktor E. Frankl, "Psychotherapy and Existentialism"

CONTENTS

ACKNOWLEDGMENTS

In writing this book I would like to acknowledge the crucial role of a few Washington bureaucrats (presumably high-positioned) who, in 1988, decided to close and disperse the Army Materials Technology Laboratory (MTL) in Watertown, MA. The Base Realignment and Closure (BRAC) Commission put this world-class research center on the list of 84 "outdated military bases" (formally we were a "military base"), and Dick Cheney (then the Defense Secretary) hastily signed the Commission's recommendations into law in December, 1988—just a few weeks before his leaving the office.

The ugly rumors, at that time, quoted a Washington bureaucrat as saying: "You have deserved it. This is for your Tip O'Neil, and for your Kennedies." I do not believe this nonsense. Years ago, my teacher, a distinguished physics professor, expressed his attitude to rumors in a joke: "I have no doubts in these rumors because I am the one who spreads them." I do not know if that "nonsense" was true or not, but it is history now.

In two years, another BRAC commission decided not to disperse the Lab, but make it a part (a Directorate) of the consolidated Army Research Laboratory. The new building for our Materials Directorate would have to be built at Aberdeen Proving Ground, MD, and was supposed to be ready by the spring of 1997.

However, Washington decided to go ahead with the 1988 BRAC decision (though already invalid), and close MTL by the end of September 1995. No arguments helped, although the simple arithmetic did show that the taxpayers would pay dearly for such a hurry (in fact, they paid over $30 million). And in due time the flag in the "outdated military base" in Watertown, MA was lowered. The once flourishing laboratory was destroyed. What was left has been transferred to a "swap space"—temporary quarters in Wilmington, DE, leased from Dupont.

I moved with the Lab, leaving my family in Boston. For almost three years, I have been commuting back "home" every other week. But I had long lonely evenings and weekends—a perfect time for writing. And that is how this book has come to life. This probably would not have happened if not for the "wise" decision to relocate the Lab to the "swap space" two and a half years before the Aberdeen building was ready. If sometime in the future those Washington people are called upon to answer for the gross mismanagement of the taxpayers' money (and that is most unlikely), I will rush to their defense.

Next, I would like to acknowledge each and every individual: star journalists and TV anchors, and even distinguished members of our Congress and Senate—fourteen of them—whose names comprise what I call "the shame list." During the six years of my desperate attempts to find a publisher or, at least, to draw the attention of influential people to the importance of the ideas that my book espouses, I have been writing letters to those people. None of them has even bothered to write in response a "thank you" note, although the US Post Office returned receipts for each letter.

I acknowledge this shameful disrespect and civic arrogance because, unfortunately, it confirms my suspicion that even our elected representatives, as well as our media, do not care very much about the most important problems—the existential problems—our society is facing today. However, in defense of those VIPs I should mention that most probably none of them read or even saw my letters, for the letters had been thrown into wastepaper baskets by the VIPs' aides after having read just a few first lines. On the other hand, the aides always know what their bosses want or do not want to read.

Thus, the main objectives of my book—to draw the attention of our society to the problems that lie at the core of most of our ills, and to initiate a discussion—have not been achieved. Most probably, this book will not be read by the thousands.

In the last sentence of the *Introduction*, I wrote: "In the summer of 1977, half a year before my family left Russia, a friend of mine—a prominent Soviet physicist who had just received an exit visa after years of struggle with the Soviet authorities, hunger strikes and home arrests—said to me: 'Do not idealize the West. Here, in Russia, you cannot speak; there you may cry but nobody will hear you.' I did not believe him then. I still do not believe him now. I hope I will be heard…"

Unfortunately, my friend's prophecy has come true. And yet, I decided to leave that sentence in the Introduction. There is still hope that eventually the voice of the ideas I am espousing in this book will have been heard.

Thus, this book is just a memorabilium. It is mostly for my friends and those who expressed their keen interest and read the book's manuscript.

And to these people my true and deepest gratitude is due. The first among them, I want to mention, and give her my love, profound respect and thanks, is Sylvia Disenhof, my voluntary editor who made the many drafts of the book readable. It is symbolic that Sylvia has become the mid-wife of this book, the main idea of which is that human life is a *mission* to be fulfilled. Sylvia's life as a teacher and activist of humane causes is a manifestation that a life has virtually no obstacles when the *mission* is great.

Quite a few people gave me the support and encouragement I badly needed. The late Dr. Viktor Frankl—one of the greatest minds of the 20th century, a philosopher, and the founder of the *Third Viennese School of Psychotherapy*— wrote the *Foreword*. His appreciation of the book is my highest reward. I will always cherish my communications with him and Fr. Ellie Frankl. I am also thankful to the late Dr. Joseph Fabry, Viktor Frankl's friend and disciple, who wrote extensively on *Logotherapy*, and whose letters and phone conversations helped me a lot.

I would like to specially mention Dr. Paul Gagnon of Boston University, the author of the 1995 *Atlantic Monthly* seminal article "What Should Children Read?" which was an eye-opener to me, and made me dig into the origins of our educational crisis. Many discussions with Paul have helped me a lot to better understand my own writings.

Dr. Mary Pipher, author of the seminal book *Reviving Ophelia*, opened my eyes on the desperate problems teenage girls face in our society.

Among the people who I would also like to thank for their encouragement years, are Prof. Robert Barnes, President of the Viktor Frankl Institute of Logotherapy; Prof. Jacqueline Black, an anthropologist; Dr. Gina Giovinco, a clinical psychologist; my old friends Dr. Thomas Krapf, a journalist (Austria), and Prof. Alec Roytburd, a physicist; Prof. Woodford McClellan, a historian; Prof. Mojmir Sob, a physicist (Czech Republic); Dr. Franz Vesely, a physicist and editor of *Journal des Viktor-Frankl-Instituts* (Vienna, Austria); Dr. John Waymouth, a distinguished physicist; Prof. Paul Wong, President of the International Network on Personal Meaning; and my new young friend, Rama (Ramadhiana Thaharani), a psychology instructor in far-away Jakarta, Indonesia.

My deep gratitude also goes to my many friends and former colleagues who have read the manuscript and shared with me their opinion and criticism.

All those people did believe in the importance, the extreme importance of the problems I have been discussing, and I am thankful to all of them for their moral support.

Above all, my gratitude to Zeya, my wife, is beyond words.

Genrich L. Krasko
December 2003,
Peabody, MA

FOREWORD

This book is a precious gift to the reader. The author guides the reader in a truly universalist spirit, that allows us, in his company, to view the present state of our culture both in depth as well as in a critical manner. I myself, as a European, could of course learn a lot, gaining new information and correcting many previous misinterpretations. Small wonder: the author is a well-recognized scientist who migrated from one world and landed in another one. Hence he could accumulate a wealth of experience, and present it in the light of his personal wisdom.

Having read the manuscript of this book, I found Genrich Krasko a sensitive, warm, and concerned man. He presents a sweeping, if very personal, view of how our society should, and in his opinion could, function. In this effort he does not heed the frontier lines between the political "right" and "left." Even more, by taking a non-conformist stance he positively invites criticism from both sides, taking them a necessary—if not sufficient—condition of being right.

Being well-versed in a wide range of sciences, the author expertly guides the reader through a series of rich and promising vistas, which for the sake of his granddaughter he wishes eventually to come true. Thus, starting out from an eminently personal motive, he finds formulations that really speak to the needs of the present time.

If this were a political book, I would not accept its dedication to me: I have always taken care to keep my brainchild, logotherapy, out of the turmoil of political discussions. But it is, as I see it, simply a positive utopia in which ideas and values that have been dismissed or forgotten are brought to mind again, not in a moralistic or traditionalist manner, but after a critical "dusting" and with a new twist.

At one point in the book, the author refers to the importance of having a role model. Well, I herewith congratulate the readers—and among them, in particular, the younger ones—for, in this very respect, being given a chance by taking up this book and devoting themselves to its careful—and fruitful—study.

Viktor E. Frankl
Vienna, June 1997

PREFACE

"For too long we have been dreaming a dream from which we are now waking up: the dream that if we just improve the socioeconomic situation of people, everything will be okay, people will become happy. The truth is that as the *struggle for survival* has subsided, the question has emerged: *survival for what?* Ever more people today have the means to live, but no meaning to live for."

—*Viktor E. Frankl, "The Unheard Cry for Meaning"*

There are already so many books about our society's ills. These books expose those ills and give indisputable statistics, but the core—the origin of our problems—has been left almost unexamined. In this book, I am not going to reiterate the accusations or support them with numbers. I shall try to address only the problems that have been left unexplored or have, in my opinion, drawn insufficient attention from the public.

Just about everybody probably agrees that the current devastating situation in America with the proliferation of violence, crime, drugs, for example, has the proportion of a serious crisis. Not many know, however, that our current crisis, or I would rather say "illness," had been first anticipated and diagnosed over 50 years ago by one of the greatest psychologists and psychiatrists of the 20th century, Dr. Viktor E. Frankl, the founder of the so-called "Third Viennese School of Psychotherapy."

What is this crisis about? In his numerous books, Dr. Frankl claims that the most important motivation of human lives is *the will to meaning*. Dr. Frankl gives solid proofs of that thesis—the most convincing of them based on his own experience as a Nazi concentration camp survivor. According to Dr. Frankl, a society becomes severely ill when the will to meaning in people's lives becomes frustrated, giving way to what he calls "the existential vacuum." This is the situation in America today: Catastrophically, in a significant segment of American society, people have lost the meaning in their lives.

Unfortunately, these ideas have been virtually forgotten, in spite of the fact that in this country millions of Viktor Frankl's books were sold in the early '80s. At the same time, the most acute problems of today: crime, drugs, greed, ugly gender polarization, disintegration of family, decay in morals, racism, and so on, are, to a great extent, the direct consequences of this crisis of meaning.

In my view, the time has come for America to look reality in the face and honestly focus on what politicians usually prefer to hide under their rhetoric—our current *existential* crisis when, as Viktor Frankl put it, "more people today have the means to live, but no meaning to live for." The healing process, which will eventually make our society healthy and ready for the challenges of the new millennium, will be possible and can begin only if our public understands the true causes of our problems, and politicians openly and honestly address these burning issues.

This is an extremely difficult task. To most people this *loss of meaning* epidemic is hidden, for it has been developing against the background of a more or less successful economy. Even mentioning this sickness and its consequences to virtually all the most serious problems of our time is "unpatriotic" and politically suicidal. This is because people do not want to be aware and acknowledge that the origin of those problems is deep within our everyday lives, in our individual perceptions of our being—that it has to do with the deepest core of our existence as human beings. And yet this sickness *must* be addressed and thoroughly discussed, because chances for "self-cure" are slim. That is why this book has been written.

Acute existential problems are typical of our time, when the structure of people's lives—their time at work and at leisure—has drastically changed with respect to what it had been some 50 or even 30 years before. Not accidentally, the crisis coincided with the onset of the high-tech era—the Information Age. We live in the *post-industrial* world. Gradually, but with ever-increasing speed, the industrial economy has been giving way to an economy based on information.

However, just as the structure of our lives is so drastically changing, with traditional jobs disappearing and new jobs requiring a new dynamism and strength, we find ourselves sick. In a sense, society is unprepared to meet the dawn of the new era. People are lost, wandering in darkness. Even the American Dream, which has been the pillar of life for generations of people, and which has made America great, seems not to lead them anywhere.

The existential crisis of our society is not something specifically American. It is a worldwide phenomenon. The ills, rooted in the meaning of one's existence, are nearly universal. As the post-industrial revolution spreads worldwide, affluent societies, welfare states, and even the poorest countries are infected. In his book *The Unconscious God: Psychotherapy and Theology* (p. 91), Frankl writes:

> "Unlike an animal, man is no longer told by drives and instincts what he must do. And in contrast to man in former times, he is no longer told by traditions and values what he should do. Now, knowing neither what he must do nor what he should do, he sometimes does not even know what he basically wishes to do. Instead, he wishes to do what other people do…or he does what other people wish him to do…."

In this situation of existential confusion, our old social philosophies also fail. Hence the bitter truth that Frankl so emphatically reveals: "Ever more people today have the means to live, but no meaning to live for."

Robert Kaplan, a noted American journalist, gives a vivid picture of the *existential vacuum* that has engulfed America ("The Coming Anarchy," *The Atlantic Monthly*, Feb. 1994):

> "When voter turnout decreases to around 50 percent at the same time the middle class is spending astounding sums in gambling casinos and state lotteries, joining private health clubs and using large amounts of stimulants and anti-depressants, one can legitimately be concerned about the state of American society. We have become voyeurs and escapists. Many of us don't play sports but love watching great athletes with great physical attributes. It is because people find so little in themselves that they fill their world with celebrities. The masses avoid important national and international news because much of it is tragic, even as they show an unlimited appetite for the details of Princess Diana's death. This willingness to give up self and responsibility is the *sine qua non* for tyranny."

Even so, the situation in America is more acute than in most developed democratic countries because of the systematic decline, in fact the degradation, of our educational system over a long period of time.

Education is an aspect of human civilization that is of a fundamentally individual character, although an effort by the whole society is necessary for its successful development. Education is also of a fundamental *existential* character simply because it is the opening of a window on the world. It allows us to see *who* we are, *where* we came from, and *where* we are heading. It gives us a gulp of fresh air, even if we feel there is no air left to breathe. It tells us something about ourselves that we did not know before. It helps us to mature—building up our souls and filling them with *meaning*. Education helps us to become members of the family called *humankind* and thus have a share in its inheritance. It leads us to feel responsible not only for our loved ones and ourselves but for the whole world—its destiny.

Attaining meaning in one's life is not necessarily a consequence of education. An uneducated individual can be happy and live a meaningful and fulfilling life. However, I firmly believe that an important factor that has allowed our lives to become devoid of meaning has been the degradation in education. Consequently, it is *education* that becomes the most important factor for restoring meaning in our lives.

We need much more than just the reorganization of our schools or the injection of more money into education. We need a revolution in the minds of people. My main concern is for our children. And we, their parents and grandparents, are primarily responsible for their future. It is we who must be the leading force in the future cultural and educational revolution.

There is no other way out of this crisis, not only in America but also in the whole democratic world, than by enhancing the educational level of the populace. Almost 80 years ago H. G. Wells wrote: "Human history becomes more and more a race between education and catastrophe." Today it is true more than ever.

In a totalitarian society, people are unimportant. In a democracy, every person matters. That is why the intellectual and emotional maturity of the majority of people in a democratic society is so important and necessary for the society to be healthy. Most of all, a healthy democracy is impossible unless people's intellects and spirits are at a level well above the level of their jobs. Raising people's culture to that level is impossible without true education.

Yes, America has the most vibrant intellectual elite, with its own culture—one that has absorbed the best achievements of at least two millennia of Western civilization. America is also in the forefront of science and technology. However, the majority of Americans are getting more and more estranged from the intellectual and emotional nourishing spring of that culture. Instead, an ugly *mass pseudo-culture* is striving to subvert that culture, like a cancer, spreading its ugly metastasis such as racism, drugs, violence, and sexual promiscuity throughout the whole society.

As a result, society is becoming polarized not only into *whites* and *non-whites* and the *affluent* and the *poor* but into what I believe is much more important—for it carries in that polarization the cause of all the other problems—the *educated* and the *ignorant*. Unlike the 19th century and the first half of the 20th century *affluent* is no longer synonymous with "educated," and *ignorant* with "poor."

Apart from the traditional *ignorance* of those who virtually have studied nothing, a new kind of ignorance has emerged—the ignorance of the professional. Though these professionals have mastered the skills of their fields, their lives are devoid of almost any connections with the humanitarian culture of Western civilization. There are people of this kind with law school, medical school and other university diplomas who are in high positions in all strata of our society: in education, healthcare, the media, industry and government. *Irresponsibility* comes with this ignorance.

Education in our society today has given way to *training*, which focuses on providing a person with specific knowledge, called *skills*, useful in getting a good or better job, rather than enlarging that person's connection with the world of humanitarian culture, and enhancing one's sense of identity with our civilization. Unwittingly, our educational system, rather than helping to develop strong personalities, in fact prevents people from acquiring *maturity*. Hence, the loss of direction in people's lives.

The mass pseudo-culture begins with our children. We have abandoned them. Nobody—neither the family which, to a large extent, has been ruined by boredom and the urge to attain affluence, nor the society with its numerous institutions—cares any more about the intellectual and spiritual health of its children. School, again, sees its main objective as providing our children with *skills*: reading skills, math skills, computer skills, and so on, rather than helping them in developing their personalities, thus gradually transferring to them the treasures of Western civilization.

Unfortunately, due to the inevitable *conflict of generations*, the transfer of both cultural and moral values from parents to children has also almost completely ceased. In order to survive, the children create their own primitive culture, which they later carry on as immature adults. The next generation of children begins again *from scratch*. This culture is fundamentally anti-intellectual and entertainment-oriented, mimicking the anti-intellectual and entertainment-oriented culture of the adults.

Against the background of the crisis of meaning that has engulfed America, our children's existential misery is unbearable. The media discuss the "alienation that grips so many teenagers." Unfortunately, it is not just "alienation." It is "To Be or Not To Be" asked in earnest. One-third of adolescents have contemplated, attempted, or committed suicide. Teenage violence and homicide (to mention only the massacre in Columbine High) is just another side of the same coin. However, we do not seem to understand the core of the problem: our children's lives are empty, they are lost, they are desperate.

It is always a crime to send children to any barricades but we are sending our children to "the barricades of the sexual revolution." Our irresponsibility destroys our children's hope for romance and love, leaving sex as the only option and a surrogate for intimacy and friendship.

We encourage children to work and as early as possible. By so doing we make them take the first step toward existential misery in the future. Too early do they learn that a job is *boring*, adding to the general boredom of their everyday meaningless lives. They then try to escape this boredom through entertainment, promiscuous sex, and drugs. The notion that any job that brings in money is good (and the more money the better) is profoundly wrong. A job is good if it brings satisfaction. With satisfaction comes happiness. But both are impossible unless a person is intellectually and emotionally mature.

In all social strata of our society, millions of those who are doomed to wander in the existential darkness of boredom and meaninglessness of their lives see illicit drugs as an ultimate remedy. People use drugs in affluent suburbs and elegant offices much more than in inner-city slums. How can these people *just say no* to drugs when an enforced *no* may mean a tragedy, for there is nothing left if the liberating state of being *high* is forbidden? If tomorrow the government succeeds in completely sealing our borders from imported drugs, domestically manufactured drugs will fill the created vacuum. The domestic drug industry is already striving to get its chunk of the drug market. In any case, a new generation of *high-tech* drugs will soon be developed making use of computer technology rather than chemical substances—to say nothing of the proliferation of intellectual drugs. There are already signs of addiction to computer games and to the Internet, of which our children are also victims. We are spending billions of dollars to stop the *supply* of drugs, but it is the *demand* for drugs that makes the problem so serious. In fact, it *is* the problem.

The internal emptiness also results in ugly gender polarization, in which an infantile, macho-obsessed man dominates a more mature, but disgruntled and subservient woman. No training can prevent sexual harassment if a man does not respect a woman as an individual. No training or *tips* can prevent "a relationship" from collapsing, unless it is based on a deep mutual respect, which is the necessary foundation for *love*. Only a true education can help to develop *maturity*, without which it is impossible to stabilize family. Reassuringly, it seems as though women are winning in the social "natural selection" against all odds.

I believe that racism, anti-Semitism and other forms of bigotry are but direct psychological consequences of ignorance. Elimination of racism in our society is impossible unless we succeed in raising the educational level of all—not only the people of color but also the whites. For social harmony is possible only if the society is *enlightened*. No training can persuade white supremacists that people of color are not inferior.

The cognitive inhomogeneity of our society, the honest discussion of which is now under fierce fire from the intellectual left, is not an obstacle to achieving social harmony. We must learn more about this phenomenon, learn how to cope with it, or how to find ways of decreasing cognitive polarization. But I firmly believe that living a meaningful life and being happy have *nothing to do* with a person's IQ.

Due to the deterioration of our educational system and the proliferation of hedonism, our society becomes increasingly more ignorant in science. Far fewer people understand how the physical world functions. But much more regretful is that they simply do not care. This ignorance and indifference are mind-boggling and very dangerous at the beginning of the high-tech 21st century.

The problem of *the indifferent* in our society is extremely important. Less than 50 percent of people of voting age care to vote in elections. Who and what are the others? Who would they vote into power if one day they decided to vote? If the society is immature and ignorant, one day it will vote into power an ignorant president. It is not an abstract threat any more. During the 2000 presidential election campaign, the idea has surfaced that a president does not have to be all that knowledgeable if he has a good *team*.

The indifference of the so-called educated but culturally ignorant—I have already mentioned that type—becomes transformed into an irresponsibility of a level virtually unheard of before in America. I mean, first of all, our so-called "interest groups," politicians and those who have money and power. In their quest for power and money, they do not stop even at abusing our Constitution. *We the people* are the victims. The abuse of the *First Amendment*—the right of free speech—is mind-boggling. As for the abuse of the *Second Amendment*—the right to bear arms—we have already been paying heavy tolls in lives of children. How many more massacres do we need before those greedy and irresponsible abusers of our Constitution are stopped?

Also highly worrisome is the gradual drift of our society's moral standards toward the realm of *relative morality*, typical of a totalitarian regime. How can we stop this trend?

This book consists of a number of essays addressing the most serious problems our society is facing today, which I have mentioned above. I have tried to arrange the essays in a kind of logical succession, although each essay is virtually independent, and may be read in any order. The opening essay is my tribute to the life and ideas of Viktor Frankl, to whom the book is dedicated.

This book crosses what may be called *party lines*. Partisanship among our politicians today has risen to proportions unheard of before in American political culture. In fact, too often a concerted partisan assault by either the Left or the Right brings about only disaster—*we, the people* becoming the victims.

Given this atmosphere of intransigence and ideological warfare, the ideas espoused in this book will too often fall in a political *no-man's land*, at the mercy of both the Left and the Right. I ask only to be heard. And what I want is *discussion*. The very important problems raised in this book have not been widely and seriously discussed; they require scrupulous analysis. Some of the diagnoses I am suggesting (or supporting) are too serious to be rejected out of hand.

In this book I often use the word "revolution." The late noted physicist and author, Abraham Pais, wrote in his book, *The Genius of Science: A Portrait Gallery of Twentieth Century Physicists* (p. 32): "In the political sphere, revolution is a rather clear concept. One system is swept away, to be replaced by another with a distinct new design. It is otherwise in science, where revolution, like love, means different things to different people." The latter also applies to the future revolution in our education. It will mean different things to different people. However, this revolution will occur—first of all in our consciousness—if and when we understand, from the bottom of our hearts, that teaching our children *skills* will, at best, help them, in the future, only to get a job—perhaps, a good job. However, it will not help them to mature, and to become responsible, thinking and creative individuals and citizens. It will not help them to begin the everlasting and unstoppable quest for meaning, which is also a road to happiness. Only a strong general academic education will set our children on a life long road to a meaningful life.

What will happen if we fail to fulfill this goal of revolutionizing our education? Even if we improve the quality of *training* in our schools and colleges (and that is what today's "educational reforms" are aiming at), we may be able to sustain, possibly even for a long time, the high-tech development of our society, but we will not be able to significantly improve our social climate. Racial strife will continue to haunt our society. The drug culture will flourish, moving into a new, and probably more devastating phase of high-tech drugs. And, as its companion, social inequity and crime will increase. But let us leave these doomsday scenarios to science-fiction writers.

Before you start reading this book, I have a request, or a suggestion to you, my reader. Sometimes what you will read in this book may make you irritated, angry, and even enraged. At that point, you will have two options. One is to return the book to the store and try to get your money back. The other is to put the book aside for a while and try to ponder what has made you so angry. At that moment, I want you to know that it is the deep pain I feel for this country, which I love, and, which is my "sweet home" and the home of my family—of my beloved granddaughter Rachel—and, I hope, of the generations of descendants to come that made me write this book. I want you to share this pain with me. Because if you as well as, I hope, many of my other readers do so, *we, the people* can make a difference. The future of your children, grand- and great-grandchildren is at stake at this crucial turning point in this country's destiny. If you are a psychologist or a social scientist, I challenge you. Some of my "accusations" are so serious that they need to be investigated by rigorous scientific methods. Believe me, I passionately wish I were wrong.

Introduction: Why This Book?

> "I feel myself a traveler on a journey that is far longer than the history of nations and philosophies, longer even that the history of our species."
>
> —*Freeman Dyson, in "Nature's Imagination"*

I was born in Russia. Seventeen years before, in a little Jewish town in the south of Russia, a squad of Cossacks of General Mamontov galloped into the backyard of a small dyeing shop. An officer shot and killed the middle-aged blind man, the shop owner, his elder son, and the son's fiancé, who were working in the yard. Two younger boys, ages sixteen and ten, managed to hide themselves behind a huge vat of boiling dye. From there, they watched the Cossacks gang rape their mother. Then the Cossacks found the boys, and tied them and their mother together. Perhaps, they wanted to do some more killing, but at that moment they heard shots and panic in the street. The Reds were entering the town. The Cossacks hastily fled.

The blind man, killed on that August day of 1919, was my grandfather, the ten-year old boy—my father. That very afternoon, sixteen-year old Zelik (my uncle) joined the Red Army. Eventually, he became a commissar and a professional soldier—all his life a devoted Communist. My grandmother never fully recovered after that horrible day.

I never heard about these events from my father. For many years, bit-by-bit, I reconstructed them; then just a few years ago I heard the whole story from an elderly man, who had lived next door and still remembered that day.

After the turmoil of Russia's Civil War (1917-1919) was over, in the late 1920s, my father graduated from a *Rabfak*—one of the thousands of new colleges opened in Communist Russia with the sole purpose of educating the formerly underprivileged classes. He became a journalist. With my mother, a schoolteacher from a peasant family, they were a "new breed" of people, to whom Communists gave everything. Their loyalty to and trust in the Communist regime were unlimited. Even the infamous Stalin purges of the thirties, and then of the late forties

1

and early fifties (which my father miraculously survived), could not have shaken my parents' devotion.

Though a talented journalist, my father was always a *deputy*—simply because in the Soviet Union Jews were never trusted, and too often openly hated and discriminated against. Being Jewish never meant being affiliated with a religion, but rather belonging to a different race, with all the attributes of the anti-Semitic tradition, rich in Russia, which was later enhanced by the Nazis.

The word *Jew* was kind of a shameful one. It was never pronounced aloud—that was sort of "indecent." Everybody knew (and it was taken for granted) that to be a Jew was *bad*. Everybody could distinguish Jews by the way they looked and talked—they were usually more educated and spoke perfect Russian. Everybody knew the rules of the game: A Jew could not complain, for any accusation of discrimination or anti-Semitism meant the slander of "the most democratic, the most humane and the happiest" society in the world, and the slanderer was ruthlessly persecuted.

Every Soviet citizen had an internal passport, where, on the very first page, after the date of birth, first and last names, and marital status, there was the infamous "fifth item:" Nationality. That is where that hated and ashamed of word "Jewish" was written. There was a joke (it could even be an anecdote) about a man who, when filling out a library card, has automatically written in the line with number 5: "Jewish." The gist of the joke was that due to a bureaucratic "negligence," unlike most of the forms in the USSR, line 5 on that card asked for marital status. Children of "mixed marriages," when they had their passport issued at age sixteen could choose between the nationalities of their parents (of course, in most cases, they preferred a non-Jewish fifth item). However, personnel departments could easily "unmask" a half-blood.

In a very popular joke, a personnel officer says to a "Russian" applicant. "Comrade Ivanov, with such a nose, we would rather hire a Jew." In real life, exactly that happened to my former Ph.D. student

---

Somehow, I do not remember much about my early childhood. But two events have been sharply imprinted in my memory. The first I see as if from the outside. A beautiful alley of tall—very tall—trees. Early morning. The sun penetrates the tops of the trees, filling the air with shining warmth. I am very small—perhaps three or four years old. I am stunned by the beauty of the gigantic trees. Joy overflows me. A young woman and a young man (perhaps teenagers) are holding hands and are approaching me. They look very happy; they are both smiling broadly. I am happy too, and I want to do something pleasant for them.

"Look what I have," I say, and show them a large, half-inch diameter birthmark on my forearm (I am very proud of it.). The girl, smiling (I still see her beautiful shining green eyes), says, almost with tenderness, "You dirty little Jewish cub." And both burst out laughing…

The recollection of the second event has been haunting me all my life. When Germany invaded the Soviet Union in 1941, I was five. We lived then in Rostov-Don, a city in the south of Russia. The Germans were advancing very rapidly, and our family had to be evacuated (my father was at the front, working for a military newspaper). There was virtually no time left. We were boarding a train (as we learned later, it was the last train before the Nazis entered the city). Our car was the nearest to the engine. When my mother was hurriedly helping me to climb into the car, the bundle of my five-month-old younger brother in her hands, I saw two small children—a girl (perhaps eight or nine), who was holding by the hand a boy of my age, or even younger. She was pleading with the train machinist.

"Sir, please, sir. Take us on the train, please. The Germans will kill us…"

I was already in the car, and the train departed in a few minutes. Were those children Jewish? Did they manage to survive? In my memory, I have been seeing this scene so clearly and so often, that now I do not know if it ever happened, or if it was a trick of my imagination.

In 1943 my father was called from the front and started working for a Moscow central newspaper. Our family moved to Moscow.

I was a shy boy, a "loser," unable to defend myself. Somehow I knew that I could not complain at home, and I never did. I heard "you dirty Jewish cub" (*zhidionok*) so many times and so often, and was so ashamed of being one, that I simply did not believe anything could be done about it.

In 1946, right after the Nuremberg Trials were over and some former Nazi leaders hanged, I was also about to be hanged by neighborhood kids ("Hitler has not finished the job."). They gagged and tied me up, and were looking for a hook, when a passerby scared them away. It was in Moscow, not in some remote obscure town.

At middle and high school, we Jewish kids tried to keep together. We knew that we had to be the best, so that no matter how hard the authorities tried, they would be unable to deny our acceptance to a university. By then I knew already that not all Jewish families were like mine. Some other parents used to discuss important matters with their kids—tell them important things, encourage them, "train" them for the struggle to come.

In high school, I had two close friends: *G* and *B*. We used to spend a lot of time together, talking a lot. *G*'s father was a former Red General. In the thirties, although he had been a deputy of the great Marshal Tukhachevsky, one of the military geniuses shot by Stalin's order in 1940, he managed miraculously to survive the purges. My friend told us the awful truth about the GULAG, about the millions upon millions of the best Communists murdered by Stalin, about the incredible and permanent lies in our everyday life.

GULAG was the acronym for the system of hard labor camps mainly located either in the far north of Russia or in Siberia. The Western world first learned about Stalin's atrocities and the huge system of slave camps much later from Alexander Solzhenitsin's *The GULAG Archipelago*. Recently an excellent book was published: Anne Appelbaum, *GULAG: a History*.

All of a sudden the impossible truth dawned upon me: the Soviet Union *was not* what the Communists were claiming it to be, but was a Fascist totalitarian state based on lies and crime. And yet we believed in Communism's great *ideals*. We read "Lenin's Will" (the letter to the Communist Party Central Committee written by Lenin before his death). Just to read it was then a criminal offense, which could cost us many years in GULAG. We believed that Lenin's cause had been brutally betrayed.

Later, already in college, B and I joined an underground group. Our purpose was to study the *unofficial* Communist ideology—in all its aspects—and to try to understand what had gone wrong with the experiment that Lenin had started. We were just a few 18-years-old boys and girls (my future wife Zeya also was with us), very idealistic and very naïve. We also did not understand how dangerous it was. However, quite soon, we came to the conclusion that the whole idea of Communism, no matter how attractive it looked, *was wrong—morally wrong*. We were not religious then, but somehow we felt that a relative morality, when *Good* and *Evil* easily change places depending on what is profitable at the moment for the "proletariat," when "the ends justify the means," is both corruptive and destructive for any society. That was just what we were witnessing in everyday life. At the same time, relative morality had been the cornerstone of Lenin's theory. Not everybody in our group shared this view, and the group somehow disintegrated. By the way, our "guru," and close friend, is now a world-renowned expert in computer science and a professor at one of the leading American universities.

Stalin died in March 1953. There was mourning all over the Soviet Union— not only an official mourning. Millions of people mourned "the father of nations," "the best friend of the Soviet children," "our hope and support." My family was no exception. My mother and elder sister were sobbing. As for me, I was about to explode, to burst with joy and happiness. The monster was dead. The end of tyranny. The beginning of a new era. I simply could not stay at home.

Hanging out in the streets, I and my friend B suddenly found ourselves in the tight shoulder-to shoulder mass of people slowly moving through the downtown

Moscow area toward the House of Councils—the hall where Stalin's casket was placed for "the nation's farewell." All of a sudden we found that we had become particles without will power, part of a dark mob, a physical mass some thirty to forty yards wide, moving slowly (a foot or two a minute.) down the steep street toward inevitable doom. It took all our strength as seventeen-year-old boys to elbow our way across the current to the safety of the boulevard's low fence. We were saved. From our position at the top of the hill, we could see two hundred yards ahead of us. On Trubnaya Square, busses were being turned upside-down, people smashed and crushed under the unstoppable incoming flow of the mob. A few thousand people were killed that afternoon on Trubnaya Square. It was the first consequence of Stalin's death. Even dead he could not stop killing.

We finished high school that summer. Very soon we knew that nothing had changed; for a Jewish kid to be accepted to a college was as difficult as before. Both my friend *B* and I finished high school with distinction: he was awarded a gold medal, I a silver one. A medal entitled its recipient to skip entrance exams to a college, with only an interview to be passed. Earning the medal was an extremely important advantage for a Jewish kid, for the entrance examinations (no matter what the college) were infamous for their cruel practices.

> The Soviet colleges were (and in the former Soviet Union still are) called "institutes," and they have, typically, a very narrow specialization. There is the Textile Institute, the Oil Industry Institute, the Institute of Steel and Alloys (I will be calling it the Metallurgical College), the Institute of the Mining Industry, the Machine and Tool Institute, the Institute of Foreign Languages, for example. And there are perhaps only a few dozen colleges called "universities" (Moscow University being the best among them), typically in large cities. Below I will be using the term "college," when speaking of a school of higher learning.

Most of the exams were oral, but at least one written exam had to be passed: Russian Composition. A typical grade for a Jewish kid would be F (two on a five-point scale), with no explanation and virtually no right of appeal (the authorities refused to show the graded compositions). An interview left a chance for success. Because the interview was typically held before a five- to ten-person examination board, there was a chance that its results would not be falsified or forged.

In spite of many warnings not even to attempt to apply to Moscow University, I still did. Even now, 50 years later, I see the angry, hateful face of the Moscow University examination board chairman: "How dare you, being morally inferior, request acceptance to the best university in the world, to become a Soviet physicist, a proud representative of your great country." My "moral inferiority" was that I did not know what had been discussed at a recent Young Communist League Congress.

Later, a friend with whom I had attended the Moscow Planetarium lectures, told me that he had been turned down by the same board after having failed to explain why the carafe with water on the windowsill was warmer on the side opposite to that turned toward the sun. It was leaked by a board member that the carafe had been turned around right before my friend was called in.

Having failed to pass interviews there, as well as at two other technical colleges, I ended up at the Metallurgical College, whose director's brother was a member of the Communist Party Central Committee. Therefore the director could afford to accept *smart Jews*.

At the Metallurgical College the interview was quite different. The board chairman, all big smiles, said, "Why does your high school diploma look as though it were 50 years old?"

I got angry. "Because it had been bent and unbent in a thousand places, and with dirty hands." "Moscow University included?" asked the chairman. And then, "I am kidding. Ladies and gentlemen, I think this boy should be accepted. No objections?"

We had quite a spectrum of talents at that college. Famous physicists, mathematicians, computer scientists, engineers, and even a movie director and a science-fiction author are among that college's alumni. We also had a constellation of brilliant professors who had been turned down or fired from other schools during the anti-Semitic campaigns of Stalin's time. Later, when the times changed for the better, they left the college and took highly deserved top and honorary positions in Academia. It is still a good college now, with its graduates successfully competing for professorships or post-doctoral fellowships all over the world.

My friend *B* was smarter. He wanted to be a computer scientist (an unknown animal at that time), and applied to a college that was just opening a Computer Science Department. There was virtually no competition for that department, and yet, *B*'s interview was difficult. After over an hour of fierce fighting and endless questions in physics and math, well above the high school requirements, the board chairman said, "I have done what I could, but may I be damned if, after all this, you will not be accepted." My friend was accepted.

Our mentor, *G*, after difficult and stressful entrance examinations, was accepted to a second-rate college. He was depressed; his spirits were very low. We did not know that he had a brain tumor. He passed away soon after.

Being accepted to a university did not mean, for a Jewish youngster, the end of fighting for survival. Though, during the five to six years of study, students did not feel strong discrimination (there were anti-Semitic professors, but one could always find ways to avoid them), one always had to keep in mind that after graduation one had to get a job assignment.

A Soviet college did not have a bachelor's degree. After five and a half to six years of study, students graduated with qualifications close to that of a master's degree in America. A graduate had to write a thesis (often a piece of original research) and defend it before an examination board. Graduate school (called *aspirantura*) usually took three to five years. After passing a number of exams and defending a thesis (in my time one had to submit at least two papers to refereed journals prior to the defense), the graduate was awarded the degree of Candidate of Sciences. This diploma is recognized in the West as equivalent to a PhD. There is a second, and higher academic degree: Doctor of Sciences. No counterpart in the American educational system exists (the closest analogy is the German *habilität*). Only six percent of those having the degree of Candidate of Sciences are in the future awarded the doctor's degree.

A Doctor of Sciences is typically a distinguished, mature, and often world-renowned expert in his or her field. Most of the leading American and European universities recognize the qualification of the former Soviet DSc as equivalent to that of a tenured full professor. Of course, as in America, the quality of education in the Soviet Union varied from college to college, but most of the Moscow colleges were in my time (and, I believe, still are) among the world's best.

Since the education in the USSR was free (needy students even received a monthly stipend), a graduate had to "pay back" society by accepting a job assignment for three years. There were no unemployed graduates. Everybody had a job assignment, but the assignments were different. An ethnic Russian (in Russia) or Ukrainian (in Ukraine) or Armenian (in Armenia), for example, had, in principle, nothing to worry about. Typically, for an "ethnically correct" graduate there was always a job he or she liked. Better grades usually meant a better job (although, the so-called *blat*—"protection"—always flourished).

For a Jewish student the story was completely different. A "round A" physics graduate could be sent to a remote Siberian village as a schoolteacher, while a "round C" non-Jew could have a position in a prestigious research laboratory right in downtown Moscow or its suburb (to be a "non-Russian" in Moscow was generally rather bad, but not as bad as being Jewish). Some courageous professors fought for their Jewish students, and sometimes won, but this was not typical.

In spite of all these obstacles, Jewish kids who were ready to fight survived. A Siberian high school physics teacher somehow found ways of writing formulas at night in his cold *izba* (a log cabin with no toilet or running water), publishing papers and keeping in contact with his colleagues in Moscow. In three years, when his mandatory job assignment expired, he might manage to get a research position in Moscow or be accepted to a graduate school.

A young Jewish doctor could, after spending a few years in the Far East or Siberia, return to Moscow an experienced surgeon or gynecologist—very often uniquely experienced because he or she had to perform operations under conditions a Moscow surgeon would never have seen in worst dreams, had to fight incredible deficiencies in equipment and basic drugs. I do know a few dramatic examples like that.

My thesis advisor insisted on giving me a job assignment to a metallurgical research center in Moscow—perhaps the best in the Soviet Union and, in many respects, unique in the world. I worked there for seventeen years until, in 1977, my family received exit visas and were catapulted to freedom and the new life.

This book is about America, not Russia. The only reason why I decided, to talk about my background in the *Introduction*, is that I wanted the reader to understand my personal anxiety—even pain—and the imminent urge to do something about the situation in America, my new home and the home of my son and granddaughter and, I hope, of many generations to come.

As I have already stated, for a Jew in the Soviet Russia, education was not just a way to get a better job. It was the only way to survive in some very broad and, I should say, existential sense.

For some miraculous reason, most of the people who, during all the decades of the Communist rule, were at the forefront of both technical research and development, and the development of all aspects of the Russian literary and artistic culture (literature, poetry, music, theater), were Jewish. Again, most of them (at least of the generations born under Communism) had never experienced any influence of Jewish cultural or religious traditions, as we understand them in America.

To survive, for me and my friends as well as for thousands and thousands of Jews in the Soviet Russia, meant not only to be the best (in order to get a job or achieve success in one's chosen profession), it also meant to live a vibrant intellectual and spiritual life. No matter how harsh the official policies toward culture were at times, there were always books or literary magazines to be read.

Both my future wife Zeya and I spent three years of our college years attending evening English courses. (To pay for them, Zeya had to regularly give her blood—I learned about that much later.) So, in our early twenties we could already read almost fluently in English, and grabbed every opportunity to obtain paperbacks from Western tourists (these encounters were often dangerous, and resulted in confrontation with the Soviet secret police—the infamous KGB).

There were also "unofficial" libraries. Our English teacher and friend (a former American who had come to the USSR with her parents on the wings of idealism in the early '30s, only to lose her parents in Stalin's purges and then, herself, to spend five years in a GULAG labor camp) had a collection of a few hundred good books, which she willingly lent to her students.

Russian literature lived a very strange life. Of course, the fiction and poetry of contemporary Soviet authors were heavily censored. Some masterpieces like Bulgakov's *The Master and Margarita* were published in Russian almost twenty years after the author's death, during the short period of the so-called "thaw" under Nikita Khruschev. Many authors were able to publish their manuscripts only either abroad or in the so-called *samizdat* ("self-publishing")—an unofficial, in fact, underground, network of production and dissemination of typewritten books.

The KGB ruthlessly punished for both these offenses. Boris Pasternak, a great poet and author, was criticized violently, humiliated, and forced to reject the Nobel Prize awarded for his *Doctor Zhivago*.

Strange as it may seem, in spite of the fundamentally anti-intellectual nature of the Communist regime, some Russian language literature was flourishing. Perhaps, as a reaction to heavy censorship, as a kind of sublimation, a great culture of literary translation emerged under the Communists' rule. Virtually all great world classics had been translated. The list of authors—from ancient times through the 20th century—translated into Russian would take many pages. Anthologies, selected works, and full collections of hundreds of authors were in the bookstores. Or to be precise, did not stay on bookstores' shelves for more then a few days. Sometimes they could be purchased only on the black market.

Among the intellectuals, there was a kind of madness—the hunt for books. Every year, new book subscriptions were announced. Often one had to bribe a bookstore clerk, or buy the subscription from a speculator. But the best of all would have been to have a *blat*—a friend in a bookstore, or a highly placed official, who had special quotas for subscriptions.

A month or two before we left Russia for good, I bought an eight-volume "academic" edition of the Russian translation of *Complete Shakespeare* from a speculator. I paid for it with my one-week's professor's salary. Five years later, at a yard sale in Danvers, MA, I bought a *1906 Cambridge Edition of the Poets* a one volume complete Shakespeare for a quarter.

Often one had to spend a night in line to get a multi-volume subscription of complete Jack London, Charles Dickens, Guy de Maupassant, Edgar Allan Poe,

Jules Verne, Fenimore Cooper, O'Henry, Theodore Dreiser, or Earnest Hemingway. In those years I discovered and immediately fell in love with William Faulkner, who is still my favorite author even now, forty years later. Comparing the English and Russian texts by Faulkner—line by line—one can see what a miracle had been performed by the translators.

Numerous editions of Russian literary classics were also being published. Of course, there were "forbidden authors," especially among the brilliant poets and novelists of the beginning of the 20th century pre-revolutionary Russia, and the first years after the revolution. For ideological reasons, Dostoyevsky was semi-forbidden during the Stalin's years. The great author Vladimir Nabokov—an emigrant (i.e. a *traitor*)—literally did not exist.

Among the Western authors, there were also those who were forbidden For example, Heinrich Böll's publications had been immediately stopped after his anti-Soviet remarks. The same happened to works of John Steinbeck and Graham Green. Of course, George Orwell was forbidden outright, although we read and discussed *Nineteen Eighty-Four*—a miraculously close picture of our society (or its nearest future).

There was probably not a single reading family, whose apartment (very often a tiny one, or even just one room in a communal apartment) was not crammed with books—endless shelves, often makeshift, with books in two rows. Of course, that did not mean that all those books were read. But that was a tradition. One *had to have* books around, in order to *belong*. Belong to what? To the free world of culture that does not know limits either in space or time? Hard to say. But books were everywhere, and people did read them.

How numerous was this reading class? During a very short period, in the '60s, subscription to the literary magazines was unlimited, and their circulation figures could give an estimate of the reading class population. The most generous number I could arrive at was two hundred thousand out of a population of two hundred million in the Soviet Union. But most of these elite was concentrated in a dozen big cities—Moscow and Leningrad being the cultural capitals.

By the mid '60s, the main concern of Zeya's and mine, as well as our closest friends, was the upbringing of our children. We read and discussed the most modern trends in child psychology and pedagogical science in the West. Of course, the role model for us was America. Dr. Spock's book was heavily read, borrowed from friends, and lent further on along an infinite line. We read somewhere that according to the latest discovery of American child psychology, a child's personality was completely formed by the ages of three to five. With our kids approaching school age, we felt that we were late in helping develop our children.

We believed that American education and child care were the best in the world. Whatever American teachers did had been scientifically proven to be optimal.

Scientifically justified tests and polls helped teachers to find optimal strategies in educating the children. We believed that education was the main concern of a free society because, in order to survive the deadly conquest of Communism, a free society must be intellectually, educationally, and culturally superior. Then military superiority would automatically follow. Almost passionately, we exchanged pieces of information from the *Voice of America* (in spite of the pitiless electronic jams), occasional books or just rumors confirming our hopes and beliefs.

Later, there appeared translations of numerous American experimental textbooks. Among them were the *Midlands Mathematical Experiment, Berkeley Physics Course, Fundamental Physics* by Jay Orear and, perhaps the best since time immemorial, the *Feynman Lectures on Physics* (the latter was published in Russian as a nine-volume set, plus two volumes of problems and solutions).

At that time emigration was unthinkable, and our friends and we saw our main and most important goal as the parents to educate our children according to American standards. This was necessary in order to assure our children's successful survival in the racist and brutal Soviet society. I am talking now of a cluster of six or seven families: scientists, engineers, mathematicians, physicians (not all of them Jewish)—close, trusted friends from high school and college days, united in our hatred of the totalitarian regime. At least in Moscow, among the intellectuals, there was a similar trend to strive for excellence in their children's education.

Perhaps, because of such pressure, the semi-private school for preschoolers (four to six-year-olds), *Orlyonok* (*Little Eagle*), was organized under the auspices of Moscow University. Three times a week, 9 a.m. until noon, on the university grounds, in the pompous skyscraper built in Stalin's time on the beautiful Lenin Hills, the children were played with and taught painting and music. The teachers were young enthusiasts, some of them just teenagers themselves. They worked for a meager salary, but were obsessed with the desire to give the children as much as they could.

That was a time of relative liberalization. Then came the dark Brezhnev era (which is now referred to as the "stagnation").

I would like my reader to understand that this atmosphere of complete devotion to the education of children was typical only of very few and scattered groups of intellectuals. In fact, since sharing views or discussing even innocent problems was extremely dangerous (for the KGB informers were everywhere), those groups of families were very much isolated. The institute of friendship in Communist Russia, and especially in Brezhnev's time, played a fundamental role in the lives of dissident intellectuals. It would, perhaps, not be an exaggeration to claim that we would not have survived without the moral and often the financial support of a few close friends.

And what about our children? In 1970 almost all the children of our friends had reached the age of seven and had become first-graders. As almost everywhere in America, in Moscow a child had to go to a public school in the district of residence. Exceptions were very rare, and in most cases required a strong *blat*. There were no private schools, but the first attempt to open special schools had been undertaken. From the political (and ideological) point of view, that was an attempt to create a special, better-educated cadre of politically loyal specialists. Communists understood that this process had to originate from elementary school on.

Thus, in the early '70s, a number of special language schools—English, French and German—were opened in Moscow. Of course, the most popular were English schools. The foreign language studies began with the third grade, and gradually, one by one, foreign language teaching in general subjects such as nature, geography, history, physics and math, were switched on.

By graduation—the tenth grade (seventeen or eighteen years of age)—the students were supposed to be fluent in the foreign language, and be ready (the ethnic and political background of their parents permitting) to enter either the Institute of Foreign Languages or the Institute of International Relations—the two main elite colleges educating the future diplomats, interpreters and the other cadre for the foreign trade or diplomatic services.

In addition, two or three special schools with enhanced mathematics and science profiles were opened in Moscow in those years. The most famous of them was *School Number 1,* organized by the world-famous mathematician, academician Kholmogorov, under the auspices of the Mathematics Department of Moscow University. There, math and physics were taught mostly by university students. The school, with its relatively liberal approach to education, also attracted brilliant historians and literary scholars who taught humanities, and again, for a meager high-school teacher's salary. One of them was so insolently daring as to include in the very rigid curriculum (of course unofficially, but none of his students reported on him) the great Bulgakov's *The Master and Margarita*, then semi-illegal. (I hope sometime, the history of this fabulous and unusual school and its brilliant teachers will be written. Most of its graduates have left Russia and are now professors in prestigious universities in America and Israel, or leading researchers in American defense and National Laboratories or industrial companies.)

At that time we thought that in the future our son would go into science, but a French school was just in our "micro-district," a ten-minute walk from our apartment. So we decided that, at least as a beginning, that would do. The only formality was an interview, which our son flawlessly passed. In spite of all the obstacles, in a miraculous way, at least ten children in my son's French school class happened to be either "directly Jewish" (an entry "Jewish" in the school papers), or "camouflaged Jews" (with innocent Aryan last names, but unmistakable physical features, which allowed them later to find "proper" friends).

Though virtually no Jews (or children of dissidents) were allowed at the higher levels of the foreign language system, a Jewish first-grader could be accepted, especially if there were somebody influential or useful—like a gynecologist, or even a theater box-office clerk—who would agree to offer his or her services to the school principal in exchange for acceptance of the child.

As usual, there was no "free lunch." Although, in general, the quality of education at our son's school was better than at the regular public school next door, the social climate there was worse. Our son did not feel very comfortable among the children of the ardent Communists or corrupt Communist bureaucrats. Fortunately—and we were proud of him—our Danny understood the situation well enough for a seven-year-old boy, and we did not have any problems.

He knew a lot about the regime under which we lived. It was a matter of rather heated discussion among our friends: Do we have the moral right to tell the truth to our children, thus making them "black sheep" and, perhaps exposing them (and, to that effect, ourselves) to permanent danger? In fact, we were actually choosing the life of dissidents for them, without their consent. And yet, we decided that it was right. Later our children would adjust their behavior if they felt it necessary, but now it was important to be honest with them.

We knew families, where parents used to listen to the "enemy's voices"—like the Voice of America, Radio Liberty or the Voice of Israel—locking themselves with a transistor in a bathroom with water running so that, God forbid, the children would even suspect them. Alas, sometimes children imbued with Communist ideas reported on their parents to teachers, and thus, unavoidably, to the KGB. As a matter of fact, teachers in school explicitly encouraged children to share with them any doubts regarding their parents. Our Danny was proud of us, and we, of him.

One of the canonized national heroes—a role model for children to follow—was Pavlik Morozov, a 10-year-old boy in a Siberian village who, in the early '20s, reported on his father to CHEKA (the then secret police). His father was executed, but his father's friends later killed Pavlik, thus placing him in the pantheon of Communist martyrs.

With the beginning of the '70s, a new era dawned for us: Jewish emigration began. Many books have been written about those heroic years. To request an exit visa at that time was like jumping from a high cliff. If the water beneath was deep, you survived; if it was shallow you broke your neck.

Officially, there was no emigration in the normal, civilized sense: If people wanted to change the country of residence, and they did it, provided the immigration quota allowed that at the time. If not, people waited for their turn. It was rather a cynical and absolutely unprincipled and immoral game, dressed as a humanitarian action: "re-unification of families."

Of course, the whole business was a consequence of *détente,* the thawing of the Soviet-West relations. In cynical terms, the Jews were the hard currency the Communists decided to pay for the benefits of good relations with the United States. However, nobody throws down money without a good payoff. The Communists were no exception. Every time they felt that the benefits of *détente* were not as good, the release of Jews slowed down. It completely stopped for many years, after the *détente* ended with the Soviet Union's invasion of Afghanistan in 1979.

On the other hand, even in the best times, from the business point of view, the release of Jews was never easy or automatic. In order to discourage the would-be applicants, the process of applying for an exit visa was made as humiliating and as painful and dangerous as possible. People were harassed at work (and children, at school), they lost their jobs, and they were arrested under all possible false pretenses, and prosecuted. And, after a sometimes lengthy waiting period, a significant percentage of applicants were refused the exit visa.

Sometimes those refusals were distributed almost at random so that nobody could be certain of the outcome of the risky enterprise. A person having had access to classified information had a much higher chance of being refused the exit visa. Sometimes quite absurd things happened: a person could be refused the visa, while his supervisor, working at the same research lab, and on the same project, was allowed to leave. This happened to my friend *B.* Later I'll say a few words about his family's heroic fight for emigration.

That is how the class of *refuseniks* was created. Thousands upon thousands of people became trapped without jobs, often unable to make their living. People lived under the threat of the infamous Law of Parasitism—a person who did not have a job (that was officially recognized as "a job"), could be put on trial, and sentenced to years of internal exile or a labor camp. The future Nobel Laureate poet Joseph Brodsky was one of many accused of parasitism and prosecuted. Professors, fired from their positions, had to do menial work. Sometimes they were hired by their loyal colleagues as fake private secretaries. People of the highest professional qualification (the wave of emigration of the early '70s consisted mostly of intellectuals) worked as movers, lift operators, baby-sitters, and janitors. Of course, without the support—both material and spiritual—of the West (mostly scientists and clergymen), thousands of these courageous people would simply have starved or become morally broken. Now that Communism does not exist any more, those events are gradually sinking into the depths of history and into oblivion.

Returning to the life of my family: From 1972 on, our closest friends began to leave Russia. For almost everybody of roughly a dozen families with whom we were close, this process was not easy. Some were refused exit visas, and became active in what the authorities called *Zionist activity*—the struggle for their human rights.

For those of our friends who, like us, were not yet ready to make that irreversible step, the question was not "shall we have to leave," but rather "when."

Of course, the interest among the Jews toward Israel had risen tremendously. Leon Uris's *Exodus* was in high demand. Sometimes, even a photocopy (there were no Xeroxes then) could be borrowed for only one night—a sleepless night for the whole family (except for children, but later the story was retold to them in all possible detail). Jewish education began—the Hebrew language (with the help of books and self-taught teachers, mostly *refuseniks*), Jewish history and culture, Judaism. Later, after Afghanistan, when the doors to emigration had been shut, the whole unofficial culture began to flourish. Jewish kindergartens and schools, drama and literature classes, celebration of Jewish and Israeli holidays, religious observance—the activity in which tens of thousands of people were involved in spite of the harassment and brutality of the KGB and the Soviet society as a whole.

The family of my old friend *B* was refused exit visas in 1973. After that, he and his wife, as well as their elder twelve-year-old son, became involved in activities the authorities strongly despised. *B*, a talented computer scientist (then already a PhD), together with a few other prominent physicists, mathematicians and engineers, organized an unofficial weekly scientific seminar. For scientists deprived of ability to work, it was a gulp of fresh air. Those people were given the opportunity to discuss their scientific ideas and, in fact, this allowed them to survive as creative individuals.

Visiting Western scientists often gave lectures at the seminar. Apartments, where the seminars were held (the locations often alternated in order to confuse the KGB), were packed; people filling every imaginable space in the tiny apartments. Gradually, the seminar became a cultural center, where not only scientific problems were discussed, but also various aspects of Jewish culture and history. Politics was an absolute taboo. That made it very difficult for the KGB to find a valid pretense for harassment or even closure of the seminar.

Gradually, my friend *B.* became involved in another activity. The unofficial *samizdat* Journal, *Jews in the Soviet Union*, had been founded, and my friend became one of co-editors of the Journal.

That is when my family became more and more involved. We lived next door, and often (especially when *B*'s telephone had been cut off), communication with the Western scientists and activists went through our telephone. Our sons were buddies, and sometimes my Danny inconspicuously rode his bicycle to *B*'s apartment with a message, right under the noses of a dozen KGB agents watching *B*'s apartment around the clock (and, as we found out later, ours too). I was also doing some editing work for the Journal.

A no-return culmination point in my family's destiny was reached in the early morning on May 4th, 1977. Right after Danny left for school, a team of KGB agents raided our apartment with a search warrant. They spent a few hours looking through every book, every drawer, even the toilet tank, and the refrigerator. Unfortunately, they found what they were looking for very quickly. On the eve of that day, my friend *B* had brought in the new issue of our Journal—a few dozen copies—just typed. The KGB knew that the new issue had just been ready for circulation, and we expected a search in the *B*'s apartment. That was a grave miscalculation. Together with the precious Journal copies, they also confiscated my two typewriters, the Bible, and a dozen books—mostly on Jewish history and culture. Among the confiscated books were *The Master and Margarita* and *Doctor Zhivago*—both books published in the West and purchased on the black market.

That very night Danny rode his bicycle to a typist a few blocks away, and brought in another part of the Journal circulation, just finished being typed. We expected that our typist's apartment would also be raided, while a second search of our apartment was unlikely.

When the KGB agents were shamelessly searching through our family archive, our letters and dear artifacts, all the obstacles for our leaving Russia miraculously vanished. We had already received an invitation from a fake relative in Israel, and immediately began the lengthy and painful process of applying for exit visas.

As a part of the application package for the exit visa was a legend, explaining who the relatives in Israel were, how the contacts with them had been established, for example We did not know who that woman from kibbutz Kfar Blum, who sent us the invitation, was, and even whether she existed at all. I made her my cousin. Our legend was as follows: On that tragic August afternoon of 1919, when my grandfather and the elder uncle and his bride were shot by the Cossacks, my uncle actually survived. He later immigrated to Palestine. The woman who had sent us the invitation, was his daughter. I had met her at a scientific Congress in Moscow...

In fact, the KGB did not care. It was a game, and one just had to follow the rules. Recalling those days now, the following six months of waiting for the exit visas, and finally, the days when we were saying good-bye to our families and beloved friends—with no hope of seeing them again—it is hard to believe it was we who did it. In spite of enormous stress, and a few occasions that required superhuman concentration, when a mistake could have been fatal, everything went flawlessly. We felt the religious feeling of God present and helping us.

We expected that, like our friend *B*'s family, we will be refused the exit visas. But, miraculously, we received them just in six months—in December 1977.

The last days were filled with sorrow and bitterness. Not only were both Zeya and I leaving our families, we were leaving our dear friends, who were the most important part of our lives, and among them, the *B*s.

We thought then, and still believe now, that we owed our freedom to the *B*s. At that time, the KGB expanded its persecution of the Journal and the Refusenik Seminar. The criminal investigation was begun against the Journal. We believe that the KGB decided to let us go in order to further isolate the *B*s—to rid them of our support, no matter how modest it was. In 1980 *B* was arrested, put on trial and sentenced to internal exile in Kazakhstan. Hundreds of influential people in the West were fighting for his freedom. But nothing helped. As in the case of the more famous prisoner of Zion, Nathan Scharanski, *B* was freed, and his family allowed to emigrate only after the Soviet Empire began to collapse. Now the *B*s live in Israel; both my friend and his wife are university mathematics professors. In 1999 and 2002 *B* was elected to Israeli Parliament—the Knesset.

Walking under the falling snow to the plane, and showing our papers for the last check to a submachine gun-armed soldier before boarding the plane, we had only one regret: that our Danny, then 14 years old, had to leave his school. Just a few months before, after a lengthy interview, he had been accepted to a biology class of the Moscow Special School No 57. The school was famous for its high quality education. But we were optimistic. We were looking forward to the new and even better educational opportunities in the West.

The first three years of our emigration were quite dramatic. Of course, we left for Israel (although, exactly half of the emigrants leaving Moscow in our plane had America and Europe as their destination). The first half-year was filled with studying Hebrew (it appeared to be easier than we had expected) and looking for jobs. We lived in an absorption center a few miles from Jerusalem, overlooking the Judean Desert—the hills where, it seemed, time had stopped, and God was ever present.

Our *ulpan* (Hebrew school) group consisted only of English-speaking new immigrants from South Africa, Rhodesia, and Argentina. We developed friendships with those people. All of them were idealists, having left the affluent life of architects, physicians and businessmen for their historic home. Perhaps due to those people, their optimism and moral support, we were happy in those most difficult months.

Danny was accepted to one of the best Jerusalem high schools. To Zeya's and my regret, we were unable to devote as much time to him as he needed. He had been certainly undergoing a cultural shock, but we were too busy trying to organize our lives to be of any significant help to him.

Zeya, a PhD in electrical engineering, and an expert in gas-discharge high efficiency light sources, found a research position at the Hebrew University of Jerusalem. She created her small lab and began developing a new lamp for treatment of jaundice in the newborn. I found a professor's position at a technical college. Both positions were temporary, with the money provided by the Ministry of Absorption. The chances for transforming my position into a permanent one were rather high. To enhance them, in 1979 I accepted an invitation to spend a year as a visiting professor at a university in Germany. We decided that Zeya and Danny would stay in Jerusalem.

During my absence, quite dramatic events developed. Zeya's new lamp was being successfully tested in the best Jerusalem hospital, when Zeya's funds were unexpectedly cut down. No matter how hard she tried to find a job utilizing her high qualifications and expertise, she failed. Quite accidentally, she saw an ad in her professional journal advertising a position *exactly for her* in the United States, and she sent her résumé.

She was given an offer without an interview. A few more offers followed from companies in the US, England and Germany, where she had also sent her résumé. She accepted the very first offer.

In July 1980, Zeya, Danny and our darling collie Lassie, joined me in Germany, and in a few days we left for the United States. Our family was granted US Permanent Residence Status ("the Green Card") in less than a year (Zeya had the highest immigration priority as a *Distinguished Scientist*), and in five more years we became American citizens.

But let me return to that day when we first stepped on American soil. From the very beginning, our main concern was Danny's education. The reality pitilessly destroyed all our crystal castles. Almost immediately we discovered that the educational process in Danny's high school not only was below our expectations, but it was below any standards we could even think of. There was virtually no homework, but a lot of free time was spent mostly on all kinds of entertainment. At that time, kids did not carry handguns and knives, but marijuana and alcohol were abundant. We were also shocked by the unrestricted promiscuity and sex among Danny's friends. And his was a high school in a rather affluent town in Connecticut.

Years passed. We have not been impartial observers of the American educational system. Becoming more and more *Americans*—beginning to better understand American life in its many aspects—we have been watching, in deep despair, the gradual degradation and deterioration of not only the educational system, but also the mass culture itself. What seemed incredible and destructive in the '50s and '60s—like Elvis Presley or the Beatles—seems now as naïve and harmless as nursery rhymes. In the beginning of the '80s, violence was not an indivisible part of American life. Sex and teenage pregnancies were not as "normal," and the society was not as tolerant toward them as now. Relatively innocent marijuana now gave way to crack cocaine, amphetamine, and the so-called ecstasy pills. The proliferation of firearms is now threatening normal life in our cities and towns. In addition, a new, previously unheard of and ugly phenomenon—American terrorism, under the disguise of *patriotism*—has emerged.

Recalling our naïve perception of America, another aspect of American life now seems very strange. Of course, we cannot read all professional journals and magazines having to do with education and culture in general. But in the media accessible to an "average American," to a "man in the street"—without special education—even the slightest attempts to find even tentative explanations to the ills of our society are missing.

A few examples:

- The conservative thesis, "welfare destroys family," was not given a serious discussion, let alone a meticulous sociological investigation. We witness only political bickering. This thesis may be true. But what destroys a non-welfare family? Over 50 percent of marriages break up.

- Is the proliferation of drugs in inner cities a result of poverty, or does poverty follow addiction to drugs?

- Is violence in our society being provoked by the indiscriminate media and the Hollywood, or is they are simply supplying what millions of Americans want to see, hear, or read?

- In 2001, three million American teenagers thought about committing suicide, and one million actually attempted it. According to medical authorities, in most cases the leading cause was depression. In the general population, 20 million Americans also suffer from depression. The use of Prozac and other psychotropic drugs skyrocketed. What is the cause of this "epidemic?" According to medical authorities, "The cause is unknown." Is it possible that the epidemic of depression—among both adults and children—is because "people are nothing to live for?"

- Another "chronic illness" among our children—a younger bunch—is the so-called "attention deficit disorder (ADD)." Children are unable to concentrate—to focus on what is taught at school. No worry—Ritalin will help. And tons of this drug are being consumed by our children today. But what is the cause of this condition? Why was not it known thirty or forty years ago? Is that because now children are raised in the atmosphere of nonstop entertainment or sports games, and preschoolers are never encouraged to quietly concentrate on something creative without jumping and throwing ball?

- America has been shocked when the unbelievable greed of executives from Enron, WorldCom, and dozens of other big and small companies were disclosed. Recently (August, 2003) *US News and World Report,* in its thirty-page

"The Ultimate Consumer Survival Guide," warned Americans of rip-offs waiting for them virtually everywhere. *The Consumer Report* has been warning us how to defend oneself from dishonest business practices for years. Sometimes, it even seems that ours is not a "market economy," but rather an "economy of greed!" And millions of Americans spend their hard-earned dollars gambling, and casinos—disguised or blatantly legitimate—are proliferating. Has it always been that way? Why has money become today the most important stimulus of American life?

When attempting to explain these and other problems, nobody even mentions their possible *existential* cause. And yet, competent and purposeful sociological research could explain many crucial aspects of these problems, as well as many others that haunt our society today. How can we seriously discuss violence, in general, and the rising violence by teenagers, proliferation of drugs (especially among the young), juvenile crime, teenage pregnancies, the epidemic of divorce, or irresponsibility of fathers, if we do not understand the societal forces behind these phenomena?

What is this book about?

As I have already said in the Preface, I do believe there is a common cause behind many problems that our society is facing today. This cause is of a fundamentally existential nature because it affects the very foundation of one's existence. I believe that at the heart of the majority of our problems today is the loss of meaning in the lives of millions people. People are like the blind wandering in the existential darkness or, as Viktor Frankl coins it, *the existential vacuum*. On the individual level, this vacuum takes the form of unbearable boredom—hence the title of my book. In my view, the only remedy that may improve the situation is a dramatic improvement of our educational system—perhaps nothing short of an *educational revolution*.

In no way is the idea original that the loss of meaning in peoples' lives is at the core of our crisis today. As I mentioned in the preface, Viktor Frankl wrote about it decades ago. In spite of the millions of copies of his books sold in this country, there is no discussion in the media of that problem, which is so vital for our society. Moreover, as I have already mentioned in the Preface, even mentioning the existential character of our problems seems to be "un-American" and politically suicidal.

The then First Lady, Hillary Rodham-Clinton said, in one of her speeches in 1993: "A sleeping sickness of the soul is at the root of America's ills." She was mocked by the press as "Saint Hillary." However, the Clintons did not have guts to confront the reality; they missed a unique opportunity to make a difference by launching a discussion of the *core* of our problems. And yet, this discussion is necessary. The present book is my modest contribution—an attempt to steer the discussion of the existential problem—perhaps the most important problem of our society today.

Some readers may accuse me of not having enough credentials or competence to discuss sociological problems. I have never been *trained* in sociology, I am a scientist, a physicist. In this respect, however, I am in a very distinguished company of scientists.

Freeman Dyson, a renowned theoretical physicist, has written a dozen of books having nothing to do with the quantum field theory in which he is an expert. In one of them he offers an "apology for a physicist venturing into biology." Over half a century before, Erwin Schrödinger, one of the fathers of quantum theory, the foundation of contemporary physics and chemistry, wrote: "Some of us should venture to embark on a synthesis of facts and theories, albeit with second-hand and incomplete knowledge of some of them, and at the risk of making fools of themselves."

I am proud to be one of these people.

In the summer of 1977, half a year before my family left Russia, a friend of mine—a prominent Soviet physicist, who had just received an exit visa after years of struggle with the Soviet authorities, after hunger strikes and home arrests—said to me: "Do not idealize the West. Here, in Russia, you cannot speak; there you may cry, but nobody will hear you." I did not believe him then; I still do not believe him now. I hope I will be heard.

MEANING OR PLEASURE?
VIKTOR FRANKL AGAINST SIGMUND FREUD

"I cannot share Freud's opinion as he stated it…: 'The moment a man questions the meaning and value of life he is sick.' I rather think that such a man only proves that he is truly a human being."

—Viktor E. Frankl, Psychotherapy and Existentialism.

To be a prophet—to tell people the truth they would not like to hear—is a difficult job. And yet, throughout the history of mankind, every time had its own prophets. At the dawn of our civilization, the biblical prophets, humble but rugged, dared to challenge both kings and the mob. Too often they were stoned. Today we do not stone the prophets: we simply do not listen to them. Besides, there were so many pseudo-prophets in Earth's history, how does one know this one is *real*?

The truth is that there is no way to know. Biblical times have gone, and we do not believe that today's prophets are God's messengers. They are just people who see beyond the easily seen, and understand beyond the easily understandable. And they do tell the truth we do not like to hear.

Perhaps, Viktor Frankl, the founder of the so-called *Third Viennese School of Psychotherapy*, did not consider himself a prophet. But how else but prophetic would one call Frankl's greatest accomplishment: identifying the "sickness of the century" and showing the ways of treating it?

This sickness is the loss of meaning in people's lives. In one of his books Viktor Frankl writes: "For too long we have been dreaming a dream from which we are now waking up: the dream that if we just improve the socioeconomic situation of people, everything will be okay, people will become happy. The truth is that as the *struggle for survival* has subsided, the question has emerged: *survival for what?* Ever more people today have the means to live, but no meaning to live for" (UCM, p. 21, italics by Frankl).(Abbreviations to references of Viktor Frankl's books are listed at the end of the essay.)

In another book (PAE, p.122) Frankl notes: "What threatens contemporary man is the alleged meaningfulness of his life, or, as I call it, the existential vacuum within him. And when does this vacuum open up, when does this so often-latent vacuum become manifest? In the state of boredom." *Boredom* is the main symptom of our illness. Too often it is *unbearable*.

All segments of our society are afflicted with this state of existential vacuum. Frankl also calls it "frustration of meaning." This is "the sickness of the century"— both the industrialized countries and less affluent societies have been infected with it. In America the crisis is exacerbated by the fact that our education does not help people to overcome the infection, but rather enhances its toll. The growing illicit drug use and crime are the direct consequences of that illness. Our younger generation is the victim who suffers most from the crisis. The feeling of *the loss of meaning* among American students is stronger than in Europe. Frankl writes (MSM, p. 129): "A statistical survey recently revealed that among my European students, 25 percent showed a more-or-less marked degree of existential vacuum. Among my American students it was not 25 percent but 60 percent."

These words, written over 15 years ago, are most probably true today. Unfortunately, I have been unable to find newer statistical data. As for juvenile violence and crime—steadily on the rise in America today—its cause is almost without exception the meaninglessness in the lives of our children.

In fact, the very foundations of the American philosophy of life have been threatened. The American Dream—the dream of affluence and wealth—does not seem to promise happiness anymore. Acquiring wealth does not add meaning to life. Among the drug users there are more who are affluent than poor.

The quintessence of this devastating crisis has been expressed in a statement by International Network on Personal Meaning (http://www.meaning.ca/):

> "In modern society, several forces and trends are converging in creating a crying need for meaning and spirituality. Prosperity without a purpose leads to disillusion and emptiness. Progress without a spiritual direction results in confusion and uncertainty. A winner-take-all economy contributes to conflict and injustice. Violence, conflict, addiction, depression, and suicide reflect an existential crisis. The paradox of prosperity without happiness reflects an unfulfilled spiritual hunger. The intense competition of the new economy results in an increasing gap between the haves and the have-nots."

Frankl's books have been published in dozens of languages. Only in the United States were millions of copies sold. But in America today his name is known only to a handful of professionals, and his ideas are either unknown or disregarded. They have not been given any serious discussion, either on the level of government and policy making, or on the level of *we the people*—the millions who suffer most from that sickness Frankl diagnosed over half a century ago.

And this is in a time when the sickness of meaninglessness has taken on the proportions and scope of an epidemic. To most people, this epidemic is hidden, for it has been developing against the background of more-or-less stable economy.

Paving a way out of our crisis, the existential crisis, would require fundamental social reforms, a radical change in our educational philosophy and educational system in the first place, to which the numerous interest groups would not agree without a fierce struggle. On the other hand, the populist politics of our policy makers, on both sides of the aisle, prevents them from doing anything that *we, the people* would not like. And the therapy that would make the society healthy again may be painful.

This essay is about Viktor Frankl—his life, his ideas and the legacy he has left.

Vienna

"There is only one Vienna"

—*A common phrase in Vienna, c. 1781*

In the second half of the 19th century and the first decade of the 20th, Vienna, the capital of the Austro-Hungarian Empire, was also a second cultural capital of Europe, second only to Paris. It was a cultural Mecca and a center of science.

It was also a powerful economic magnet, attracting numerous immigrants. Among the notable immigrants were composers Johannes Brahms and Gustav Mahler, the founder of Zionism Theodore Herzl, and the great Sigmund Freud.

The decline of the Empire, reaching its nadir after Austria's defeat in World War I, was also the time of triumph and fame of the new school of psychiatry named *psychoanalysis*. In 1920, the 64-year-old Sigmund Freud was the dominant and most authoritative international figure on the scene of psychological science and psychiatry.

Vienna was boiling with multiple ideas, originating from the Freudian revolution in psychology. Not only the university campuses, but also numerous discussion clubs in schools were caught in this process of learning and discussion.

Passionately absorbed by this sea of ideas was young teenage boy named Viktor Frankl. Just 15 in 1920, he still remembered how his family, immigrants from Moravia, was on the edge of starvation, begging for food at the farmers' market. The Frankls could not afford an expensive private school for their son, but in a Volkshochschule (free public school, attended mostly by children of poor people), Viktor was an active speaker in youth and discussion clubs. He writes in his autobiography (RCL): "More and more my speech exercises and school papers became treatises on psychoanalysis. More and more I supplied my schoolmates with information in this field." This was right after Freud had published his epochal work *Beyond the Pleasure Principle*. It was on everybody's tongue.

"I was still in high school," recalls Frankl, "when the wish of my early childhood to become a physician became focused, under the influence of psychoanalysis, on becoming a psychiatrist." Actually, when the time of decision came, Frankl, for a while, "toyed with the idea to turn to dermatology or obstetrics."

Frankl recalls that the final decision—to become a psychiatrist—came after a friend of his, in their argument about the future, quoted from Kierkegaard: "Don't despair at wanting to become your authentic self."

A few years later, as a university medical student, Viktor Frankl was a witness and participant of the battle of psychiatrists in the atmosphere that "made Vienna a city of couches as much as a city of dreams"[1]

Ideologically, psychiatry was not an untroubled and peaceful kingdom. In 1912 Freud expelled from his inner circle—and, as a matter of fact, from his kingdom altogether—his most talented follower, Alfred Adler. Adler later became the founder of *The Second Viennese School of Psychotherapy* (the *First* was the Freudian school).

As a medical student, Frankl began to correspond with Sigmund Freud. "I sent him material which I came across in my extensive interdisciplinary readings and which I assumed might be of interest to him. Every letter was promptly answered by him." As a matter of fact, Freud personally presented Frankl's paper of 1924—his second scientific paper—to the *International Journal of Psychoanalysis*.

In spite of the fact that Frankl's psychoanalysis professors were two exceptional followers of Freud, the young medical student began to drift away from the *canonical* Freudism. He felt that Freud's *Pleasure Principle* was lacking a human dimension, and began developing his own theories that contradicted Freud's *Principle*. He also felt that the whole Freudian philosophy was somewhat nihilistic. This feeling brought him into the Adlerian camp.

---

[1] W. B. Gould, *Frankl: Life With Meaning*. Books/Cole Publishing Company, Pacific Grove, CA 1993

Unlike Freud, Adler saw a person's freedom of choice as a fundamental factor in the decision-making process. This idea became a starting point, and, in fact, a cornerstone in Frankl's own theories. Ironically enough, history repeated itself. Having been expelled by Freud fourteen years before, Adler insisted on Frankl's leaving his circle after the latter openly supported the dissenting view of two Adler's followers.

After graduating from the university, Viktor Frankl became a practicing psychiatrist. He passionately wanted to help people. Apart from taking patients, he spent a lot of time giving lectures and counseling. Since 1927 he had been teaching a weekly class at the adult education school. For many years—until the dreadful day when Frankl, together with his family and thousands of Viennese Jews, was deported to a death camp—he worked at clinics for the poor.

Seeing hundreds of patients and watching the symptoms and development of neuroses, his new approach had crystallized. He even suggested a method of treating some neuroses, the so-called "noögenic neuroses," the ones to do with frustration of man's spirit (noös). Psychoanalysis gave way to a *Meaning Analysis*.

This approach, by 1929, grew into the whole philosophy that revolutionized both psychology as a science and psychiatry as a branch of medicine. Frankl named his new approach, *Logotherapy* (*logos* is Greek for meaning), showing a new way of treating neuroses and, in fact, exposing the origin of the many ills of contemporary society.

In his autobiography (RCL) Frankl writes: "…as a psychiatrist, or rather a psychotherapist, I see beyond the actual weaknesses…I can see beyond the misery of the situation, the possibility to discover a meaning behind it, and thus to turn *an apparently meaningless life into a genuine human achievement.* I am convinced that, in the final analysis, there is no situation, which does not contain the seed of meaning. To a great extent, this conviction is the basis of logotherapy's subject and system" (italics by Frankl).

Frankl's school of thought was later named *The Third Viennese School of Psychotherapy*. In a nutshell, the difference among the three Viennese Schools of Psychotherapy is as follows: the Freudian and Adlerian psychologies are centered respectively on the *Will to Pleasure* and the *Will to Power*. Frankl argues that it is "the striving to find a meaning in life" that "is the primary motivational force in man." Moreover, Frankl claims that "Actually, 'pleasure' is not the goal of human striving but rather a by-product of the fulfillment of such striving; and 'power' is not an end but a means to an end. Thus, the 'pleasure principle' school mistakes a side effect for the goal, while the 'will to power' school mistakes a means for the end" (*ibid.*). However, society gets sick when the two latter *wills* take over: they bring society into a state of *existential vacuum*. That is our situation today.

Here are the *Logotherapy's* central affirmatives (Ref. 1, p. xii):

- "Life has meaning
- We have the will to meaning, our central motivation for living
- We have the freedom to find meaning in how we think and in what we do
- We are mind, body and spirit. These dimensions of the self are interdependent. The key is the spirit (*noös*); it enables us to exercise our will to meaning, to envisage our goals, and to move beyond our instinctual and sexual needs to self-transcendence."

But let us turn back. The year was 1933. The Nazis had just taken over in Germany. But it was still quiet in Austria, although the Nazi party became more and more noisy. Vienna, Austria's capital, was still the capital of world psychology and psychiatry. The great Sigmund Freud was still a ruling emperor. But life had changed. Anti-Semitism was on the rise and the annexation of Austria by Germany (*Anschluss*) seemed imminent.

The world of ideas and aspirations together with all hopes for the future collapsed 12 March 1938, the day of *Anschluss*, when Nazi Germany invaded Austria. Two days later, Sigmund Freud's apartment and his university offices were searched and his passport revoked. With great difficulty and only after the interference of the international scientific community and the American President personally, was the 82-year-old and terminally ill Sigmund Freud allowed to leave Austria.

It was the collapse of Viktor Frankl's world also. Since 1937, Frankl had had his own practice as a specialist in neurology and psychiatry, at the same time continuing to work in hospitals and youth counseling centers. Gradually he became renowned internationally. He was being invited to give lectures at international conferences throughout Europe.

However the future looked grim. Frankl was thinking of emigrating, but was hesitant. He hoped, that as a psychiatrist, he would be able to support his parents, his younger sister and brother and his fiancée. But, he also knew that in spite of his international standing, nobody would be able to defend his family against possible Nazi persecution. Eventually he submitted an application for an immigration visa to the American embassy—a visa he was not destined to use.

That is how Victor Frankl recalls those dramatic events (RCL). "I had to wait for years until my quota number came up that enabled me to get a visa to immigrate to the United States. Finally, shortly before Pearl Harbor, I was asked to come to the US consulate to pick up my visa. Then I hesitated: Should I leave my parents behind? I knew what their fate would be: deportation to a concentration camp. Should I say good-bye and leave them to their fate? The visa was exclusively for me."

When he came home that day he found his father in tears. "The Nazis have burned down the synagogue," said his father, and he showed him a fragment of marble he had salvaged. That piece of marble had just one letter of the Ten Commandments engraved on it, the beginning of the commandment "Honor thy father and thy mother." Frankl called the American embassy and canceled his visa. "It may be that I had made my decision, deep within, long before, and the oracle was in reality only the echo of the voice of my conscience," concludes Frankl.

As a part of the infamous *final solution*—complete extermination of the Jews from the face of the earth—the turn of the Austrian Jews came in 1942. The late Dr. Joseph Fabry, a most distinguished student and disciple of Viktor Frankl in the United States, and the translator of his autobiography into English, wrote[2]: "The deportation of the Jews from Austria was no different from that from other countries, perhaps more severe because of the innate anti-Semitism of many Austrians. Up to 1942 the deportations were somewhat selective and exceptions were made for a certain class of Jews, such as doctors in the Jewish Hospital (Frankl), nurses there ([Frankl's wife] Tilly), or people recruited to help clean up apartments of deported Jews (Tilly's mother), and often their immediate families. From the Wansee Conference on (1942) where the 'final solution' was decided, there were no more exceptions."

The Frankl family was deported to the Theresienstadt camp in July 1942. Almost all the family perished. Frankl's father died in Theresienstadt; his mother was gassed in Auschwitz; his wife Tilly died in Bergen-Belsen after she had been liberated by the British; his younger brother died in a branch camp of Auschwitz, working in a mine; only his sister survived (she managed to emigrate to Australia before the deportation).

Frankl's experience, as a death camp prisoner, was described in his first book written after the liberation. First published in 1946 in Vienna as *Ein Psycholog Erlebt das Konzentrationslager*, it was later translated into many languages and

---

2 Dr. Fabry was also the founder of the *Institute of Logotherapy*—a research and educational institution dedicated to promoting the meaning-oriented methods of Viktor Frankl and his followers. The current Institute's address: Hardin Simmons University, P.O.Box 15211, Abilene, TX 79698. I deeply appreciate Dr. Fabry's assistance: sending me the manuscript of Viktor Frankl's autobiography prior to its publication, and very helpful correspondence (the above quote is from one of Dr. Fabry's letters).

sold in millions of copies. In the English translation it is the most popular Frankl's book: *Man's Search for Meaning* (MSM).

Today, after over half a century of that world tragedy, the *Holocaust*, the tragedy that the human brain simply refuses to comprehend, thousands of accounts of people's first encounter with the Nazi extermination machine are known. And yet, Viktor Frankl's account is special. His is that of a scientist, a medical doctor, a soul healer—almost devoid of emotion but full of sober analysis and meaning.

The generation of Holocaust survivors is gradually leaving this earth, taking with them the agony of their memories. For us, who have never felt what it was to be jammed into a cattle car slowing down at an obscure place named Auschwitz, a semi-mad woman screaming: "Fire, I can see fire" (Elie Wiesel, *Night*), there is only imagination. The gift of conscience that does not allow us to forget, that reminds us how fragile our civilization is and how thin is the layer of our humane culture. Frankl's account is extremely important for all, who are distressed that that layer of humanity in our civilization is so thin. It is a source and a symbol of hope that we, the humans, can be superior beings, can challenge the animal in us, and thus win against all odds.

The train, overloaded with humans about to lose their human identity in exchange for a tattooed number (if lucky enough not to turn into a burst of black smoke in the crematorium chimney); German shepherds and SS men with submachine guns; the selection—those on the right will get their numbers and will live and, at last, will have the real shower and striped *uniform* of the previous owner who does not exist any more. Frankl writes: "While we were waiting for the shower, our nakedness was brought home to us: we really had nothing except our bare bodies—even minus hair; all we possessed, literally was our naked existence. What else remained for us as a material link with our former lives? We knew that we had nothing to lose except our so ridiculously naked lives" (MSM, pp. 33-34).

That is what Frankl writes in his autobiography: "I have never published what happened at the first selection at the Auschwitz train station. I have never published it, simply because I still am not sure whether I perhaps only imagined it. This was the situation: Dr. Mengele turned my shoulders not to the right, that is to the survivors, but to the left, to those destined for the gas chamber. Since I couldn't make out anyone I knew who was sent left, but recognized a few young colleagues who were directed to the right, I walked *behind Dr. Mengele's back* to the right. God knows where the idea came from and how I had the courage." This episode has an almost mystical flavor—as if the mission Viktor Frankl was destined to fulfill had been secured and enforced.

Among the things that Frankl left behind, was the manuscript of his book on the foundations of *Logotherapy*—his first book—hidden in the inner pocket of his coat, of all the material things the dearest to him. During the endless two and a half years of his imprisonment, page by page, chapter by chapter, he reconstructed his book in his memory. This book: *Ärztliche Seelsorge, The Doctor and the Soul: From Psychotherapy to Logotherapy* (DAS) was published after the war, translated into nine languages and in 57 editions.

In the Introduction to the book (p. xv) Frankl writes: "Life is a task. The religious man differs from the apparently irreligious man only by experiencing his existence not simply as a task, but as a mission. That means that he is also aware of the taskmaster, the source of his mission. For thousands of years that source was called God." This feeling of an important mission to be fulfilled, of the responsibility before himself, his family (he did not know that he would never see his parents, brother, and wife again), and his fellow prisoners never left Frankl. This is that mission, that was with him all his life, till the very last breath. Viktor Frankl passed away in Vienna on September 2, 1997.[3]

Auschwitz

"Our generation has come to know man as he really is: the being that has invented the gas chambers of Auschwitz, and also the being who entered those gas chambers upright, the Lord's Prayer or the *Shema Yisrael* on his lips."

—*Viktor E. Frankl, Psychotherapy and Existentialism*

A Freudian man, having been put into conditions of endless suffering and deprivation, would have had to turn into an animal with the lowest possible instincts taking over whatever *civilized* and *humane* qualities had been implanted during the previous life. Often, that was the case in the Nazi concentration camps. People betrayed each other or stole precious food from their comrades, even when that could hasten the unfortunate's death. All the means were good if

---

[3]   On the date of the first anniversary of Dr. Frankl's death, 2 September 1998, I put an essay, based on the present chapter, *Viktor Frankl: The Prophet of Meaning*, on the Internet: www.mit.edu:8001/people/gkrasko/Frankl.html).

they helped to save their own lives. And yet, in his account of the psychology of the concentration camp (*Man's Search for Meaning*, MSM)) Viktor Frankl gives quite a few examples of human behavior that disprove Freud's theory.

They do not, in fact, quite disprove. Those examples rather prove that one can elevate oneself, rise from that abyss of the animal to the heights of the human. "In the concentration camp,…in this living laboratory and on this testing ground, we watched and witnessed some of our comrades behave like swine while others behaved like saints. Man has both potentials within himself; which one is actualized depends on decisions but not on conditions" (p. 157).

In his book, Frankl again and again quotes Nietzsche's words: "He who has a *why* to live for can bear with almost any *how*." If one understands the *why* of one's existence, one will be able to cope with the *how*, no matter how impossible that would seem. Understanding the *why* simply meant that people were able to make sense of, and thus find a meaning in their sufferings, and even probable death.

"It can be said that they were worthy of their sufferings; the way they bore their suffering was a genuine inner achievement. It is this spiritual freedom—which cannot be taken away—that makes life meaningful and purposeful" (p. 87). If, on the other hand, people were unable to take that challenge of turning their lives into an inner triumph; if they believed that life was over, that all the real life opportunities had disappeared for good, then their days were numbered. They vegetated—progressively sliding down toward the imminent end.

"Under the influence of a world which no longer recognized the value of human life and human dignity, which had robbed man of his will and had made him an object to be exterminated (having planned, however, to make use of him first—to the last ounce of his physical resources)—under this influence the personal ego finally suffered a loss of values. If the man in the concentration camp did not struggle against this in a last effort to save his self-respect, he lost the feeling of being an individual, a being with a mind, with inner freedom and personal value" (p.70).

The understanding of the new *why* did not come easily to those people. And any piece of advice was precious. Frankl recalls one of the first lessons given to them—newcomers in Auschwitz—by an already seasoned inmate: "Don't be afraid. Don't fear the selections….But one thing I beg of you…shave daily, even if you have to use a piece of glass to do it…even if you have to give your last piece of bread for it. You will look younger and the scraping will make your cheek ruddier. If you want to stay alive, there is only one way: look fit for work" (p. 38).

Those who were unable to find the inner strength to cope with the *why* were doomed. That victory over inhuman suffering seems almost unbelievable today, over half a century later, when entertainment and pleasure are the most important components of people's lives. But it *was* a real triumph of human spirit, another proof of that which God made of us was *good*.

Everyone who is trying to understand the *why* of our so comfortable and safe life must read Frankl's book—at least those one hundred pages of the concentration camp chapter. In a new school curriculum, I would recommend this book for our teenagers as one of the most important textbooks.

A long column of inmates, the walking skeletons, suffering from hunger, exhaustion and, on top of everything, edema of their legs and feet. Some do not have socks—their frostbitten and chilblain feet are so swollen, that there is no space for socks, even if they had them. Suddenly, the man marching next to Frankl whispers: "If our wives could see us now. I do hope they are better off in their camps and don't know what is happening to us." Frankl continues: "And as we stumbled on for miles, slipping on icy spots, supporting each other time and again, dragging one another up and onward, nothing was said, but we both knew: each of us was thinking of his wife" (p. 56).

Thoughts of their beloved ones were an important part of that "will to meaning" that enabled people to survive. "...for the first time in my life I saw the truth as it is set into songs by so many poets, proclaimed as the final wisdom by so many thinkers. The truth is that love is the ultimate and the highest goal to which man can aspire. Then I grasped the meaning of the greatest secret that human poetry and human thought and belief have to impart: *The salvation of man is through love and in love.* I understood how a man who has nothing left in this world still may know bliss, be it only for a brief moment, in the contemplation of his beloved" (p. 57; italics by Frankl).

In that marching column, and on hundreds of other occasions when Frankl and his comrades were uniting in thoughts with those whom they loved, they did not even know if their loved ones were alive. "I knew only one thing—which I have learned well by now: Love goes very far beyond the physical person of the beloved" (p. 58).

This escape into the past from the emptiness, spiritual poverty and physical suffering of the inmates' existence was possible only due to the enormous intensification of their inner life. Of much greater importance for acquiring a meaning, in comprehending the *why* of one's existence, was one's ability to find both hope and strength in the future—to find a goal to which one could look forward. "The prisoner who had lost faith in the future—his future—was doomed. With his loss of belief in the future, he also lost his spiritual hold; he let himself decline and became subject of mental and physical decay" (p. 95).

Frankl recalls how, in the moments of frustration with the current situation and overwhelmed with thoughts of trivial but important things—like where to find a piece of wire to substitute for a rotten shoe lace—he forced himself into thoughts about his future after the liberation. He saw himself standing under bright lights in a lecture hall, before a friendly audience, and giving a lecture on the psychology of concentration camp. The manuscript of his first book on *Logotherapy*, his new theory and method, had been lost with his coat upon arrival at Auschwitz. At the very first opportunity, he began reconstructing the manuscript. He writes in his autobiography: "In my own mind, I am convinced that I owe my survival, among other things, to my resolve to reconstruct my manuscript. I started to work on it when I was sick with typhus and tried to keep awake, even at night, to prevent a vascular collapse. For my 40th birthday an inmate had given me a pencil stub and 'organized' a few small SS-forms. On their empty backs, still having high fever, I scribbled shorthand notes which I hoped would help me reconstruct the *Ärztliche Seelsorge.*"

For a concentration camp inmate, to lose faith in the future was a tragedy, resulting in death. That happened quite suddenly, in the form of a crisis. Its symptoms were familiar to the inmates, and its consequences were unavoidable. People knew "who was going to be the next."

By the end of war, the loss of faith in the future took an almost mystical form. Frankl recalls that a friend of his—a fairly well-known composer and librettist—told him in February 1945, that he had had a dream in which a voice had told him the exact date of their liberation: March 30th. At that time the man was still full of hope, and believed that the prophecy was true. The promised day approached, but no signs of imminent liberation were seen. On March 29th, he developed a high fever. On the day of the prophecy, March 30th, he became delirious and lost consciousness. Next day he was dead. To Frankl and to the camp doctor, there was no doubt he had died of typhus.

"To those who know how close the connection is between the state of mind of a man—his courage and hope, or lack of them—and the state of immunity of his body, will understand that the sudden loss of hope and courage can have a deadly effect. The ultimate cause of my friend's death was that the expected liberation did not come and he was severely disappointed. This suddenly lowered his body's resistance against the latent typhus infection. His faith in the future and his will to live had become paralyzed and his body fell victim to illness—and thus the voice of his dream was right after all" (p. 97).

That case of an unexplained death was not a unique event. Between Christmas 1944, and New Year of 1945, the death rate in Frankl's camp increased beyond all possible expectations, and that was against the background of no visible deterioration of either working or living conditions in the camp. "It was simply, that the majority of the prisoners had lived in the naïve hope that they would be home again by Christmas. As the time drew near and there was no encouraging news, the prisoners lost courage, and disappointment overcame them. This had a dangerous influence on their powers of resistance and a great number of them died" (p.97).

Both the *past* and the *future* of the prisoner were instrumental in his or her survival in a concentration camp. What about the *present?* The present was filled with suffering, both physical and spiritual. But for someone who had already acquired the strength and inner freedom, even that dreadful present became full of meaning.

Perhaps some of the prisoners who had been religious in their previous lives lost faith. But in those who had not lost the faith, or had even just acquired faith in the camp, religious feelings were "the most sincere imaginable."

"The depth and vigor of religious belief often surprised and moved a new arrival. Most impressive in this connection were improvised prayers or services in the corner of a hut, or in the darkness of the locked cattle truck in which we were brought back from a distant work site, tired, hungry and frozen in our ragged clothing" (p. 54).

Art existed in the camps. Tired, hungry and frozen people composed music, drew pictures, wrote poetry. There were even makeshift concerts, with good music, songs and even humor.

Against all odds, the aesthetic feeling—the ability to see the beautiful in nature—had not disappeared. An exhausted man might draw the attention of a friend working next to him to a view of the setting sun through the trees of a winter forest. Frankl recalls: "One evening, when we were already resting on the floor of our hut, dead tired, soup bowls in hand, a fellow prisoner rushed in and asked us to run to the assembly grounds and see the wonderful sunset. Standing outside we saw sinister clouds glowing in the west and the whole sky alive with clouds of ever-changing shapes and colors, from steel blue to blood red. The desolate gray mud huts provided a sharp contrast, while the puddles on the muddy ground reflected the glowing sky. Then, after minutes of moving silence, one prisoner said to another, 'How beautiful the world *could* be.'"(pp. 59-60; italics by Frankl).

But perhaps the most important feature of the *present* in the inhuman conditions of the concentration camp was the feeling of *responsibility* that was so strong in the inmates who had not lost their inner freedom—responsibility for their own future, for their beloved ones, and for their fellow prisoners. The camp authorities issued new regulations: death for even any petty violations of the regime that could be interpreted as sabotage. A few days before, a semi-starving prisoner had stolen a few pounds of potatoes. Many prisoners knew who the "burglar" was. The authorities threatened that if the guilty man was not given up, the whole camp would starve for a day. "Naturally, 2,500 men preferred to fast." It was not quite natural in those conditions. Just imagine, there was not a single man who decided to betray his comrade, although a reward—some benefits—perhaps extra food or easier work could have made a difference in the life-death race.

Frankl writes (UCM, p. 52): "Sigmund Freud once said, 'Let us attempt to expose a number of most diverse people uniformly to hunger. With the increase of the imperative urge of hunger all individual differences will blur, and in their stead will appear the uniform expression of the one unstilled urge.' In the concentration camps, however, the reverse was true. People became more diverse. The beast was unmasked—and so was the saint. The hunger was the same but people were different. In truth, calories do not count."

And, of course, the strong helped the weak. On quite a few occasions Frankl himself tried to do his utmost to strengthen his comrades' resistance to the physical and moral decay and degeneration that the camp existence promulgated: from unobtrusive conversations to collective psychotherapeutic (in fact, *Logotherapeutic*) sessions, at the outcome of which people thanked him with tears in their eyes (MSM, pp. 103-105).

Although Frankl modestly notices that "…only too rarely had I the inner strength to make contact with my companions in suffering and that I must have missed many opportunities for doing so" (p. 105), he was doubtlessly one of those who "…walked through the huts comforting others, giving away the last piece of bread. They may have been few in number, but they offer sufficient proof that everything can be taken from a man but one thing: the last of the human freedoms—to choose one's attitude in any given set of circumstances, to chose one's own way" (p. 86).

In order to prove that something is *not,* one has to prove that every possible example of that something is not. While, if one wants to prove that something *is,* just one example would be enough. Viktor Frankl's account of his experience as a concentration camp prisoner gives these examples, and not just one, but many. The examples of people whose will to meaning was stronger than death.

Meaning

"…there is a meaning in life…it is available to everyone and, even more…life retains its meaning under any conditions. It remains meaningful literally up to its last moment, up to one's last breath."

—*Viktor E. Frankl, The Unheard Cry for Meaning*

Meaning. What is it? In his autobiography (RCL) Frankl writes: "As early as 1929 I developed the concept of three groups of values, three possibilities to find meaning in life—up to the last moment, the last breath. These three possibilities are: 1) a deed we do, a work we create, 2) an experience, a human encounter and love, and 3) when confronted with an unchangeable fate (such as an incurable disease, an inoperable cancer) a change of attitudes. In such cases we still can wrest meaning from life by becoming witness of the most human of all human capacities: the ability to turn suffering into human triumph."

These three *sources* of meaning seem to be so simple and easy to understand. However, a meaning cannot be learned or taught or shared. As a matter of fact, there is no such a thing as a universal meaning for everyone. Meaning is always personal, *the* meaning. Frankl writes: "In other words, life gives the person an assignment, and one has to learn what that assignment is. But what is important...the true meaning of life is to be discovered in the world rather than within man or his own psyche, as if it were a closed system" (MSM, p. 133).

Frankl stresses that finding a meaning in life inevitably requires what he calls *self-transcendence*—rising above one's own self. "Being human always points, and is directed, to something, or someone, other than oneself—be it a meaning to fulfill or another human being to encounter...The more one forgets himself—by giving himself to a cause to serve, or another person to love—the more human he is and the more he actualizes himself."

In another book (PES, p. 24) Frankl writes: "What man is, he ultimately becomes through the cause, which he has made his own."

A reader may ask, "OK, it is all declarations, slogans. But how does one acquire that *meaning*?"

Joseph Fabry devoted his book *Guideposts to Meaning* [4] to the difficult task of step-by-step guiding the reader toward understanding what really matters in one's life. Joseph Fabry suggests that one should involve oneself in *Socratic dialogues*—the dialogues inside oneself—that would facilitate finding the meaning. Five guideposts should be probed in the areas where the meaning is most likely to be found. These areas are:

> "1. Self-discovery. The more you find out about your real self behind all the masks you put on for self-protection, the more meaning you will discover.
>
> 2. Choice. The more choices you see in your situation, the more meaning will become available.

---

[4] J. Fabry, *Guideposts to Meaning: Discovering What Really Matters* Institute of Logotherapy Press, 1988.

3. Uniqueness. You will be most likely to find meaning in situations where you are not easily replaced by someone else.

4. Responsibility. Your life will be meaningful if you learn to take responsibility where you have freedom of choice, and if you learn not to feel responsible, where you face an unalterable fate.

5. Self-transcendence. Meaning comes to you when you reach beyond your egocentricity toward others" (p. 10).

And yet, there is no easy and ready prescription for everyone. Frankl's advice: listen carefully to what your life requires of you. Listen to your conscience. Think. Be patient; do not hurry. One day you will know. But this may be a long and difficult road till you have reached your destination.

> "By its very nature this ultimate meaning exceeds man's limited intellectual capacity. In contrast to those existential writers who declare that man has to stand the ultimate absurdity of being human, it is my contention that man has to stand only his incapacity to grasp the ultimate meaning on intellectual grounds. Man is only called upon to decide between the alternatives of 'ultimate absurdity or ultimate meaning' on existential grounds, through the mode of existence which he chooses. In the 'How' of existence, I would say, lies the answer to the question for its 'Why.' Thus, the ultimate meaning is no longer a matter of intellectual cognition but the existential commitment. One might as well say that a meaning can be understood but that the ultimate meaning must be interpreted" (PAS, p. 46).

Work We Create

We spend over a third of our time working. To most people, a job is a necessary and unavoidable way of earning one's living. Americans work hard. If you wish, it is an American tradition to work hard. It began first with the colonists and then was taken over by the generations of immigrants who came to America in search of a new and better life. The American Dream of affluence and wealth has been driving millions of people to work hard.

At the beginning of the 21st century, working hard, for most people, does not mean merely fighting for survival any more. The American middle class has emerged; the majority of Americans live in their own homes. Even the American "poor" are believed to be "the richest poor in the world." In spite of accusations fired at each other by politicians, the living standard of an average American family is higher than that in Europe, although it is steadily going down.

Americans are still working hard, even more than before, but their work has lost the original existential meaning of necessary effort for survival. In the beginning of the 21st century, the principal aim of hours upon hours of work (today full-time working Americans work on average 47 hours a week) is either sustaining rather high material standards of living, or simply making money for its own sake. Americans still believe that any work is good that brings in money—and the more the better. But this belief is no longer valid. It has been destroyed by the boredom of a dull, unfulfilling job. And yet not many understand that a job is only *good* if it is *fulfilling*. In addition, jobs have become more and more difficult to find—for jobs require an educational level that most people do not have, and losing a job becomes a tragedy. But this boredom does not originate from the jobs themselves. It is a result of our attitude.

Logotherapy claims that work, a process that takes so much time from our life, may be a source of meaning, direction and fulfillment. For many, it's an important source of meaning; for some the only source.

The job becomes that well of meaning and fulfillment if it is *creative*. The word itself means creating something new that did not exist before—not only in the sense of revolutionizing technologies, discovering new principles in science, or creating an art masterpiece—but most often just participating in a modest and unambitious process of gaining knowledge, trust, kindness, love. This quality is of a fundamentally subjective character. The job does not contain creativity in itself. A white-color job can be boring, and a job of volunteer helping kids to cross the street, fulfilling and exciting. The one who is doing the work can make it *unique*—creative and interesting or dull and boring. It is only a matter of attitude.

In 1979-80 I spent a year in Germany doing research at a university. Every day, at about 5 p.m., I heard a knock on my office door and an elderly lady janitor entered with a broad smile and a "Guten Abend, Herr Professor." Then she began her daily routine: cleaning my office. She knew that her job was extremely important, for without it, we, the *eggheads* of the fifth floor, would perish in the dirt and disorder of our offices. She lifted every single sheet of paper on my desk and dusted beneath. Whatever papers were scattered around were carefully piled up and secured on the desk corner. I did not speak German, she did not speak English, but we both knew that what she was doing was *important*. Of course I could live without the daily dusting of my papers; she could not. And I agreed with her. From the existential point of view we—the *eggheads* in the offices around, and herself— were equal: we each did the work we loved and believed to be important. And, whenever a party was held, she was always a part of it: a loved and respected member of the fifth floor community.

For a work to be creative, one does not need a high IQ or be highly educated. One has only to find *the meaning* in the work; make it a part of one's personality. The only role education plays in this process is facilitating the finding of this unique meaning. One's horizons are wider, one's understanding of the world is better, one's identification with society is deeper through education.

The role of education is important. I do firmly believe that one of the factors that have exacerbated our crisis, is the degradation of our educational system. It simply has been failing to raise a person above the level of immaturity. And *maturity* means meaningfulness. That is why a way out of the crisis—quite possibly the only way—is in a dramatic improvement in our educational system.

Today, creative fulfilling work is the destiny of only the few. To the rest, work is an unpleasant and boring duty. Fifty million Americans *hate* their jobs. Perhaps the most regretful aspect of our life is that we teach our children that a boring job is all right. We encourage them to start working as early as possible, learning how to make money being the only purpose. In 1991, five million teenagers were working. I wonder whether anybody knows how many our working children are among those fifty million job haters.

However, even a boring job has an important quality—it fills (or, rather, kills) time. When even this dull and boring work is over (and the work may be difficult, requiring the concentration of both mental and physical energy) a person feels lost. Frankl, in one of his books, describes a "Sunday neuroses"—people do not know how to *kill* time. (Now, with a five- rather than a six-day working week, Frankl would speak of a "weekend neuroses.") Typically, people have two options: shopping and the reliable and never failing TV. The new, high-tech options— computer games and surfing the Internet—become more and more addictive. Frankl writes (DAS, p. 127): "…people who know no goal in life are running the course of life at the highest possible speed so that they will not notice the aimlessness of it. They are at the same time trying to run away from themselves—but in vain. On Sunday, when the frantic race pauses for twenty-four hours, all the aimlessness, meaninglessness, and emptiness of their existence rises up before them once more."

Of course, there are jobs that are very difficult to make creative. Among them, the jobs requiring monotonous repetition of a similar operation, such as a job at a conveyer belt. With the development of new computerized technologies and robotics, these jobs will gradually disappear, giving people virtually unlimited opportunities to realize their innate creativity. This, however, will require an educational level which, unfortunately, the American school today does not give.

With the advancement in technology, the amount of leisure time is increasing. This is both a curse and a blessing: It is a curse if an individual has not discovered a *mission* in his or her life. Then any means of killing that leisure time will be good, from meaningless TV watching, computer games and Internet surfing to gambling and drugs. It will be a blessing if a mission *does* exist. Then it will require the concentration of one's abilities, and will demand more time than the individual can normally afford. No time will be enough. A good education will give an individual the basis—the foundation—for the future meaningful and happy life.

Human Encounter and Love

The basis—the core of a meaningful life—is one's *singularity*—one's *uniqueness*. But one can actualize the creative values of one's personality only through the external world—through something done *for* people. In response, the world—the *community*—rewards the individual's uniqueness and singularity with *meaning*. In fact, the external world becomes an indispensable part of one's personality.

It enters one's personality in two ways: through the *impersonal* effect of nature, books, music, art and culture, in general (recall the role of these factors in strengthening the will to survive in the Nazi concentration camps), and through encounters with people.

Martin Buber, one of the most distinguished Jewish religious philosophers, once said: "Behind every meeting, every encounter—responsibility."

To those who agree with Buber, there is only one answer to the question "Am I my brother's keeper?"—spewed by Cain in self-defense: "Yes, I am the keeper of my brothers—all over the world."

The fact that most people do not think that way does not mean the idea of *global responsibility* is idealistic delirium and nonsense. Thousands upon thousands of young men and women, in 1936-37, left their families and jobs and joined the International Brigades in Spain to fight fascism. Too often, those brave people were accused of being Communists. Not all of them were. George Orwell, the author of the immortal *1984*, who hated all kinds of totalitarianism, fought in Spain. His book, *Homage to Catalina*, is a legacy of those years. Then, the world was indifferent, but those people knew that Spain was just the beginning.

They were right. The Second World War erupted just a couple of years later. After Pearl Harbor, thousands upon thousands of young Americans volunteered for the armed forces to fight the Nazis, although they could have gone on with their studies or with civilian work important for the military. Two decades later, thousands upon thousands of Americans of the next generation joined the Peace Corps to fight disease and illiteracy in the Third World.

In the everyday life of most people, the idea of *global responsibility*—even if the individual does subscribe to it—is pushed aside by small deeds and smaller responsibilities. And it is all right as far as the responsibilities exist. But too often the feeling of responsibility—in encounters with people—is frustrated. It is only partly to be blamed on the individual. Erich Fromm, one of the greatest psychologists of the 20th century, writes in his immortal book *The Art of Loving*[5]: "From birth to death, from Monday to Monday, from morning to evening—all activities are routinized, and prefabricated. How should a man caught in this net of routine not forget that he is a man, a unique individual, one who is given only this one chance of living, with hopes and disappointments, with sorrow and fear, with the longing for love and the dread of the nothing and of separateness?" (p. 14)

This is exactly the *existential vacuum* that Viktor Frankl discusses in his books. But it is up to the individual to escape from this vacuum into the freedom of meaning. Then "the nothing" and "the separateness" will disappear, giving way to constructive and creative encounters with people, with their "hopes and disappointments, sorrow and fear."

Love, the main object and concern of Erich Fromm's book, is something that cannot be compared in its importance to any other existential category in human life, except, perhaps death. It has been the object of discussion and analysis of the greatest philosophers and scientists since the human race has distinguished itself from the animal horde. Poetry is almost exclusively about love.

The great Sigmund Freud attempted to reduce love to elementary instincts originating from the "pleasure principle." Viktor Frankl returned to love its *human, existential* character.

Discussing the meaning of love, Frankl writes (DAS, p. 135): "Loving represents a coming to a relationship with another as a spiritual being. The close connection with spiritual aspects of the partner is the ultimate attainable form of partnership. The lover is no longer aroused in his own physical being, nor stirred in his own emotionality, but moved to the depths of his spiritual core, moved by the partner's spiritual core. Love, then, is an entering into direct relationship with the personality of the beloved, with the beloved's uniqueness and singularity."

---

5   Erich Fromm, *The Art of Loving*. Bantam Books, 1963

Frankl stresses that, although love is as primary a phenomenon as sex, normally sex is only a mode of expression for love. "Sex is justified, even sanctified, as soon as, but only as long as, it is a vehicle of love. Thus love is not understood as a mere side effect of sex: rather, sex is a way of expressing the experience of the ultimate togetherness which is called love" (MSM, p. 134).

On the societal level, this confusion inevitably brings about a devaluation of sex: "Like any kind of inflation—e.g., that on the monetary market—sexual inflation is associated with a devaluation: sex is devaluated inasmuch as it is dehumanized. Thus we observe a trend to living a sexual life that is not integrated into one's personal life, but rather is lived out for the sake of pleasure. Such a depersonalization of sex is a symptom of existential frustration: the frustration of man's search for meaning" (USM, p. 93).

The confusion of sex for love in the psyche of millions of people, resulting in the degradation of love and proliferation of sex, both in America, and in all the industrialized societies, is doubtless a manifestation of the frustration of meaning and the deep existential crisis. I also discuss this problem at length in other essays in this book.

The Unchangeable Fate

In his book *Psychotherapy and Existentialism* (PAE) Viktor Frankl writes: "We have seen that there exists not only a will to pleasure and a will to power but also a will to meaning. Now we see further: We have not only the possibility of giving a meaning to our life by creative acts and beyond that by the experience of Truth, Beauty, and Kindness, of Nature, Culture, and human beings in their uniqueness and individuality, and of love; we have not only the possibility of making life meaningful by creating and loving, but also by suffering—so that when we can no longer change our fate by action, what matters is the right attitude towards fate."

This third avenue to meaning is perhaps the most important one. Too often we forget that suffering is an unavoidable and ineradicable part of human life. Without it, life could not be complete. Suffering—albeit in unequal degrees—accompanies us through all our lives, eventually terminating in death. Finding meaning in suffering is not as much the ability to cope with suffering and not letting it destroy oneself, but the possibility of *"rising above oneself,"* *"growing beyond oneself,"* and thus *"changing oneself."*

In *Man's Search for Meaning* (MSM, p. 88) Frankl writes: "Here lies a chance for a man either to make use or to forgo the opportunities of attaining the moral values that a difficult situation may afford him. And this decides whether he is worthy of his sufferings or not." And a few pages over: "When a man finds that it is his destiny to suffer, he will have to accept his suffering as his task; his single and unique task. He will have to acknowledge the fact that even in suffering he is unique and alone in the universe. No one can relieve him of his suffering or suffer in his place. His unique opportunity lies in the way in which he bears his burden" (p. 99). Frankl proves that a human being "may turn a personal tragedy into a triumph."

The Nazi concentration camps witnessed thousands of examples of such human triumph that a Freudian man with his *will to pleasure* is incapable of. Our everyday life also gives us examples of this unbreakable will to meaning. Among them is the professor of Cambridge University and perhaps the most distinguished theoretical physicist of our time, Dr. Stephen Hawking—a victim of Lou Gehrig's disease, almost completely paralyzed, and unable to speak (a computer helps him communicate).

Stephen Hawking's mother, Isobel Hawking writes[6]: "He says himself that he wouldn't have got where he is if he hadn't been ill. And I think it is quite possible"

America is proud of Helen Keller. However, not many remember another name—that of her teacher, Anne Sullivan. Helen was able to overcome her handicaps—she was blind, deaf and mute—to become an author and one of the most cultured people of her time. Her teacher Anne Sullivan was not handicapped, but she made the tremendously difficult, seemingly impossible task of turning a frightened and angry little animal, seven-year-old Helen, into a *human being*—that became her mission. That mission filled all Anne Sullivan's life and became her only objective. This is an almost mystical example of a person who "had grown above herself," who made the life of another human being more important than that of her own.

Another hero—also the one America will always be proud of—is its great President Franklin Delano Roosevelt, whose imprint on this country's destiny simply cannot be overestimated. A disabled man—a tragic victim of polio that struck when his political career was only beginning—he, by nonhuman willpower, was able to turn his disability into the most powerful stimulus of his life. Smiling broadly—as he always did—when he, with the help of a bodyguard or one of his sons,—*walked* toward the podium, most of the nation did not know

---

6 *Stephen Hawking's A Brief History of Time: A Reader's Companion.* Bantam Books, 1992, p. 110.

that he actually *was unable* to walk. It was an imitation, a pretense forced by FDR's enormous physical and moral strength.

I will never forget seeing a blind man skiing on a downhill slope in New Hampshire (with an assistant skiing before him with a sign: "Attention, a blind person skiing"), or a smiling and excited young woman with paralyzed legs, being helped by two volunteers in loading her sledge to a ski lift on Mt. Attitash; later I saw her "skiing" down a difficult slope. I am proud to belong to the same species as those two people and many thousands of others, who have won over their disability and turned tragedy into a human triumph.

The list of people, who have turned their suffering into human triumph is long, and each of them deserves a monument in the pantheon of humankind. The examples above were just names from the books and magazines scattered on my desk while I was writing this essay.

While inhuman ordeals of extreme handicap is the fate of relatively few, the everyday sufferings of millions are the reality of *normal* life. In his books, Frankl gives quite a few examples of how people can "rise above themselves" and "grow beyond themselves." He also shows how the ideas of *Logotherapy*—the school of thought and psychotherapy he had developed—can help people understand the *why* of their suffering and thus give them the *how*, which enables them to cope with that *why*—from personal tragedy of the loss of a beloved, to the tragedy of a prison inmate whose life seems to be over.

Frankl relates his conversation with a patient—a physician who could not overcome the loss of his wife whom he loved above everything in the world. Two years had passed since the death, but the patient's depression would not subside. Here is the conversation:

F.: "What would have happened, Doctor, if you had died first, and your wife would have had to survive you?"

P.: "Oh, for her this would have been terrible; how she would have suffered."

F.: "You see, Doctor, such a suffering has been spared of her, and it was you who have spared her this suffering—to be sure, at the price that now you have to survive and mourn her."

Frankl concludes: "He said no word but shook my hand and calmly left my office. In some way, suffering ceases to be suffering at the moment it finds a meaning, such as the meaning of sacrifice" (MSM, p. 135).

In his book, *The Unheard Cry for Meaning* (UCM), Frankl also quotes two letters from inmates of American (Florida) prisons: "I have found true meaning in my existence even here, in prison. I find purpose in my life, and this time I have left is just a short wait for the opportunity to do better and to do more." Another letter: "During the past several months a group of inmates has been sharing your books and your tapes. Yes, one of the greatest meanings we can be privileged to experience is suffering. I have just begun to live, and what a glorious feeling it is. I am constantly humbled by the tears of my brothers in our group when they can see that they are even now achieving meanings they never thought possible. The changes are truly miraculous. Lives which heretofore have been hopeless and helpless now have meaning.... From the barbed wire and chimney of Auschwitz rises the sun...My, what a new day must be in store" (p. 47).

Homo Patiens

The urge to have a meaning in one's life, the *will to meaning*, is an indispensable quality of a "*homo patiens*"—the term coined by Frankl—"the suffering man, the man who knows how to suffer, how to mold even his sufferings into a human achievement." Frankl. writes (UCM, p. 46): "Usually, man is seen as the *Homo sapiens*, the clever man who has know-how, who knows how to be a success, how to be a successful businessman or a successful playboy, that is, how to be successful in making money or in making love. The Homo sapiens moves between the positive extreme of success and its negative counterpart, failure."

However, there is another dimension to human life. The *homo patiens* moves on an axis perpendicular to that of the *Homo sapiens*. It extends between the poles of fulfillment ("plus") and despair ("minus"). The fulfillment of one's self through the fulfillment of meaning and the despair over the apparent meaninglessness of one's life.

This visual interpretation of our existential stand (see the diagram below) is very helpful in understanding real-life situations. A wealthy individual who has achieved complete success in his or her life may find himself or herself in the extreme negative on the *homo patiens* scale, if his or her life is devoid of meaning and direction. It may be not only a rock-, movie-, or athletic star, but also a successful medical doctor or a lawyer, or even an elected official.

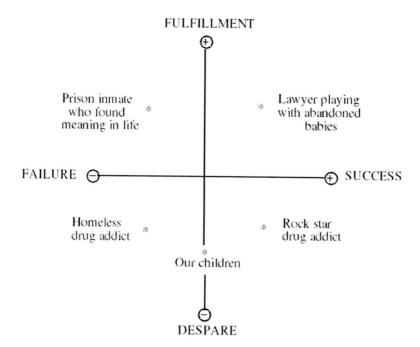

On the other hand, a modest individual who can hardly exist on a meager salary or a pension—and is, of course, far from achieving *success* from the point of view accepted in our society, perhaps is even a *loser*—may be fully content and happy doing his or her work that is *unique* and *important*—as did my modest janitor, nameless hospital volunteers, people giving their time to charity. An extreme case is, of course, a prison inmate who can find a new meaning in his or her suffering.

The upper right-hand corner of Frankl's diagram is not empty either. I have read of a successful lawyer who found time in his busy schedule to help out in the maternity ward of a hospital. They needed "human hands"—just to lull babies abandoned by their mothers, in order that they might feel a "mother's warmth."

In 1995, a story made headlines in the Boston press. A factory owner who, after his factory had been destroyed by fire, continued paying salaries to his workers until the factory began functioning again. Thousands of prominent leaders of industry, culture and sports selflessly give their money and their time to projects, making life on earth better.

The lower left-hand corner of the diagram is occupied by the underclass: people who were unable to achieve either material success or meaning in their lives.

If we suppose that our younger generation—our children—are *neutral* with respect to success-failure in society ("zero" on the *Homo sapiens* axis), most of them occupy the *homo patiens* axis well below, in the negative. Their lives are empty and devoid of meaning. They are abandoned by our society. They drift, creating their own ugly "culture," and nobody is out there to help them.

Happiness…

It is always difficult to talk about the fundamental *existential* problems. They are too personal and intimate. We rarely discuss them even with people who are close to us. In our everyday life there is not much time when, left alone with our own soul, we can ask ourselves: "Where am I? What am I? What do I live for?" And yet, it is important to go on asking these questions again and again, even if only to prevent our souls from "falling asleep."

We do not talk much about meaning. Somehow it is believed to be an abstract category that does not make much sense. But we do talk a lot about *happiness*. The American Declaration of Independence proclaims *pursuit of happiness* as one of the unalienable rights of human beings, together with the right to life and liberty. To most of us, pursuit of happiness is one of the most important aims of life.

However, as Frankl has convincingly shown in his many books, happiness is evasive. Happiness is a by-product of meaning. It cannot be pursued; it must be attained. Frankl writes (MSUM): "Happiness—is the side effect of living out the self-transcendence of existence. Once one has served a cause or is involved in loving another human being, happiness occurs by itself. It is the very pursuit of happiness that thwarts happiness. The more one makes happiness an aim, the more he misses the aim."

For a skeptical reader who still thinks that what Frankl is saying is just an abstract philosophy, which is difficult, if not impossible, to implement in everyday life, I would like to quote from an article published sometime in the middle '80s in a Boston North Shore newspaper. In my files I found one page—a photocopy of just some fifty lines (two short columns) from that article.

I do not know what newspaper it was published in. The author's name is also missing. But I am deeply grateful to that person for what he or she wrote, and I regret that I do not know the name and am unable to personally express my gratitude to that person. That article was important to me at that time. When I read it, I did not know of either Viktor Frankl or *Logotherapy*. Perhaps, the article's author did not know either. But that article is an excellent and thoughtful interpretation of Frankl's ideas. Let me reproduce here the whole text as I have it on that photocopied page:

"In the television series *Late Night America*, I learned from experts that only twenty percent of Americans are happy, which prompted me, during the last year, to talk about happiness with psychiatrists, psychologists, educators, religious leaders and many other successful Americans. All agree that happiness comes to us as a direct result of high self-esteem, a positive attitude, and the way in which we relate to other people. It's not as complicated as we make it out to be. But happiness may be different from what we think it is.

Happiness, I have learned, is a feeling of contentment and peace of mind. Life is a mixed bag of joy and sadness, laughter and tears, pain and growth. Happy people accept the whole package, realizing that happiness is only a part of life's puzzle.

Unfortunately, too many Americans have swallowed a bill of goods which states that happiness can be achieved 24 hours a day and will be found in success, fame, possessions, and marrying or having a relationship with the right person.

I've discovered that to be happy we must have something to do, someone or something to love, and something to hope for. Our work must give us a sense of pride and satisfaction, use of our special talents and abilities, and provide us with the opportunity for recognition and contribution. If we work only for money at a job we hate, we deny ourselves the chance to be happy.

To be happy we must live for something outside ourselves—another person or people, a cause, a belief in God. To live only for ourselves is to exist in a world of one—and that brings misery. To be happy we must have hope, which is our commitment of time and energy to the future. We need to dream. To have no dream is to have no hope, and to have no hope is to have no reason to live."

The above may be, in essence, summarized as a formula of ultimate happiness. This is also the Frankl formula. Like any mathematical formula, which does not make sense unless some numbers are put into it, the formula of ultimate happiness, in order to work, requires the actions of a whole life. It is simple:

Live a life that multiplies good, so that when you are about to leave, the Earth is better—even though just a little bit—than it was when you came to this world, and this because of the life you have lived. If, though only once in your life, you saw tears of gratitude in the eyes of a stranger who you may never see again, the formula worked.

Years ago, after a lecture at an American university, a student asked Viktor Frankl: "You talk so much about meaning. But what is the meaning in *your* life?"

"What do you think the meaning in my life is?" Frankl addressed a student standing next to him.

"I believe the meaning in your life is to help people find meaning in theirs," was the answer.

And I would like to finish this essay with the words of Viktor Frankl (DAS, p. 139): "We must never be content with what has already been achieved. Life never ceases to put new questions to us, never permits us to come to rest. Only self-narcotization keeps us insensible to the eternal pricks with which life with its endless succession of demands stings our conscience. The man who stands still is passed by; the man who is smugly contented loses himself. Neither in creating nor experiencing may we rest content with achievement; every day, every hour makes deeds necessary and new experiences possible."

References to Viktor Frankl's books:

MSM: Viktor E. Frankl, *Man's Search for Meaning*, Washington Square Press, New York, 1985

UCM: Viktor E. Frankl, *The Unheard Cry for Meaning: Psychotherapy and Humanism, Washington* Square Press, New York, 1985

PAE: Viktor E. Frankl, *Psychotherapy and Existentialism*, Washington Square Press, New York, 1985,

DAS: Viktor E. Frankl, *The Doctor and the Soul: From Psychotherapy to Logotherapy*, Vintage Books, New York, 1973

RCL: Viktor E. Frankl, *Recollections: An Autobiography* (English translation by Joseph and Judith Fabry), Plenum Publishing House in London, 1997

MCUM: Viktor E. Frankl, *Man's Search for Ultimate Meaning*, Insight Books, New York, 1997

TRAINING OR EDUCATION?
AMERICA'S CULTURAL DILEMMA

"…ours is the only educational system in the world, vital segments of which have fallen into hands of people who joyfully and militantly proclaim their hostility to intellect"

—*Richard Hofstadter, Anti-Intellectualism in American Life*

Our education system is sick. No secrets about it. Dozens of books and, perhaps, hundreds upon hundreds of articles in journals, magazines, and newspapers suggest treatments to our sick education. Now it is on all the wavelengths. It is *urgent*.

As a matter of fact, the problem has been urgent for quite a while. Over twenty years ago (1983), the report of the National Commission on Excellence in Education, *A Nation at Risk*, disclosed the shameful state of our education. One sentence was extremely striking: "If an unfriendly foreign power had attempted to impose on America the mediocre educational performance that exists today, we might well have viewed it as an act of war."

Since then, not much has happened or changed. The very recent years, however, have seen an increased activity among school reformers. Obviously, the educational establishment has felt that we cannot procrastinate any longer.

Why is this problem so urgent? We are told that if our educational system undergoes no fundamental changes, in ten years most of high school graduates will not find jobs in spite of the fact that the economy will desperately need workers. This is simply because the high school graduates will be unqualified to fill the jobs the economy will require.

Apart from the already "mature" industries like computer software and hardware and telecommunications, among the "youngsters" are artificial intelligence, robotics and, of course, biomedical technology. The industries of the future—virtually without exception—will be high-tech intensive.

Most of the jobs in today's industries (especially in those still quite young), already require a college education. Today's high school graduate, with virtually no general education or even basic knowledge of contemporary mathematics, physics, chemistry and biology, cannot think of getting even the lowest-paying job, other than that in a packaging department. And in ten to fifteen years, those jobs will disappear, having been taken over by robots. Even the jobs in the predominantly low-tech service industry are becoming increasingly more demanding, requiring high levels of computer literacy.

> As statistics show, it is not just the skills in concrete fields of knowledge that today's students are lacking. They are lacking something much more important—the ability to be responsible and to communicate with people. Tragically, they also do not comprehend their deficiencies. The figures below show a dramatic gap in the opinions of high school seniors in comparison with those of their potential employers on whether the students are "very well" prepared in various job skills (the first figure is the students' evaluation of themselves; the second, the employers' evaluation): ability to work in diverse groups (66 percent-13 percent); oral communications (57 percent-9 percent); written communications (45 percent-6 percent); ability to meet deadlines (62 percent-8 percent); basic math skills (62 percent-8 percent); basic computer skills (28 percent-14 percent).[1] Even in the field of computers, where the students are less arrogant, the situation is still quite hopeless. In a radio interview, the owner of a small computer business said that out of 100 applicants for a job, he had hired two, but only one was able to work as the job required. Is it because playing computer games is fundamentally different from understanding and be able to learn programming?

Thus, we are told, in order to secure future jobs for our children and to sustain and enhance the ability of our economy to compete in the international market, we must dramatically improve teaching our children the necessary practical *skills*. This is the objective of education as seen today, not only by our educational establishment but by most Americans throughout the social and economic strata, from the bottom to the very top.

In 1989, in one of his first addresses as Vice President, Dan Quayle, speaking to an audience of young people said that they should study *in order to get better jobs*. This concept—that education's sole purpose is giving a person the necessary

---

[1] *USA Today*, 26 June 1997, quoting from the findings by Roper Starch Worldwide, Inc.

set of skills to be able to find a good job—is believed, in America, to be an absolute truth. However, it is *wrong*.

When we speak of education, we, almost inevitably, use the word *training*. One was trained as a technician; one was trained as a manager; one was trained as a chemist, one was trained as a poet, one was trained as a pianist, one was trained as a medical doctor, and on and on, and on.

Actually, using the term *trained*, rather than *educated*, when referring to what and how it is taught in America, is, in most cases, right. Because what in this country is called *education* has, in fact, been *training*.

The Dilemma

That confusion—and unfortunately not only on the level of word meaning— has come so far that people have simply forgotten the difference between these two concepts. However, one can open any dictionary to see what the difference is.

The *Webster's New International Dictionary of the English Language*, Second Edition, G. & C. Merriam Company Publishers, Springfield, Mass., USA, 1958, explicitly stressed, in a note, the difference I am focusing on. Symptomatically, this note is absent from the *Webster's Third New International Dictionary of the English Language*, same publishers, 1994.

Here are the definitions:

> TRAIN: "to make proficient by instruction and practice, as in some art, profession or work, to develop or form the habits, thoughts or behavior; to give the discipline and instruction, drill, practice, for example, designed to impart proficiency; to teach so as to make fit, qualified, or proficient."

> EDUCATE: "to develop and cultivate mentally, morally or aesthetically; to expand, strengthen, and discipline, as the mind, a faculty, for example"

The difference between these two concepts is striking. Education brings understanding of the world we live in. It tells us who we are, where we have come from, and where we are heading. It helps us understand ourselves; helps us to identify our place as individuals among other people. Education makes us intellectually and morally strong. It fills our souls with meaning. It helps us to develop the ultimate treasure of our personalities: *maturity*.

Education allows us to deal with novel and complicated situations. The variables we can ultimately understand and handle may be almost infinite. And our understanding should range from the most concrete to the most abstract. For example, the educated person can thoughtfully discuss the natural or physical world, the social world, or the spiritual world. The educated person can range the universe and construct questions appropriate to a member of a civilized society. The educated person can and should "rock the boat" in a democratic society and see that it remains democratic. An educated person does not elevate the trivial to a position of importance, and does not trivialize what really matters.

As for training, it only helps us to acquire the necessary skills to find and do a job, but does not help a tiny bit either to identify our place in our culture or to understand who we are personally, or even to find the fortitude to do our job well in difficult times.

We confuse information with knowledge. Training does provide one with new *information*; however *knowledge* can be obtained only through education. And yet, Americans believe in training. It seems that in our country all that anyone needs to get along is a training—and not only professional training, but also all kind of "social skill-building" training, including "self-esteem boosting skills," "relationship skills," for example.

But *why* do we humans need something more than just having a good paying job?

A "Three-Dimensional" Human

According to Viktor Frankl, a human being lives simultaneously in three dimensions: bodily, mental, and spiritual[2]. The first two dimensions are obvious. We have bodies, and we have minds. Animals also have them. As for the third dimension, it often has a religious connotation, but Frankl stresses that "spiritual" in this concept refers only to the dimension that distinguishes humans from the other living world. "Spiritual is what makes human beings human."

Borderlines between the mental and spiritual dimensions are somewhat fuzzy. Animals have a lot of "mental" capacities. Most of what we call "being smart"— knowledge or a gut feeling of how to do something—is still within the *mental* dimension. However, the imagination, the ability to think in abstract terms and

---

[2]   See, e.g., Viktor E. Frankl, *The Doctor and the Soul*, Vintage Books, New York, 1965, p. x.

solve abstract problems, and the ability to make moral choices, are already a part of the *spiritual.* Self-consciousness, the ability to judge our own behavior and analyze our thoughts and, ultimately, what we call *conscience* are the important parts of that dimension.

In order to survive in this world, one obviously has to be able to "navigate" through these three dimensions. When a baby is born, he or she has only *potential* abilities of acquiring the navigational *skills.* These skills must be developed and do gradually develop with time.

The *bodily* dimension is the lowest on the cognitive scale. Here, a human being is not different from an animal. A baby will learn how to walk, run, and use its body for multiple purposes, even without any influence from human society.

For developing *mental* abilities, a society is already necessary. Children abandoned or completely neglected for a long time are unable even to speak. Their ability to think concisely is also severely impaired. This handicap may become irreversible. Kipling's *Mawgli* is, of course, just a brilliant fiction.

The development of *spiritual* dimension requires special and very intense efforts. As I mentioned above, these efforts, although directed to an individual, require active participation of the whole society. And they must be *thoughtful* efforts.

What I am actually saying is that each of the three dimensions requires its own "education." And, of course, a *right* educational system should provide for an adequate development of people's abilities to navigate through all three dimensions.

Now, how does our school accomplish this difficult task? Apart from the "unconditional" and "natural" development of the body, a special training in sports is necessary for both improving body function and sustaining a healthy metabolism Even this is not being provided in our schools. We only have to observe the increasing obesity among American children to illustrate that we can't deal with the least complicated of these dimensions.

For some twist of semantics, developing body is called "physical education," although it has nothing to do with the true education whatsoever. In spite of the failure by our schools to help a child develop a strong and healthy body, sports are the most loved in this country by children and parents. In commercials everyday we see boys catching footballs, with happy parents at the background (girls are usually hugging moms!), and never a girl or a boy reading a book! Sport is the most desirable and widespread extra-curricular activity of our children. More and more often we hear about "soccer moms," and never about "library moms!"

Physical education virtually does not require any *spiritual* or even simple *mental* effort. It requires, however, persistence and willingness to compete and win. Nobody would probably deny that this is important. And yet, the latter qualities are of relatively low intellectual and spiritual value. In our reality, however, being proficient in sports is often one of the most important prerogatives of being accepted to a university, and being able to navigate through it without significant intellectual efforts and, very often, virtually free financially.

It is easy to see that what is called *education* in this country, and is, actually, just *training*, is directed only at developing our children's *mental* abilities. Almost nothing has been done to help children develop a strong *spiritual* core of their personalities.

But, as badly as we do in these first two dimensions: bodily and mental, we do even more poorly in the third dimention, since we do not approach the spirit at all. Almost nothing is done to help children develop the strong intellectual, spiritual core of their personalities.

No doubt, a good training directed at building skills is needed. It helps people to find a place in society. One acquires a profession—a role in society's financial and social hierarchy. However, important as they are, the skills acquired during all the years at school and even college, do not help a tiny bit to survive the *existential vacuum*, which, in our post-industrial, post-modern, information-avalanched, high-tech society, inevitably engulfs one's life if one is lacking a strong spiritual foundation.

On the other hand, real education fundamentally deals with the person's deep spiritual core. An individual can survive solitary confinement or a death camp or a debilitating illness, and still be happy and fulfilled, and even create masterpieces of science or art out of incessant sustenance from the individual's spiritual core.

The high spiritual level of a human being may not necessarily correlate with his or her job, wealth, or social status, although it can make any endeavor more easily achievable. But it is necessary. Because, in a human society, *every member* must have human qualities, not merely those of automatons or computers. Most of all, a healthy democracy is impossible unless people's intellects and spirits are at a level well above the level of their jobs. Raising people's culture to that level is impossible without true education.

Let me stress again: the skills that we want our children (and then adults) to master have almost nothing to do with their souls, their human spirit.

If what I am saying is true—and in this book I present quite a few striking examples of that—it is simply mind-boggling. Just think, ours is the educational system that completely (at best, almost completely) neglects spiritual development of our children. For over a hundred years—generation after generation—our educational system has been sentencing American society to life of spiritual poverty, with almost no chance for parole.

We have reduced human beings to the lowest common denominator—the body and sexuality. Our entire society operates against a background of self-indulgence and vicious propaganda of sex and violence in virtually all spheres of human life.

Should we not stop to ask ourselves why the f-word has become an indispensable part of our literature and art, and our language in general; why our culture is so violent and, especially, why "all of a sudden" violence took over our children?

We do not care if the children (and later adults) feel any attachment to the civilization that has been built for over three thousand years on the shoulders of hundreds of generations of people desperately wanting to know what a human being is, where we came from and where we are heading.

If we cared, the so-called "popular culture"—poisonous, ugly and destructive—would not be what it is today. If we cared, children (and adults) would want to know more about the physical world we live in. They simply do not care. Our scientific ignorance is beyond any comparisons.

If we cared, children (and adults) would want to know more about themselves, their souls, and their lives. Today they do not care.

If we cared, children (and adults) would read a lot. Reading would be an important and necessary mode of their lives rather than just a source of entertainment or emotional excitement.

If we cared children (and adults) would not use drugs, and would not even attempt to "experiment" with them. Their lives would not be boring, sometimes unbearably boring.

Below I will address the important question of when and how our problems all began, but now I would like to return to our "education" reality.

Educating About...

Against the background of an almost total absence of *spiritual* education that develops personality, *education about* is the main mode of "education" in our society today.

A huge blunder permeates not only our education, but also our society at large. I mentioned it already: we confuse *information* with *knowledge*. Knowledge is impossible without information. But in order for information to become *knowledge*, the appropriate information must be first transformed by our cognitive mechanisms into something that will fit our intellectual level, our previous experiences, and our ability to comprehend, in general.

Americans believe that our children *must* have access to the Internet as early as possible. Millions upon millions of dollars are being spent to provide every classroom with computers. American presidents endorse and praise this strategy. However, not saving our children from and even throwing them into this information jungle may be the worst—the most irresponsible thing that we adults do to our younger generation. Our children are unable to consume most of the information they receive over the Internet; some of it is harmful to their souls; some of it is bluntly criminal.

Actually, an adult on the Internet is not very much different from a child. Most of the information is either useless or dangerous or harmful, especially if one's ability to navigate the spiritual dimension is underdeveloped. But the Internet exists. It is like a genie offering to fulfill a wish. One may only hope that one really understands the wishes one wants fulfilled.

Most of us believe that what we need is information. This is what the *education about* is about. This is what most of trainings or "refreshing trainings" are directed toward.

Now, this is the world of adults. Since we feel a lack of *knowledge*—the important nutrition for our souls—and there is no *true* education that could supply us with knowledge from the early age on (Americans do not even know if such an education may exist or exists anywhere)—we firmly believe that this deficiency can be compensated for by *training*. As soon as there is a demand, there is a supply.

It is rather difficult to estimate the amount of money private citizens, commercial companies, and the government spend every year paying for this or that training. Of course, I do not mean technical training in fields such as safety, security, property accountability, or computers. This kind of training is necessary and justified. However, even training directed at "improving managerial skills" is already questionable. Today, training courses and books directed at improving self-confidence, boosting intimate relations, improving sexual performance, for example, are in enormous demand. *Amazon.com* responds to the request of books on "self improvement" with 78,300 titles! (and this is without the key word "sex!"). People who buy these books and attend these courses (or listen to them on tapes in the privacy of their cars), usually feel a lack of maturity and a kind of deficiency typical of underdeveloped personalities.

It is doubtful that one can be *taught* how to respect his or her partner, or how to discuss family problems calmly and constructively without a fight. But people expect that some sort of training will fill this gap.

Two quite "innocent" examples: An ad promises that you will speak a foreign language "like a diplomat" if you buy a taped foreign language course and follow all the instructions. Nobody tells you, however, that to speak a foreign language like a diplomat is possible only if you have already read at least as many books in that foreign language as has the diplomat with whom you are going to compete. What about your vocabulary in your native English? Another course promises to dramatically improve your mastery of English so you will soon be "speaking like a Harvard graduate" However, this is, again, impossible unless one reads—and reads a lot—of good, serious literature. There is simply no "free lunch" when culture and maturity are the issues.

A few more examples, this time more serious. The host of a talk show comments on communications between spouses: "People do not know how to talk with each other. They simply have not been taught." Another discussion on teenage mothers: "Someone has to teach them how to be mothers—they do not know." An article in *US News and World Report,* titled, "Marriage Proposal" (March 11, 2002) presented interesting facts regarding attempts in Oklahoma to decrease the enormous divorce rate. There, an initiative had been funded for "relationship-skills education for welfare recipients." Obviously, officials in Oklahoma believe that (quote) "marriage is a skills-based relationship, and these skills are teachable."

As was noted in the above-quoted article, the Oklahoma program "hasn't shown much progress yet, but it has gained at least one admirer: President Bush who last week presented a plan to spend $300 million to promote marriage." And here is the truism that, in the president's view, justified this expenditure: "Strong marriage and stable families are incredibly good for children." Would not it be much better for children if that money were spend on educational needs?

Of course, one can be instructed not to yell at each other or not to abuse little ones, but it is naive to believe that such training will teach people responsibility, empathy, and compassion. Here again, even professionals dealing with important social issues honestly believe that a short training may be a substitute for the long and painful process of maturing.

Respecting each other or being a good and caring parent cannot be taught, just as, during a one-hour training session, a male chauvinist cannot be taught to respect a woman, or a bigot to respect a minority colleague. And yet, government periodically pays for training its employees in the "prevention of sexual harassment" or "understanding diversity" (meaning diversity in race, culture, sexual behavior and culture in general). The 1996 revelation of sex abuse in the army shocked America. What was the reaction of government? Apart from reprimanding and punishing the guilty, it was to provide "extra training in ethics and values." It looks quite obvious, but not to those administering and financing expensive training sessions, that respect of cultural and racial diversity comes only with maturity and as a result of serious and true education and development of personality.

Once, during my long commute, I listened for a few hours to tapes of such a course on enhancing self-esteem. The authors suggested, apart from some ideological recipes, a kind of *auto-training*: closing your eyes, completely relaxing, breathing deeply, for example. This could or could not work. But I was struck by something quite unexpected in a "psychology-based" course. According to the tape, if you follow all the instructions and, as a result, have your self-esteem and self-confidence strongly enhanced, then you will never have problems finding a parking space. Imagine! You go shopping on Saturday morning, and your supermarket's parking lot is overfilled. If you really have a strong will and self-confidence, then, when you arrive at the parking lot, *there will be* a car just leaving to give you a space. Of course, this example is ridiculous. But most of the instruction courses do typically promise something that the majority of people will never achieve, although, again, they will most probably blame themselves for the failure.

The invincibility of the industry invites all kinds of impostors. I also happened to listen to a tape on "love and intimacy in relationships," by a former alcohol and drug abuser. His background was an obvious plus, since he could share his experience and *educate about* important problems. It contained very uncouth, strongly slangy language, and simplistic thoughts—as if Erich Fromm's *The Art of Loving* had never been written.

I do not know if there are any statistics on the success or failure of all those courses having to do with cultural or personality problems. These data are very difficult to obtain, and that is what makes the industry providing such training practically invincible. People who attend (or listen to) these courses feel distressed and, too often, even depressed, and would probably blame themselves, rather than the meaningless course for any failure to achieve improvement in their standing *vis-à-vis* their problems. This is exactly the situation described by the great Hans Christian Andersen in his immortal parable *The Emperor's New Clothes*.

What is much more serious and may have really grave consequences is that we apply the same strategy when dealing with our children and adolescents. We Americans believe that in order for the youngsters to be less aggressive, we have to teach them some "conflict resolution" methods. Just explain to children that violence is bad, that they have to negotiate and respect each other's opinions, and the problem will be solved. It seems so easy.

Of course, we *must* explain to children that violence is bad, that they should respect each other, and that experimenting with drugs is dangerous. Unfortunately, even if the children listen to us rather than succumb to peer pressure, which would probably push them in the opposite direction, it is unlikely that our exhorting a "magic incantation" will make our children civil, responsible and unscathed by the counterculture of their peers. And yet, we *do* expect that these naive measures will solve serious existential problems, for we do not see these problems as *existential* in the first place.

Teenagers experiment with alcohol and drugs. Just explain to them that drinking and sniffing glue are harmful. Sex is everywhere? Train children in "safe sex." We believe that "sex education" has to begin as early as possible. A highly positioned health official in the Reagan Administration even suggested that fifth-graders must be instructed on how to use condoms while involved in anal sex. It would seem that we are completely ignorant as to how much of an explanation children actually need and are able to comprehend; how much and what information their brains are able to transform into knowledge.

I want to share an old joke with you. A boy returns from his first Boy Scout meeting, and asks his father, "Daddy, what is abort?"

Father decides that what his son means is "abortion," and therefore it is better that he himself explains this touchy subject, rather than somebody else. So he, in great detail, explains what he knows, including the *Roe v. Wade*. And then he asks, "But why did you ask?"

The boy answers, "When we all gathered, the Boy Scout leader said, 'Welcome aboard.'"

And, of course, the sex education in our schools is but a sort of training—a set of instructions to follow. In order for girls not to get pregnant, instruct them in the physiology of a woman and how children are conceived and, of course, teach them to "just say *no.*" In order to avoid AIDS, instruct the boys in how to use condoms (also in anal sex).

An alternative to these *preventive instructions* is preaching abstinence. Preaching abstinence to youngsters, whose bodies are waking up and in whose blood hormones are raging, is simply naïve. It is as naive as preaching abstinence to drug users. The "Just Say No" campaigns, in both cases, have been proven to have low success in spite of their high costs. Of course, something must be done about proliferation of sex among our teenagers, but it is not an easy problem, and we even seem not to understand how to approach it. We are just doing what we have been doing in looking for solutions to most of our problems. And it is what a drunken man who has lost his wallet is doing—looking for it under a street-light, not where he has lost it.

The bitter truth is, however, that the whole so-called "sex education" in our schools is misguided at any age, particularly if the teenagers are not mature enough to understand the role of sex in society and everybody's life on a fundamental level, not just on the level of a few hours of instructions (with giggles and blushes) and their miniscule experiences. And this is against the background of unrestricted and sometimes simply vicious sex propaganda in virtually all spheres of our society. Just watch MTV or look into magazines directly addressed to adolescents, *YM* or *Seventeen*, for example.

What is far worse is that our "sex education" is devoid of *any* moral judgment or position. It is your body, experiment with it. Want pleasure and fun? Sex is OK, just be careful not to get pregnant or contract a disease. Of course, the moral relativism in sex training is not accidental; it is a cornerstone of our whole *postmodern* educational ideology and mass culture devoid of any spiritual content.

Once again, I want to stress my point. Our educators *must* talk with children a lot about the dangers of violence, drugs, and sex, as much as of the moral criteria of children's behavior. However, only a thoughtful true *education* directed at developing personalities and building up a strong spiritual core—not utilitarian information-transferring training—will gradually help our children to acquire maturity, and with it, a strong character based on responsibility and moral values.

When people say, "Our schools do not teach moral values," most people do believe that some classes in "moral values" should and must be provided. Again, the answer is that although classes on moral values are doubtlessly necessary, acquiring moral values must be tightly interwoven with the whole educational process. No matter what is taught—literature, history, and even science—the teacher must have a strong moral position. That position must be an implicit part of the knowledge the teacher wants children to absorb.

Acquiring moral values is an integral part of the process of bringing up children from the earliest childhood. If children do not have these values as an essential part of their personality, something is wrong with their family and society as a whole. Due to the infamous *conflict of generations*, there is a good chance that children from families who treasure both "family traditions" and spirituality in life, in general, will refuse to accept these treasures. Instead, they join a "reference group" of directionless teenagers lacking meaning in their lives. Under this nihilistic fire, the role of school as the bearer and enforcer of moral values is extremely important, but not on the level of "training in values."

A Bit of History

It is time now to turn to history. How and when did it happen? When did our true education disappear? Did America ever have it anyway?

If a reader wants to get a concise picture of the history of American education, I recommend a brilliant article by Boston University professor Paul Gagnon, *What Should Children Read?*[3] This article is an eye-opener and very shocking. An "unprepared" reader will be astonished to learn that the problems of our education are not a result of some "screw-ups" or tricks of demographics, but are the direct results of the implementation of an educational ideology that was born in America in the 19th century, but has been rejected in other developed countries many decades ago. We are still sticking to it, and it brings us deeper and deeper to the abyss of intellectual, spiritual, and cultural inadequacy.

One can find a broader and very detailed picture of how we happen to get where we are now in an excellent book by Diane Ravitch, *Left Back: A Century of Failed School Reforms* (Simon & Schuster, 2000).

A lot has been written about the failure of our education. As a matter of fact, a kind of war is—and has been for years—raging between the supporters and opponents of the "true" (usually called "traditional") education. This "war," however, involves mostly university professors. Our general public, who does not read those books, is completely unaware of the problem. The media brings up to the surface only primitive solutions and judgments devoid of serious analysis and responsibility. As for our schools, they are impenetrable fortresses of that ideology.

Actually, quite a few books by the opponents of the existing educational system have been written in the '80s and '90s. Among them, the books by Virginia University professor E.D.Hirsh, Jr.: *Cultural Literacy: What Every American Needs to Know* (Vintage Books, 1988) and *The Schools We Need and Why We Don't Have Them* (Anchor Books, 1999). Dr. Hirsh is also a founder and editor of *The Core Knowledge* series. I would like also to mention the seminal book by the University of Chicago professor Allan Bloom, *The Closing of the American Mind: How Higher Education Has Failed Democracy and Impoverished the Souls of Today's Students* (Simon & Schuster, 1987). The list of authors who contributed to the thoughtful and comprehensive critique of our failed educational system is long. I only want to mention one more of them—perhaps I should have put this name at the head of my list. This is one of the greatest political historians of the 20th century, the late Dr. Richard

---

[3]   *The Atlantic Monthly*, December 1995.

Hofstadter, whose 1964 Pulitzer Prize-winning book, *Anti-Intellectualism in American Life,* [4]did, in fact, explain the origin of our disaster.

However, let us return to our history lesson. When I was pondering over this essay I felt quite proud. "I seem to have understood what the most fundamental problem of our education is, and I will impress my reader with how smart I am." The only missing link in my logical thinking was the understanding of when all this began (probably in the '60s, due to the Baby Boom, the lack of good teachers and the rise of political radicalism?). To me, a newcomer, this was quite a vital issue. I also felt very uncomfortable, rather like an impostor, writing about something that I had never experienced in my life, and therefore did not have any "gut" feelings about—so important for any researcher.

My euphoria vanished, giving way to a deep depression when I found in my mailbox the December 1995, issue of the *Atlantic Monthly*. The above-mentioned Paul Gagnon's article, *What Should Children Read?* was both a shock and an eye-opener to me, who, in my "previous" life had worshiped American education. I learned that the problem I "had discovered" already existed in America, and was recognized as such, over 100 years ago.

At that time, nobody discussed the educational problems in "existential" terms. But thoughtful educators did understand that strong general education—they called it "academic education"—that develops a spiritual core in man, is necessary irrespective of one's profession, walk of life or social status. Dr. Gagnon writes: "The idea that a democratic education requires a rigorously academic core for every student is not new. The report of the illustrious Committee of Ten, published in 1894, forcefully articulated it, calling for the established academic curriculum for all high school students, *whether or not they were going to college*" (p.68; italics by P. Gagnon).

For a more detailed picture of the defeat of "the Ten" and the triumph of the ideas of so-called *Progressive education* that were fatal for the national standards movement at that time and, in fact, had the disastrous consequences for the future of education in America—we are suffering from these consequences today, and they became only worse with time—Dr. Gagnon directs the reader to Richard Hofstadter's book I just mentioned.

First of all, the dilemma: *Training* vs *Education* may be introduced from a slightly different aspect and, I would say, on a more fundamental level, as an *intelligence* vs. *intellect* dilemma. This aspect is important, for it helps us understand why America's educational establishment has been against broad academic education for over a century.

---

4   Richard Hofstadter, *Anti-Intellectualism in American Life*, Vintage Books, New York, 1963.

America is no exception. Virtually in all "civilized" countries there is and always has been a deep disrespect toward people of intellect. In America, it has acquired a special meaning, and has resulted in most dramatic consequences, because anti-intellectualism has infected the whole educational system.

John Dewey, one of the founders and apostles of *Progressive education*, wrote in the preface to his *Characters and Facts* (1929): "If we once start thinking, no one can guarantee what will be the outcome, except that many objects, ends and institutions will be surely doomed. Every thinker puts some portion of an apparently stable world in peril, and no one can wholly predict what will emerge in its place."

Now, what are the definitions of these two "antagonists"? (R. Hofstadter, p. 25; quotations below are from this book, unless stated otherwise.)

> INTELLIGENCE "is an excellence of mind that is employed within a fairly narrow, immediate, and predictable range; it is a manipulative, adjustive, unfailingly practical quality...Intelligence works within the framework of limited but clearly stated goals, and may be quick to shear away questions of thought that do not seem to help in reaching them. Finally, it is of such universal use that it can daily be seen at work and admired alike by simple or complex minds."

> INTELLECT "is the critical, creative, and contemplative side of mind. Whereas intelligence seeks to grasp, manipulate, reorder, adjust, intellect examines, ponders, wonders, theorizes, criticizes, imagines. Intelligence will seize the immediate meaning in a situation and evaluates it. Intellect evaluates evaluations, and looks for the meanings of situations as a whole. Intelligence can be praised as a quality in animals; intellect, being a unique manifestation of human dignity, is both praised and assailed as a quality of men."

One can see that Viktor Frankl's *mental* dimension is the realm of *intelligence*, while *intellect* is an indispensable part of man's *spiritual* core.

The above definitions of intelligence and intellect also exactly correspond to Webster's definitions of training and education. This new aspect of the educational dilemma enables one to understand the evolution (or rather, the decline) of American education as a logical development of definite ideas, rather than a result of changing social conditions, political cataclysms, or just screw-ups.

Where was the origin of these ideas? Dr. Hofstadter writes: "During the nineteenth century when business criteria dominated American culture almost without challenge, and when most business and professional men attained eminence without much formal education, academic schooling was often said to be useless. It was assumed that schooling existed not to cultivate certain distinctive qualities of mind but to make personal advancement possible. For this purpose, an immediate engagement with the practical tasks of life was held to be more usefully educative, whereas intellectual and cultural pursuits were called unworldly, unmasculine and impractical…This skepticism about formally cultivated intellect lived into the twentieth century" (p. 34).

Unfortunately, this is 100 percent true today, as well, at the beginning of the 21st century. America was one of the first in the world to organize a common school system—"education for everybody," and yet, Dr. Hofstadter writes (p. 301): "Americans would create a common-school system, but would not balk at giving it adequate support. They would stand close to the vanguard among the countries of the world in the attempt to diffuse knowledge among the people, and then engage drifters and misfits as teachers and offer them the wages of draymen."

Since pragmatism was the cornerstone of American educational ideas, this type of low-quality education has become deeply rooted into American life. In America's honor, there were always, among educators, daring men and women fighting the mediocrity of their colleagues, irrespective of their ideological standing. R. Hofstadter gives an impressive chronology of those efforts—all, as we now know, pitilessly defeated. The fight began well before the *Progressive* era.

1826: State of Massachusetts, first in the development of a common-school system. Educational reformer James Gordon Carter warns that "if the legislation did not change its policies, the common schools would be extinct within twenty years" (p. 302).

1837: Secretary of Massachusetts Board of Education writes a report in which he exposes the blatant neglect of public education. He writes, among other things: "The schools have retrograded within the last generation or half generation in regard to orthography…more than eleven-twelfths of all the children in the reading class in our schools do not understand the words they read…neglectful school committees, incompetent teachers, and an indifferent public, may go on degrading each other" (p. 302).

Today, over a century and a half later, our schools are not much better: "Large proportions, perhaps more than half of our elementary, middle, and high school students are unable to demonstrate competency in challenging subject matter in English, mathematics, science, history, and geography. Further, even fewer appear to be able to use their minds well"[5]

1870: William Franklin Phelps, head of a normal school in Winona, Minnesota, and later the president of the National Education Association wrote that the elementary schools "are mainly in the hands of ignorant, unskilled teachers. The children are fed upon the mere husks of knowledge. They leave school for the broad theater of life without discipline; without mental power or moral stamina…Hundreds of our American schools are little less than undisciplined juvenile mobs" (p. 303). Is this not also true today, over 130 years later?

The system definitely needed improvement. Gradually, what was later called *Progressive Reform Movement* began its activity. On the surface, it really looked very "progressive." It called for improvement of education quality and focus on the individual child. At the same time, the reformers viewed subject-centered education as the main evil. Children are not empty vessels into which knowledge should be poured, they claimed. Rather, the child must be allowed to "flow" according to the internal compass and innate and natural urge for knowledge. Unfortunately, the resistance of thoughtful and responsible educators, as we shall see below, was unable to change the course of American education.

1893: The National Education Association's *Committee of Ten* (already mentioned above), under the chairmanship of Charles William Eliot, President of Harvard University, recommended the secondary schools have "as a minimum, four years of English, four years of foreign language, three years of history, three years of mathematics, and three years of science." The Committee, in its recommendations, insisted that the proposed curriculum in no way was a preparation for college education. They stressed that even if only an insignificant percentage of high school graduates should go on to colleges, "every subject which is taught at all in a secondary school should be taught in the same way and to the same extent to every pupil so long as he pursues it, no matter what the probable destination of the pupil may be or at what point his education is to cease"(p. 330-331).. The majority of schools did not accept these recommendations.

1902. Nine years later: A complaint in the *New York Sun*: "When we were boys, boys had to do a little work in school…Spelling, writing and arithmetic

---

[5]   National Assessment of Educational Progress, 1990; quoted in: William J. Bennett, *The Index of Leading Cultural Indicators: Facts and Figures on the State of American Society*, 1994, p. 89.

were not electives, and you had to learn. In these more fortunate times, elementary education has become in many places a vaudeville show. The child must be kept amused, and learns what he pleases. Many sage teachers scorn the old-fashioned rudiments, and it seems to be regarded as between a misfortune and a crime for a child to learn to read" (p. 303).

1908. National Education Association—already strong and influential—adopted a resolution rejecting outright any claim that public schools should prepare their students for colleges (Committee of Ten also rejected that notion.). Instead, the resolution urged that the public high school "be adapted to general needs, both intellectual and industrial, of their students." Moreover, it suggested that the colleges and universities should follow the same suit (p. 333).

1911. A new committee of the National Education Association: the *Committee of Nine on the Articulation of High School and College.* Noted scholars and experts in education who were leading the Committee of Ten now gave way to school administrators and bureaucrats. Not a single authority on any subject matter was on the Committee. The objective of the public high school, the Committee argued "was to lay the foundations of good citizenship and to help in the wise choice of a vocation." And further, "An organic conception of education demands the early introduction of training for individual usefulness, thereby blending the liberal and the vocational…"

I may stop quoting from history at this point. By 1918, the American public schools were completely "reformed" and "liberated" from any ideas and practices having to do with broad academic education.

Not coincidentally, at that very time—in 1915—John Dewey's major work, *School of Tomorrow,* was published, and in 1919 the *Progressive Education Association* was founded. It had taken the movement almost thirty years before its vague ideas were eventually clearly formulated in the Dewey's book. By the early '20s the *Progressive movement* began making an impact, and in no time completely took over American education. The history of the 20th century is a sad manifestation of what a wrong educational idea can do to the greatest nation in the world.

Progressivism

Just a few words on the movement's educational philosophy. When one reads numerous articles and essays written by *Progressive* philosophers and educators, one can get a completely distorted impression. (Just, for curiosity's sake, search the Internet. You will find dozens of articles.) One may feel as if *Progressive* education has liberated America from elitism and the educational deprivation of the poor. The articles' authors are also proud of these achievements and see the proliferation of the computer and its appeal to the individual child as a new tool for completing the educational revolution (another controversial idea whose implementation, as I already mentioned, may cost America dearly).

I have chosen, however, to present a more objective and unbiased view by an education historian and scholar. I am quoting from: George F. Kneller's article, "Contemporary Educational Theories."[6] Here are the *Progressive* education's maxims:

- The whole educational process is "child-centered." The process of teaching and learning is determined not so much by the teacher or the subject matter as by the individual child.

- The teacher's role is not to direct but to advise, because the child's own needs and desires determine what the child learns.

- No absolute value or goal is acknowledged, unless it is social progress attained through individual freedom. The school must reinterpret the basic values of Western civilization in the light of scientific knowledge now at our disposal.

- Knowledge is a tool for acquiring experience in handling the various and changing situations in society.

- Children learn properly only when they can relate what has been learned to their own interests.

One of the practical consequences of the above ideology is that "subject-based" education is being rejected. It is believed to be unproductive, besides, while studying "subjects," the connection to child's "social experience" is completely lost. In stead, education must be "issue-based."

---

[6] *Foundations of Education* (edited by George F. Kneller), John Willey & Sons, 1967, pp. 99-105, 113.

Well, it is, of course, impossible to completely get rid of "subjects." You can get rid of geography simply by ignoring it. In fact, it is extremely difficult to attach any "social" or even "practical" meaning to geography. A travel agent—to say nothing of a cab driver—always knows where the city you want to go is..

You can teach the history of ancient Greece and Rome within the framework of "social studies" rather than a specific history course. In fact, it is very convenient, because then it is easy to discuss slavery and make an important connection to America or the Civil War, for example, in a completely "politically correct" way.

With the science subjects it is more difficult. It is impossible to give any social interpretation to Newton's laws. Their practical values are also questionable (unless, of, course, one acknowledges that hitting one's head against a car's windshield upon braking is not a matter of "bad lack" but just a manifestation of Newton's second law.) Therefore, *physics* (or *chemistry* for that matter) may appear in a high school curriculum but only as *elective* courses.

But is it really necessary that children study *subjects*? What if the *Progressives* are right, and studying "abstract" subjects unconnected to everyday practical "issues" is not necessary, and even harmful for children's self-esteem and feelings in general? Perhaps a layman would not answer this question. However, psychologists, and those who study human cognition, have something to say.

It happens that the initial "natural" learning of a child, during the first years of his or her life, is *intuitive.*[7] The child sees that the sun moves across the sky, and that the earth is "flat." At the age of two, it is impossible (and also unnecessary) to explain that the earth is a huge sphere that moves around the sun.

Thus the objective of school education (or home schooling for that matter) is to introduce the *true,* non-intuitive understanding of the world. This process has to begin as early as possible. The later it begins, the more difficult it is for a child to abandon the intuitive.

However, it is very hard to do if the educational system rejects teaching subjects. If the science courses are just stories about nature (of course, with emphasis on practical application of science-based technologies), then millions of children (and then adults) will not understand the most fundamental principles of our physical world. As a result, our scientific ignorance today is mind-boggling.

---

[7] Here I refer the reader to the book by a distinguished psychologist and professor of Harvard University, Dr. Howard Gardner, *The Unschooled Mind: How Children Think and How School Should Teach.* (Basic Books, 1991). Dr. Gardner, who has been the first to explain the early child's learning as *intuitive,* is however, an ardent supporter of *Progressive* education, and I strongly disagree with his suggestion of *How School Should Teach.*

People do not understand why "all of a sudden" (bad luck!) they hit their car's windshield upon braking (hence the resistance to buckle up). People do not understand why we have seasons on earth, and they do not understand at all what electricity is and how it is produced. ("It is mostly produced from coal."—a TV anchorwoman recently informed us. How has this been interpreted by millions Americans?)

Returning to the *Progressives'* ideology, one can see that the above principles are just the ones on which our contemporary education is based. The concept "education through entertainment"—of "*having fun* while learning" is just the logical development of child-centered ideas. As for the rejection of absolute values (and, for that matter, "traditional values" or "family values")—an important ideological principle of the *Progressives*—it has had, perhaps, the most devastating effect on America. And, of course, here are the roots of moral relativism permeating our society.

An Alternative

What are the alternatives to the *Progressives'* point of view? Philosophers and educators of various ilk resisted *Progressiv*ists. To me, the most attractive alternative, which completely corresponds to my gut feeling of what education should be, is the point of view espoused by the existential philosophers of education. Today,educators who espouse similar views are sometimes called *traditionalists*. Here are their main principles of education (from the above-quoted article by George F. Kneller, pp. 121-124; italics are added):

- "The freedom to have children entails the responsibility for their fullest genuine development. Parents should not give up responsibility for the education of their offspring and expect the school to do their job for them."

- "…knowledge, properly conceived, brings freedom, since *it delivers man from ignorance and prejudice* and enables him to see himself as he really is."

- The school "must cease to regard subject matter as an end in itself or as an instrument to prepare the student for his future career, and must consider it instead as *a means for the cultivation of the self.*"

- "Of all the persons, the teacher is best placed to promote the growth of free, creative manhood in those who come before him, *inspiring them with a passionate concern for the meaning of life and the quality of their own life*"
- "It is vital for the student of science to study continuously in the humanities to prevent his mind and sympathies from narrowing."

Compare these statements with the maxims of *Progressive* education, and you will see the bottomless pit separating our education today from what is needed in order to give our children understanding of this world, help them on the difficult climb to maturity, and help them acquire direction and meaning in their lives.

A Future Educational Reform

If now one takes a broader view of our educational problems and the reforms necessary to resolve them, one can see that only a concerted effort, both to change the attitude toward our children and to strongly enhance the curricula, can bring tangible results. Unfortunately, in the heated discussions on *what* should be taught in our schools, in order to bridge the gap between the intellectual and spiritual levels of our children and the requirements of society, virtually no voice is heard on *how* the children should (nay, *must*) be taught.

And, again, changing the attitude toward our children's education or, if you wish, changing the educational philosophy, is even more important. Both the school and the college curricula have degenerated, because the *Progressives'* ideas are incompatible with serious academic education and spiritual development. Their attitude toward students simply paralyzes both the everyday educational process and the innate but hidden process of acquiring maturity.

Unfortunately, the cancer of *Progressiv*ism has contaminated, with its metastasis, not only the education, but also virtually the whole culture of our society. It is not for me, a layperson, to explain how and why this could have happened and could not have been prevented from happening in this country. Perhaps a psychologist or a political scientist could provide a plausible explanation. What is important: unless our educators and the public understand the origin of our problems, there will be no progress, no matter how heavily the curriculum at our schools has been enhanced. This statement, however, is only partially true. Educators most probably *do* understand the problem—hence their stubborn resistance to changes—while the public is innocently ignorant of the problem's origin.

And please do not forget that the shameful state of our education today is not the result of insufficient funding. In 1990 we spent $414 billion on education; in 2000-2001, the funding was $678 billion, more than twice our national defense budget ($429 billion). In fact, in absolute terms, we spend more on education than any other nation. Ironically enough, while from 1972 the expenditures on elementary and secondary education have more that tripled, the combined SAT scores have dropped from 1039 to 1020 (not accidentally, this drop is due to the drop in verbal SAT, from 530 to 506; the math scores insignificantly improved by some 5 points, from 509 to 514).

In 1994, Congress passed the legislation *Goal 2000*. This document was envisioned as a foundation for the future educational reform. The goals of this reform, as formulated in this legislation, are daring and revolutionary—against the background of today's stagnation in education. But, the year 2000 came and passed. And it is doubtful that those goals can be *ever* achieved unless a revolution in our understanding of the necessity of strong general education—as opposed to strong job-oriented training—also occurs.

Unfortunately, however, America is as far from understanding the necessity of that revolution as could be. Both American educators and politicians are feverishly at work to redirect the mission of the public schools from teaching children knowledge and raising their intellectual level to training them to fit the global economy.

The very recent years, however, have seen increased activity among would-be school reformers. Everybody understands that radical education reforms must be implemented. Today, educational reforms are on everybody's tongue. The Presidents' "educational summits," the endless "cross fires," radio and TV talk shows—everybody discusses the *goals* and *means* of possible reforms. But we are still too far from a constructive consensus.

Our public education is today comprised of 15,000 independent school systems, each of them with a tremendous amount of autonomy. Should there be 15,000 independent "school reforms?" Unfortunately, the anti-government, anti-centralist ideas are too strong in our society today to bring about a consensus even on the fundamental goals of the pending educational reforms.

One of the most popular words of our politicians' jargon is "reinvent." We *reinvent* virtually everything: the government, health and human services, business, marketing, communications, public relations. We even *reinvent* America and ourselves. Now we are going to *reinvent* education. Unfortunately, what we have been doing is mostly reinventing the wheel. And at that, with no guarantee that the new wheel will be able to function as a wheel.

As was mentioned before, the ideas of child-centered "egalitarian democratic education" put forward by the *Progressive education movement* had immediately won popularity among liberal educators in Europe. Europe, however, had stopped short in broad implementation of these ideas. The cataclysms of the '30s and the devastating second World War have taught the Europeans a serious and important lesson.

Let us listen again to Dr. Gagnon. While American educators were "perpetuating elitism by denouncing liberal education as elitist," and "treating the majority of our children as though they were learning-disabled," their European colleagues, "out of revolution and class conflict...had raised wariness to a high art, looking behind words for consequences. In Europe the schools had been battlegrounds for ideas about human nature, religion, history, national honor, and democracy itself. European democrats who had suffered Nazi occupation were not about to accept the notion that schools could be different but equal." The battle had been won. "As European secondary schools were opened to all, the political parties of the left resolved that children of workers and the poor should gain whatever personal and political power they could from the same academic curriculum formerly reserved to the few."

Paul Gagnon worked for the Department of Education and was a witness to our absurd attempts to reinvent education. He writes: "Had we looked overseas after mid-century, we could have learned from our allies and our enemies in the second World War. But we did not and still do not. Those most reluctant to look abroad are the promoters of giddy educational fixes that no foreign country would take seriously, from subjecting schools to the 'free market' all the way to killing off academic disciplines in favor of "issue-based inquiry."

"We used to say," Paul Gagnon writes, "and too many educators still say—that we cannot compare our schools with those in other countries, because they educate only an elite and we try to educate everybody. Untrue for thirty years, this is now the opposite of the truth. They educate the many and we the few. To our shame, a disadvantaged child has a better chance for an equal and rigorous education, and whatever advancement it may bring, in Paris or Copenhagen than in one of our big cities."

In his article, Dr. Gagnon suggests a step-by-step approach to educational reform. Quoting from Albert Shanker, the former president of the American Federation of Teachers, Paul Gagnon, in just a few sentences summarizes the main idea behind a *true* educational reform from which America is still infinitely far away. "Americans tolerate a 'marked inequity of opportunity in comparison with Germany, France, or Japan.' Why do students work harder in those countries, with the same TV and pop culture to distract them? It's because their educators have decided what all students should know by the end of high school, Shanker says, and they have 'worked back from these goals to figure out what children should learn by the time they are ages fourteen and nine.' Standards are universal and known by everyone, so 'few students are lost—and fewer teachers are lost.'"

Universal standards seem to be the first thing to begin with. In fact, some attempts to set such standards have been made in the past, but they have failed. Paul Gagnon tells us the dramatic story of how that happened. "President George H. W. Bush and the nation's governors launched a movement to set national standards for course content at meetings in Charlottesville, Virginia, in 1989. Goal three of their statement insisted that course content be academically 'challenging,' comparable to that in the best schools here and overseas, and—for equity— that all students be offered such content and be expected to master it. Polls showed the overwhelming public support, even for a national curriculum."

The task of developing that recommendation for the unified school curriculum was handed off to the US Department of Education. "The stage was set to open equal opportunities for learning, to tamper with curricular chaos of 15,000 school districts, so that children would no longer be entirely at the mercy of where or to whom they were born." Ten years later the work is still "in progress." In 1994, four of the national projects—the arts, civics, geography, and history—were completed and their documents were issued. A math project had been completed in 1991, while science and foreign language projects are still in work. As for the English project, after spending over $900,000, it has been scrapped. Our educators "were unable to do for our language and literature what other nations have done for theirs."

These words were written eight years ago. Fifteen since the beginning of the project; and this is an enormous term, but Americans still do not see any results. (Should it take a generation?) Paul Gagnon is probably right in claiming that "the national version of standards-based reform is dead of multiple wounds—some self-inflicted, others from our culture wars, still others for congressional antipathy to any federal initiative, and most from American educators who have long resisted establishing a common core of academic learning."

The efforts to do something about the educational standards were watered down by the later Democratic administration. In 1994, as a part of the already-mentioned legislation *Goal 2000*, the establishment of two councils—the *National Educational Goal Panel* and the *National Educational Standards and Implementation Council*—were authorized. Both councils would have to function under the presidential auspices, but all their decisions, i.e., standards, tests, criteria, would have only the status of *recommendations*. Accepting them by states would be *voluntary*. (But can non-mandatory standards at all be called *standards?*)

The functioning of these two bodies—even against the background of general anarchy and disarray of opinions and suggested measures—would be definitely useful. But so far, ten years after the legislation has been passed, no results are in sight. Moreover, the discussion in the media proceeds as if no such legislation existed. Now, setting standards is in the hands of the states. And, again, Paul Gagnon is probably right. "Having fifty sets of standards need not mean disaster.

But the Committee of Ten was right: something close to national agreement on a vital common core is indispensable to educational equity, to dislodge and replace the empty, undemanding programs that leave so many children untaught and disadvantaged. Without some such agreement, the much-heralded devolution of reform leadership to the states could make things worse."

Unfortunately, in the present political climate, any bipartisan agreement on this important issue seems to be even more impossible than before. The idea of universal standards is hostile to politicians and activists on both sides of the aisle. The liberals are against any *standards* (obvious violation of individual freedoms), while the conservatives hate anything *universal* (do not let the government—the *big brother*—tell us what to do and what not).

Hence impossible is a centralized school reform. However, in the present situation when both the philosophical and actual standards of our education are so dismally low, and when the mere existence of our society as a competitive and democratic body is at stake, the decentralization of the reform may be tragically counterproductive.

Here I would like to say a few more words about the decentralization of American educational system and its dreadful consequences for the whole educational process, not only the curriculum. As I already mentioned, although there is a Federal Department of Education—and the corresponding departments in all 50 states—the real authority over the schools lies with approximately 15,000 local school boards. The funding of schools is also fundamentally decentralized. Over 90 percent of public school funding comes from state and local taxes; the federal government's share is less than 10 percent.

Such decentralization, which can even be called "extreme federalization" hinting that the public school system is but a "federation" of independent schools, immediately results in the most tragic consequence. The main slogan of American public education—the one America has always been proud of—"Equal Opportunity through Equal Education"—is, in practice, nothing but a mockery of the great idea and, actually, is a big lie.

Educational efforts have three components: what should be taught (curriculum), how it should be taught (quality of teachers) and where it should be taught (quality of teaching environment, i.e., school buildings, teaching material, equipment, for example).

Each of these three components of American education contradicts in its ability and everyday practice to that propaganda slogan of "equal opportunity." Not only is there no unified curriculum (as I already discussed), but—and this is really *bad*—there are no unified standards of educating and certifying teachers. As a result, in many—very many schools, if not in the majority of schools—teachers are not adequately qualified to teach their subjects.

The way France educates its public school teachers, or the way Denmark educates its kindergarten teachers is incomparable to the methods America uses—as if these two counties and America are on different planets.

Any attempts to improve the quality of teachers making use of the well-understood (in America) *market* mechanism—firing bad teachers and promoting good ones—runs into fierce resistance by the American Teacher's Union.

Actually, the situation is even worse. "We simply do not have nearly enough teachers prepared to carry schools, whether public or private, charter or conventional, to high standards, Dr. Gagnon, wrote in his recent article, *School Reform: Are We up to It?*—turned down by a leading magazine. Dr Gagnon continues: "The obstacle here is Academe, whose arts and sciences and education faculties do not work together but are equally responsible for the academic weakness of the American teacher corps."

But it is not just the teaching colleges' professors who do not do "good job." It is, again, like the whole state of our education, not a result of college faculties' "screw-ups," but an ideological problem. According to the *Progressive* ideology, the teacher is only an observer of a child's development rather than the one who directs it. Dr. Gagnon writes: "If they [teachers] are now unready for high standards, the fault is not theirs. University teachers of prospective teachers saw no reason to educate them as scholars."

Dr. Gagnon then contrasts education of our teachers to that abroad. He gives very striking examples of how much our teacher's education and licensing is different from those in France. The gap begins in high school, the *lycee*. "Their *lycee* years give them the basic humanities, science, and social sciences once required in our college freshmen and sophomores, but no longer. What young Americans often miss in high school they miss again in college, where in return for four years and tuition money, they rarely get a liberal education. If they do, it is by their good sense of lucky advising, not institutional integrity."

In Dr. Gagnon's view, "our colleges will not soon prepare undergraduates who could pass French qualifying tests for teachers." John Silber, the former president of Boston University wrote [8] that, to his belief, very few American college graduates could pass the A-Level examinations required in England of students who wish merely to enter a university.

---

[8]   John Silber, *Straight Shooting: What Is Wrong with America and How to Fix It.* Harper & Row, New York, 1989.

The French qualifying exams are extremely rigorous, and "are less cushioned than ours by easy grades. Upon graduation, teacher candidates are expected to write and speak on their subjects at several levels of sophistication in the Education Ministry's qualifying tests. For history/geography/civics, they write two four-hour essays—one based on historical documents furnished by examiners, the other on geography. If successful, they later take oral exams before a jury: a school inspector, a university scholar, and a senior school teacher." But that is not all. "They present a model lesson on a jury-chosen topic. They have four hours to prepare, from material furnished on the spot. Second and third discussions are on analysis and usage of documents, with two hours to prepare for each. In the words of the Ministry, these talks allow the candidate to 'demonstrate that he knows the content and structure of his discipline, that he has reflected upon the significance and evolution of the discipline, and upon its relations to the other disciplines in the curriculum.'"

In contrast to what is required from the future French teachers, our teacher college examinations "barely test the basics of old-style freshmen courses." Dr Gagnon is quite pessimistic regarding a reform that would radically improve the education of future American teachers. And again, the main obstacle is ideology. "Letting students ignore the events and ideas that shaped them and the world is called freedom of choice. Amnesia is liberation." And, ultimately, ignorance is but a freedom from knowledge.

So much for the *what* and the *how* our children are taught today. A unified curriculum—or even mandatory unified standards, as well as professionalism and high qualification of teachers—are pipe dreams today.

Now about the *where*. The complete autonomy of local educational establishment over total school budgets, including maintaining old or building new school buildings, creates a major inequity in the quality of education throughout the country.

On the other hand, the European countries understand but too well that there can be no *equal opportunity* unless there is *equal financing* of the educational efforts. And that can only be achieved if the nation as a whole voluntarily takes responsibility for the education of *all* its children, no matter whether the school is in an affluent suburb or in a poor minority town.

The recent interference of the federal government—George W. Bush's *No Child Left Behind* reform—is the unspoken acknowledgment of the failure of the decentralized educational system. It is not a revolution, completely transferring the school system under government control, but it is a serious interference with the local school autonomy. But this interference is fundamentally based on the major requirement that the accountability of schools for the quality of teaching satisfies the *market* criteria. The "better" the school, the more federal support. If the school is "bad," the support disappears.

Is it possible that the intellectuals behind the market-type educational reforms in America do not understand that in order for the education to be truly that of "equal opportunity" it must have nothing whatsoever to do with market and its forces? When a mismanaged company goes broke, it disappears. However, a mismanaged school cannot be allowed to be left without support and rot: Children cannot be "laid off." The reformers' argument that the parents should be given the opportunity to transfer their children from the decaying schools to those more economically successful is false because there may be not enough schools to accommodate the "laid-off" students, and the quality of teaching in the "good" schools will inevitably fall under the pressure of the flow of "bad" students leaving "bad schools." To say nothing of the fact that, in rural areas where the schools are almost inevitably "bad" because of implicitly poor financing, most probably, there may be no other, "better" school within many miles.

On the other hand, if the country has a high-quality, unified curriculum—mandatory for all states and all schools—and if the requirements for educating and training the teachers who have adequate qualification to teach this curriculum are also unified and very strict; and if every school's budget is guaranteed by the federal government and directly linked to the number of students and the necessary number of teachers, the necessary number of classrooms, textbooks, computers, for example, then the "equal opportunity" of getting high-quality education will be guaranteed to every student, regardless of his or her race, social status or the location of the school the student attends. These principles have been realized—albeit not in all their fullness—in democratic countries of Europe. Unfortunately, the efforts of educational reformers in America, including the recent president Bush's *No Child Left Behind* initiative, most probably will have been futile, unless the true *equal opportunity* reform has been implemented. And this is also but a pipe dream today.

Now I would like to return to say a few more words about the new *No Child Left Behind* educational initiative. In the foreword to the document, President Bush writes:[9] "In a constantly changing world that is demanding increasingly complex skills from its workforce, children are literally being left behind. It does not have to be this way."

One can see, even before reading the initiative in its details that this is the same old song: building the skills necessary to compete in the global economy. And even though a few lines later the President says: "Taken together, these

---

[9]   Quoted from www.whitehouse.gov/news/reports/text/no-children-left-behind.html.

reforms express my deep belief in our public schools and their mission to build the mind and character of every child, from every background, in every part of America," we should not deceive ourselves. *Teaching skills does not build character.* Even if "funding for character education grants to states and districts to train [sic.] teachers in methods of incorporating character-building lessons and activities in the classroom would be increased" (Title V, Part B), no "character-building lessons" can possibly build human character. It is a long and painful process that only a true academic education can accomplish.

The initiative does have some goals that look promising, such as the Reading First program. But here again, what is meant is improving children's *reading skills*, which would be necessary for an adult to be able to read a newspaper and comprehend a manual for equipment or an IRS instruction. Nowhere is it mentioned that children must be *encouraged* by teachers and parents to read much more at home and in reading clubs. Were these mentioned, we could have hope.

Reading interesting and exciting books would gradually revive children's imagination (drained away by TV), develop their ability to empathize with book characters, and tremendously increase their *knowledge* about the world and themselves. Books alone could *build character* without any special classes.

I wish the new initiative to be a success. But it is very unlikely, in spite of the huge amount of money that will be allocated to its numerous programs. The future will tell us.

Educational reform, nay, *educational revolution*, is a necessity today. However, as I already stressed in the *Preface*, "this revolution will occur—first of all in our consciousness—if and when we understand, from the bottom of our hearts, that teaching our children *skills* will, at best, help them only to get a job in the future—perhaps a good job. However, it will not help them to mature into responsible, thinking and creative individuals. It will not help them to begin the everlasting and unstoppable quest for meaning, which is also a road to happiness. It is only a strong general academic education that will prepare our children for this lifelong road to a meaningful life."

Nobody can predict when and how the breakthrough in our stagnant education will happen. The true reformers will definitely run into the resistance of teachers, parents, and students. But what we, those who feel responsible for the future of our children and grandchildren, must realize is that there is no time left for procrastination and wishful thinking. If in the 19th and the 20th centuries, those who fought our stagnant educational system wanted just better education for Americans, now it is a matter of the intellectual, cultural, and spiritual survival of the nation. What used to be just a headache is now a cancer slowly killing our society.

ABANDONED: OUR CHILDREN

"America is a country of young men"

—*Ralph Waldo Emerson, "Society and Solitude"*

Four o'clock in the afternoon. March. Bumper-to-bumper traffic on Boston's Storrow Drive. I am crawling by a scarlet convertible with four youngsters in it. The thunder of rock music pierces my ears through the closed windows of my car. The thunder fades away, only to return in a minute or two, when the red car accelerates by and abruptly stops almost nose by nose with my car. Now I can better see its passengers. Two teenage boys (17-19?) in the front seats; two girls in the rear. All are in T-shirts in spite of the chilly March weather. The boys and one of the girls wear baseball caps. The girl's cap is turned backward, one of the boys' caps is turned only halfway. The girl in the rear seat smokes. She is just four or five feet away from me. If I opened my window, I could talk to her. She is quite pretty—blonde, with long hair. She turns and glances at me—an indifferent, bored glance. I smile back. She throws a bat. It pirouettes in the air and hits my car's fender. She did not mean to hit it, she just did not care. Then she says something to the boys (I wonder how they could hear her through the thunder of the rock music). The four burst out laughing. They turn to me. The boy at the wheel gives me the finger. I smile and give them the *V*. But they do not see it. They have already lost a few seconds on me. Their car jumps forward, emitting blue smoke from under its wheels, and squeals away—only to stop abruptly after some 50 yards, almost hitting the car ahead.

The "V" I showed them—well, it was an automatic reaction, but what I really meant was "I want you to win, win against all odds, win back your own souls."

This essay is about out teenagers—about how indifferent, unfair and sometimes cruel our society is to them. Often one can hear parents lamenting to each other: "They were so sweet and nice when they were little. And all of a sudden, *bang!* They are teenagers. They are out of control, They seem almost crazy, and you almost lose them."

This "all of a sudden" is nothing else than the onset of *puberty*. Not coincidentally this onset is also the onset of *adolescence*. The former signifies the fundamental changes in the bodies and accompanying changes in the attitude both to these "new" bodies and the "new" world. The latter has a more social connotation, but the essence of this new period in our children's lives is that they begin a difficult struggle to find *a self*, to understand the meaning of their mere *being* in the external—and allegedly hostile—world. They have to *accommodate* their past, their relations with their families and their friends into the *new* "universe." Having, perhaps for the first time, recognized themselves as *separate* and *unique*, the children are desperately trying to find their place in this universe.

The onset of this crisis also signifies the beginning of the infamous *conflict of generations* that, for a long period of time will be separating parents and children. This "conflict" is of a rather special character. It is not that the generation gap is so huge that the parents are unable or unwilling to understand the ideas and aspirations of their children as *a new generation*. The conflict—the real conflict—is rather that the children do not represent a new generation yet. They are in a severe crisis, and they are trying to rebuild from scratch what has already been built by their parents. Later, when the crisis has been overcome, the conflict of generations may have even completely disappeared, although its traces may be felt for years, simply because, due to the negative societal influence, the process of children's maturing may be severely hampered.

Most pre-adolescent children are lively. They are interested in everything: sports, active games, adventure. With adolescence, these interests fade away, overshadowed by one huge dark cloud—*sex*.

Puberty *is* about sex. Girls begin to menstruate; boys discover erections and suffer nocturnal emissions. In the past, however, this period of youth development was never so painful and so destructive for teenage souls as now. This is the culture of adults—the culture where sex dominates all aspects of our life, from relations in the family to selling no matter what. Our children are an indispensable part of this culture. Moreover, teenagers obsessed with sex do contribute to the proliferation of a junk culture—the proliferation that is ruthlessly exploited by greedy adults. As a result, the children find themselves in a vicious circle. They need a culture to express themselves, but the adults, instead of helping them to find their place in the "universe," supply them with surrogates that are *easy* to swallow and thus easily edible by teenagers, but which are poisonous to their souls.

The roles of boys and girls in this developmental quagmire are different. The society, through its sexist culture, begins shaping the boys into future *men*, "doers," masters, the *Martians*; while the girls begin to learn to be good-looking, slim, obedient, and wordless: *the Venusians* (see the essay *Men are from Mars, Women are from Venus*).

Dr. Mary Pipher, a clinical psychologist, who for many years has been helping girls overcome their adolescent crises, in her book *Reviving Ophelia*[1], writes: "Adolescents are exposed, via music, television, movies and pornography, to models of sexuality that are brutal and callous. Girls are caught in the crossfire of our culture's mixed sexual messages. Sex is considered both a sacred act between two people united by God, and the best way to sell suntan lotion" (p. 71).

The place where the developmental drama unfolds is junior high. Dr. Pipher calls it a "crucible," where "...many confident and well-adjusted girls were transformed into sad and angry failures" (p. 11). Boys begin to learn first lessons of sexual harassment. "...70 percent of girls experience harassment and 50 percent experience unwanted sexual touching in their schools. One-third of all girls report sexual rumors being spread about them, and one-fourth report being cornered and molested" (p. 70).

"Girls are taunted about everything from oral sex to pubic hair, from periods to the imaginary appearance of their genitals. The harassment that girls experience in the 1990s is much different in both quality and intensity. The remarks are more graphic and mean-spirited. Although the content is sexual, the intent is aggressive, to be rude and controlling" (p. 69).

The most common sites for sexual harassment are the classrooms and hallways of our schools—it happens virtually before the teachers' eyes, but they seem not to notice it. Of course, not all boys are "bad," and not all girls are miserable. What is important is that the spiritual (and sometimes even physical) health of the adolescents depends on their standing *vis-a-vis* their reference group. The effect of their reference group is termed "peer pressure."

Lilian R. Rubin, in her book *Erotic War: What Happened to the Sexual Revolution?*[2] writes (p. 67): "The question of peer pressure is not quite so simple...But generally it also is not the kind of direct, one-on-one pressure the adult world so often envisions. Instead, the pressure resides largely in the atmosphere itself—pressure that permeates all facets of teenage life, whether the style of dress, the language used, the music listened to or the initiation into sexual activity....For adolescents who are struggling to separate from the family, to find a self-in-the-world that's uniquely theirs, a reference group is a must."

The reason for such strong dependency on the reference group is obvious. "The growing and developing youth, faced with this psychological revolution

---

[1]   Mary Pipher. *Reviving Ophelia: Saving the Selves of Adolescent Girls,* Ballantine Books, New York, 1994.

[2]   Lilian R. Rubin, Erotic *Wars: What Happened to the Sexual Revolution?* Harper Collins, New York, 1990.

within them are now primary concerned with what they appear to be in the eyes of others as compared with what they think they are."[3]

The requirements of conformism are quite ruthless among both girls and boys. It is, however, much more severe among girls. If, among boys, most of the requirements are *attitudinal* (swearing, smoking, drinking, chasing girls or scoring points in the sexual contest), a girl is additionally under severe "lookism" pressure. A girl may become a total outcast among her peers, "a germ"—if she is not beautiful enough or not slim enough. Of course, being a *nerd* or refusing to smoke and drink is also intolerable. This pressure disorients girls, suppresses their will and their ability to fight for their authentic self. Studies quoted in Dr. Pipher's book (p. 27) showed that 40 percent of all girls in a Mid Western city were considering suicide. In Atlanta, the suicide rate among children age ten to fourteen rose 75 percent between 1979 and 1988.

Adolescents desperately need and seek help. But nobody is there. Parents—the first "line of defense"—are completely impotent and feel like failures. Contact with their children has been almost completely lost. Teenagers do not trust them. Often teenagers blame their parents for their problems. The parents were supposed to sense that their child needed help and give this help, but they failed. In most cases, these accusations are both true and false. True because, unfortunately, we, parents and grandparents, do not understand the origin of the adolescent crisis. Even if we understand that it has something to do with puberty, we completely fail to see the connection of the most severe manifestations of the crisis with the contemporary culture, the educational system, societal institutions, and our own lives.

A typical example: Parents are usually angry with teenagers. Although teenagers can hardly speak with parents, they spend hours talking with their friends over the phone. But these conversations are absolutely necessary. "Talking to friends is a way of checking the important question, 'Am I okay?'" (*Reviving Ophelia*, p. 68)

It is false because, with the lines of communications cut off, it is extremely difficult for a parent to be on a constant alert. Besides, a teenager may refuse the help he or she is seeking because of being angry with his or her parents—this anger is actually the anger with himself or herself and therefore unjustified from a rational point of view. However, as Dr. Pipher stresses, "without some help, the loss of wholeness, self-confidence and self-direction can last well into adulthood."

---

[3] E. Erikson, *Childhood and Society.* W.W. Norton & Company; 1993, p. 261.

In spite of complex relationships between the two "sub-species"—the boys and the girls—they are melted together by the power of sex. Their main objective is to be together, which, in the language of our entertainment-oriented culture, inevitably means "having fun."

Having fun seems to be an easy way out also because, since early childhood, our children live in the atmosphere of permanent and endless TV entertainment. However, for adolescents, having fun becomes the obsession of one's life. It is not only parties and dating (sometimes innocent, but more often with real sex relations), but also just hanging around with friends, like a *herd* doing whatever is considered to be *funny*. Sometimes it is quite innocent; sometimes it is already marginally criminal, and too often it is truly a crime. Smoking and drinking are the norms. Most teenagers try drugs by seventh grade, and not only marijuana— a normal substance at rock concerts. They also actively experiment with chemicals that can help them to get high.

The atmosphere among today's teenagers and the "rules" of their subcultures are profoundly anti-intellectual. Among the boys, the rules are dominated by *machismo*. Among the girls, it's by *lookism*. Almost inevitably, teenagers' grades at school (and even their IQ scores) drop significantly. Study and learning, being difficult processes requiring the necessity of concentration (both physical and intellectual), are fundamentally alien and hostile to a rebelling and entertainment-seeking individual. This is exacerbated by a general *anti-educational* atmosphere in our schools, where the leading pedagogical idea is that learning must be easy, effortless; hence the decline in the quality of education in public schools. There is virtually no homework, no core curriculum in high school. Serious subjects, such as math and science, are ignored. As a result, there is an enormous amount of free time. Typically teenagers have jobs for a few hours every day. The rest of the time they *kill*. And there is no better weapon for that than having fun.

Children are desperately looking for role models, for somebody's advice, direction. Parents are rejected both as *role models* and as *advisors*. On the other hand, intellectual, emotional, and moral underdevelopment prevents teenagers from overcoming the obstacles toward finding a real meaning in their lives—toward achieving an *internal equilibrium*, and thus paving a road to their full and interesting life. But there is nobody around to help them out of this quagmire.

It is at this point that society should be expected to take over by creating and supporting institutions that would serve teenagers as "locks," distracting them from the destructive influence of sex, and gradually allowing them to acquire self-confidence upon entering the world of exciting learning, the world-opening reading and accomplishments outside the realm of fun and pleasure. But society is *indifferent*.

The conflict was not that severe in the past, since children, from early childhood, knew that life was tough. They shared responsibilities with their parents. Very early they began to work in order to support the family. There was a permanent connection with the parents—both spiritual and emotional—which enabled the children to cope with the hardships of life while, at the same time, acquire the experience necessary for their own struggle for survival.

In this struggle, the crisis of adolescence did not result in rejecting the values. The transfer of both experience and knowledge, or wisdom, between generations was more or less smooth. In more affluent classes, the conflict was not severe either, due to good education, and transferring the moral and intellectual wealth of the previous generation through both the family and the intermediaries, i.e., good teachers. The intellectual atmosphere in the families also taught children the basic values of the future life: the necessity for perseverance, hard intellectual work, and moral strength. Both in poor and affluent families, religion played an important role in the foundation for survival and moral development.

At the end of the 19th and the beginning of the 20th century, America was experiencing a few powerful waves of immigration, mostly from Europe and Russia. Many descendants of those daring men and women are now among the intellectual and cultural elite of this country. And mind you, there were no special organizations, then, with the sole objective of helping the new immigrants.

They had to find their own, and often unique, ways of survival. Most of them, poor people, immigrated to America in search of a better life for their children (both material and spiritual), or even simply in search of a life free of persecution. Many of them were semi-literate or even illiterate. The country was still "young" and there were (almost) no sophisticated theories of optimal education. People were doing what their "guts" were telling them to do. And the children knew that only *education* would bring them out of poverty. What we now call *The American Dream* led both them and their parents.

Reflecting on those times from the beginning of the 21st century—against the background of disgruntled children bored and lacking meaning in life, with disintegrated families, and with the proliferation of crime and drugs—one can but ask oneself in astonishment, "*Why*, and *how* could this have happened?"

Viktor Frankl answers this question. Let me quote again his words that I have quoted already:[4] "For too long we have been dreaming a dream from which we are now waking up: the dream that if we just improve the socioeconomic situation of people, everything will be okay, people will become happy. The truth is

---

[4]   Viktor E. Frankl, *The Unheard Cry for Meaning: Psychotherapy and Humanism.* Washington Square Press, New York, 1985, p.21.

that as the *struggle for survival* has subsided, the question has emerged: *survival for what?* Ever more people today have the means to live, but no meaning to live for" (italics by Frankl).

The crisis of adolescence is not something invented in the 20th century. It has always existed. The fundamental difference between search for meaning of the previous generations and the desperate attempts of today's girls and boys to make sense of their existence, is that today's society is their worst enemy. In fact, the majority of our children find themselves intellectually and emotionally unprepared for the adolescence crisis when it strikes. As for society, through its sex- and entertainment-oriented culture, it does its utmost to exacerbate the crisis and prevent the children from successfully surviving and surmounting the devastation of the crisis.

Adults can somehow control and fix their existential problems. They can resist being taken over by the flow of our society toward the abyss of meaninglessness. Children cannot. As Viktor Frankl has pointed out, our inner life may be thought of as represented by a diagram. In his diagram (see p. 46) the horizontal axis, failure-success, represents the traditional standing of an individual *vis-à-vis* society, while the vertical axis measures the individual's inner state from despair to fulfillment. On this diagram, our children may be placed only at the "negative" despair area. They have not started moving along the failure-success road. They have no bank accounts or career, but they already know what despair is. Their lives are boring and empty.

In this essay, I am going to address at least some of the problems, as I, "a man in the street," see and understand them—the problems that prevent our children from acquiring the necessary intellectual and emotional strength that would enable them, in the future, to develop their ability to think constructively and to make decisions, thus pave the road to their maturity and an interesting and fulfilling life. Some "experts" may disagree, but I believe my arguments, at least in their essential part, do make sense.

Sweet Little Fingers

"Ten little fingers—I love you so.
Sweet little fingers—I kiss you all…"

—An English song

Before I begin, let me present a lengthy quote from a book that, I believe, is one of the best written in this country about education and the "American

Dream," and which every parent should read. This is Betty Smith's *A Tree Grows in Brooklyn*.[5] (pp. 70-72; italics belong to the quote).

Katie, a young woman, who just gave birth to a daughter, talks with her elderly mother, Mary Rommely, an immigrant from Austria. Listen:

> "Mother, I am young. Mother, I am just eighteen. I am strong. I will work hard, Mother. But I do not want this child to grow up just to work hard. What must I do, Mother, what must I do to make a different world for her? How do I start?"

> "The secret lies in the reading and the writing. You are able to read. Every day you must read one page from some good book to your child. Every day this must be until the child learns to read. Then *she* must read every day. I know this is the secret."

> "I will read," promised Katie. "What is a good book?"

> "There are two great books. Shakespeare is a great book. I have heard tell that all the wonders of life are in that book; all that man has learned of beauty, all that he may know of wisdom and living are on those pages..."

> "And what is the other great book?"

> "It is the Bible...That is the book, then, and the book of Shakespeare. And every day you must read a page of each to your child—even though you yourself do not understand what is written down and cannot sound the words properly. You must do this that the child will grow up knowing of what is great— knowing that these tenements of Williamsburg are not the whole world....And you must tell the child the legends I told you—as my mother told them to me and her mother to her. You must tell the fairytales of the old country. You must tell of those not of the earth who live forever in the hearts of people—fairies, elves, dwarfs and such. You must tell of the great ghosts that haunted your father's people...And the child must believe in the Lord God..."

> "Mother, I know there are no ghosts and fairies, I would be teaching the child the foolish lies."

---

5   Betty Smith's *A Tree Grows in Brooklyn*. Harper & Row, New York, 1947.

Mary spoke sharply. "You do not *know* whether there are not ghosts on earth or angels in heaven."
"I *know* there is no Santa Claus."

"Yet you must teach the child that these things are so."

"Why? When I, myself, do not believe?"

"Because," explained Mary Rommely simply, "the child must have a valuable thing called imagination. The child must have a secret world in which live things that never were. It is necessary that she *believe*. She must start out by believing in things not of this world. Then when the world becomes too ugly for living in, the child can reach back and live in her imagination. I, myself, even in this day and at my age, have great miracles that have come to pass on earth. Only by having these things in my mind can I live beyond what I have to live for."

"The child will grow up and find out things for herself. She will know that I lied. She will be disappointed."

"That is what is called learning the truth. It is a good thing to learn the truth one's self. To first believe with all your heart, and then not to believe is good too. It fattens the emotions and makes them to stretch. When as a woman life and people disappoint her, she will have had practice in disappointment and it will not come so hard. In teaching your child, do not forget that suffering is good too. It makes a person rich in character."

This just a page long quote is a bottomless well of wisdom. I believe that no better manual of how to shape up the beginning life, how to fill it with treasures that will never be exhausted, has ever been written.

Unfortunately, these days, you will not find many families who follow the elderly woman's wise advice. Even if you forget about "the fairytales of the old country"—something that a third- or fourth-generation American does not remember any more—how many parents do read to their children every night? To say nothing of Shakespeare or the Bible. I bet no "sane" parents would ever read those "two great books" to their children.

And yet, the elderly woman's advice has a profound meaning. It is almost like a parable, but it makes sense even if taken literally: a child listens to a great language, and gradually begins to respect the written word—even if the child does not completely understand it—as an absolute and unquestionable part of life.

Respect. For in our today's life books are not respected, unless they are a source of entertainment; but the latter can be obtained with much less effort just by turning on a TV set.

Abstractly, everybody agrees that the development of a child begins from the very first days of life. Since people typically do not read books written by experts in teaching (and often it is good that they don't.), they intuitively believe that a little one is not *a personality yet,* that an important stage of the child's upbringing will begin *later.* Unfortunately parents do follow this *gut* feeling. But that "later" never materializes. If parents did not do something directly related to the development of their children when they were toddlers, they most probably would not do anything "pedagogically specific" later either.

The taken-for-granted belief is that if the family is *good,* the children will be *good*—like the motto: "In a healthy body, a healthy spirit." This belief has been inherited from the generations of hard work and perseverance that I mentioned above. When parents believed that in order to achieve a better life, children had to study a lot, to read a lot, to work hard, the children knew that that was what they had to do, and they did it.

Unfortunately, so many today's families *are not good.* Over half of the marriages break up. In 1995, women headed 18 percent of American families. Single mothers, in order to sustain their children, work hard—very hard. Their jobs are typically low paying and not gratifying. Even if a family has two parents, and has achieved relative affluence, it often drifts in time without direction. TV is the only source of emotional relaxation and, in fact, of connection to the external world. All their life outside of jobs is entertainment directed. The children are of course around. In fact, their parents, unwillingly, give them their first lessons of "enjoying life" through entertainment.

But let me return to the time that, on a grass-roots level, is widely believed to be *unimportant* for the child's upbringing—the toddler time. Of course psychologists know this is wrong. To challenge that view, it was discovered that children adopted at birth from families of low socioeconomic environment and low IQ into families having a more favorable environment develop an IQ appreciably higher than that of their parents.[6] As I discuss elsewhere (see the essay *The Bell Tolls*), the IQ *per se* is not a magic quality that makes people happy or unhappy, fulfilled or despaired. But that study has shown something very important: you cannot ignore the toddler age. Moreover, those years, when a child just learns to walk and talk, may be the most important years for building up the personality

---

6   Richard J. Herrnstein and Charles Murray, *The Bell Curve: Intelligence and Class Structure in American Life.* Simon & Schuster, New York, 1994.

and character and paving the way for the future happiness of the individual. Psychologists know that nothing in our society has been done to inform the public about this important fact, however.

The presumed *unimportance* of early childhood for building up the personality of a child also finds its manifestation in how easily we entrust our children to people absolutely unqualified for teaching them. What I mean is our institution of baby-sitting.

Obviously, if adults have to leave home, the most important thing for their children's safety is that somebody stays with them. This "somebody" is typically a neighborhood teenager. Of course, the teenager should be older than the child. How much older? Perhaps the most important baby-sitter's quality is *responsibility*. What age may be considered adequate for this kind of responsibility? Nobody knows. Actually, what is implied is that the main function of the baby-sitter is to provide for the child's physical safety. For this purpose a twelve-year-old girl may be adequate.

Do teenage babysitters provide safety? This belief is questioned widely today. Recent studies have shown that in close to 50 percent of cases there is some kind of abuse—if not direct physical abuse by a sadistic teenager, then the abuse of the parents' trust in the babysitter. The babysitter invites teenage guests, or even hosts a party, to the total neglect of the child to be cared for.

Even if teenage babysitters do provide the needed physical safety, their effect on the intellectual and emotional development of small children is in most cases negative. Watching a TV program that *the babysitter* may be interested in, as, for example, an MTV show or a "cool" movie (most probably an "action" movie—and thus inevitably violent), is a typical occupation during the adults' absence. Even the relatively innocent watching of cartoons directed at children may be harmful, for, alas, cartoons are also full of violence. Reading a book to the child, or doing something that will push the little one out of the realm of entertainment is unheard of. But you cannot expect that of a teenager who does not like (and possibly even hates) to read books, and whose all aspirations are focused on having fun.

In general, it is a grass-roots belief in America that the younger the child, the lower the pedagogical qualification is required of a babysitter or a teacher. Unfortunately, this applies to many day-care facilities as well.

My granddaughter Rachel, when she was three, for a short time attended a "private" kindergarten. A neighborhood woman with three children of her own took another two or three little ones for five to six hours a day. A few times, when I picked up my Rachel, I was struck by the poor, slangy English the woman spoke, and by the whole *anti-educational* atmosphere of the house. Rachel could never explain what they were doing during those hours. Most likely, they were left on their own. At least Rachel never mentioned a book read to them or a story told. I presume the woman had a "license." But do the licensing authorities care about the educational and pedagogical level of the childcare provider? In fact, they believe that a short training course is enough.

Here are the licensing requirements for *Family Child Care*—exactly the type of care I just mentioned (care for up to six children not related to the care provider). They are the excerpts from brochure: "Licensed Family Child Care: Caring for Children," issued by the Massachusetts Office of Child Care Services:

- You must be at least 18 years of age.

- A criminal record check will be conducted on you and all household members.

- You and all household members must be in good physical and mental health.

- You must have at least one year of full-time experience or the equivalent caring for children under age seven. Training may be substituted for some experience. Parenthood is considered experience.

As one can see, no education credentials are required.

This picture of small children spending hours with people unqualified—by any, even the lowest pedagogical standards—to participate in children's upbringing, is quite typical of this country. And since, allegedly, the most important years for development of child's personality are the years from two to four, then we actually committing a crime against our children by entrusting them to unqualified hands.

This is a difficult problem. A possible way to partly solve the problem would require a sort of revolution in grandparents' minds resulting in their active desire to give their help in this difficult process of bringing up their grandchildren. This would make a world of difference in the lives of our women. It would make a crucial difference in the lives of the elderly and retired grandparents also. Grandchildren bring much more meaning and fulfillment to life than everyday golf or hours of TV watching. It would also make a tremendous difference in the lives of children.

A child psychiatrist Arthur Kornhaber who spent 30 years studying attachment between grandparents and their grandchildren claims that "kids raised by their grand-parents are broader and deeper people. They have a sense of the past.

They know other languages. They do better at school. They have a good sense of family and family values."

Arthur Kornhaber has written 13 books on grand parenting.[7] He and his wife Carol also created Foundation for Grand-Parenting (www.grandparenting.org), with the objective to promote and nurture inter-generation relationships. The Foundation supports various programs, among them a grandparent-grandchild summer camp in upstate New York.

And yet, according to Kornhaber, only 20 percent of grandparents in America have close emotional links with their grandchildren. Retired grandparents prefer to live alone, seeing their grandchildren only occasionally, especially if they retire to some other part of the country, like Florida. To many, the golf they play every day, and the TV they watch for hours are kind of drugs that helps them kill time, leaving their lives even more meaningless than before they retired. Less affluent retirees find some other occupations to fill the vacuum of their lives, rather than begin a new full and fulfilling life caring for their grandchildren. But only very few retired people (still in good health and full of energy) have chosen to devote their time to helping their children to raise the grandchildren.

However, grandparents cannot completely solve the problem of the preschool education of children. In the first place, not all children have grandparents in good health, able physically and willing to spend time with them. An ideal solution would be a wide network of *high-quality* day-care centers. Developed European countries like Denmark do have such networks.

Let me quote from an American journalist's report on the child-care system in Denmark:[8]

"In Denmark, it is generally accepted that no woman, whatever her circumstances, should have to pay a price for combining career and motherhood, and that is the way society's organized from the moment women return to work after six months' paid maternity leave. It's considered anti-social and anti-family to work late. Most Danes, women and men, stop work at 4:30 and

---

7   His three most recent books: *Grandparent Power*, 1995; *Contemporary Grand-Parenting*, 1996; *The Grandparent Guide*, 2002.

8   Vera Frankl, *All Things Considered.* National Public Radio, 27 April 1993.

get to spend three hours with their children before putting them to bed."

Aarhus, Denmark's second largest city: "It's 8:00 on a weekday morning. In the state-run kindergarten across town, a baby is having his nappy changed on a state-of-the-art, electronically operated changing table. Elsewhere, as the sun streams in the windows, 40 children between the age of three months and six years play under the watchful eyes of a dozen highly skilled staff. Most of the children have been here since the doors opened at 7:00. I watched the mothers drop them off and walk out without a backward glance. They told me that's because they go to work knowing their children are in the best of hands."

"Solveg and Kirsten are both professional, middle class women. But there's nothing special about the kindergarten their children attend. It's just one of hundreds of local child care institutions ranging from nurseries to after-school centers set up and subsidized by the municipality. The children of doctors and factory workers enjoy the same facilities, and all parents have an equal say in the way they are run. The only difference is that the better off pay one-third of operating costs. The poorest pay nothing at all, and nobody seems to resent that."

And who is that *highly skilled staff?* "A college for child-care workers in Aarhus, one of 33 around the country—in a gleaming building of glass and steel, a group of students is having a music lesson. It's a part of a three-year course that's compulsory for all Danish child-care workers. The reason music is on the curriculum is not because the students will be expected to teach it which, to judge by this little lot, is just as well. It's more in the hope they'll be able to convey a love of music to the children in their care. That may seem a touch indulgent to some of us, but the Danes don't believe in doing things by halves, and for them, the children and working mothers are high priority."

Unfortunately, the social climate in the United States—the greatest and the richest country on Earth—is completely different. The proportion of married women aged 24 to 35 in the work force increased steeply from 32 percent in 1965 to over 70 percent in the late '90s. As I mentioned above, in 1995, 18 percent of American families were headed by women. Since it is very difficult (although not impossible) to find in America a day-care center that would be a substitute for mother's care, conservative media insists that "mothers should stay home." They blame working mothers for all the societal problems with children, including juvenile crime, teenage drug and alcohol abuse, and teen pregnancies, for example.

It is hard to argue with these facts since no serious sociological research seems to have been done on the consequence of women going into labor force. I would only like to make two points.

First of all, as I mentioned above, the quality of "mother's care" in America has dropped significantly during the recent three decades. Even if a mother can afford to stay home (either for material or spiritual reasons), she does not spend much time with her children—unless they claim immediate attention having to do with their health or physical safety. In fact, parents shy away from actively interacting with children. They spend more time watching TV than actively communicating with their children. As I mentioned elsewhere parents in America spend only 13 minutes a day interacting with their children.

It is this lack of contact that is the core of the crisis that almost every child undergoes at the threshold of adolescence, and that leads later to the complete loss of trust and the infamous *conflict of generations*. Developing a role model— developing the basic ideas of *why* one lives, what one should strive for—begins not at the age of thirteen for by that time the crisis is already about to burst out. Staying home and watching TV together is not a way out of this situation.

My second point is that the call "Mothers, Stay Home," is simply naïve. I do not think that feminist movements or an alleged *Motherhood Revolution* (as conservative media claims) have been the motivation behind women going into labor force. In most cases, women had to go to work either in order to sustain their families or to preserve their intellectual and spiritual health, rather than as a response to some feminist theories and ideas.

In fact, the argument of whether mothers should stay home, is irrelevant, as, unfortunately, is irrelevant the argument of should or should not fourteen-year-old children be involved in sex. Mothers have left home and joined the work force. It is a fact.

Recently, I came across a book by Rosaline C. Barnett and Caryl Rivers,[9] *She Works/He Works: How Two-Income Families Are Happier,*

---

9   Rosaline C. Barnett and Caryl Rivers, *She Works/He Works: How Two-Income Families Are Happy, Healthy, and Thriving.* Harvard University Press, Boston, MA, 1998

Healthier, and Better Off. This book, based on a long and serious soci-ologic investigation involving the interviewing of hundreds of married couples, proves a very simple fact: People respecting each other, shar-ing their duties in both the household chores and the upbringing of their children, create a happy, loving family. Their life is full; their children are healthier and happier than are those in families where the mother does not work. The fact that a two-income family is economi-cally much better off and less vulnerable to the economic cataclysms of the society is an important factor, also stabilizing relationships among all the family members. However, the *success story* told in this book relates only to people having a relatively high educational level: mostly whites of the "middle or working class" (not very untypical of the Boston area where the study had been conducted). By the way, the authors note: "Not until we accept the working woman as the norm can we adequately prepare our sons and daughters for the lives they will really be leading. Our study conclusively proves that holding up the rigid and outdated lifestyle of the 1950s, as a sacred icon will only add stress to their busy and often difficult lives. On the whole, we do not help young women prepare for the flexible jobs that will protect their economic futures and that of their families if we plant in their heads the idea that what they really *ought* to be doing is staying home. We don't prepare young men for the deep involvement they are going to have with their families if we create in them the idea that the *real man* doesn't change diapers or drive the kids to nursery school" (p. 11; italics by the authors).

No question that today's American day-care system is not a high-quality sub-stitute for high-quality mother care. The question is how it can be improved, and how it can be made affordable to an American family, even the one that failed to realize the "American Dream." Perhaps a step in the right direction would be cre-ating day-care centers affiliated with factories, companies, universities, for exam-ple, where people working at these institutions could leave their children when they come to work in the morning, see them at lunch break, and return home together. It would make a tremendous difference. And this is only a matter of active involvement of the parents and the institutions' management: the govern-ment has nothing to do with it. Although, in some cases, a kind of subsidy, or tax credits will be needed. I do know one example of such a day-care center: the kindergarten at New England Bio-Labs in Beverly, Massachusetts. Hundreds of others may already exist, but they are not yet an essential and integral part of our society. When we feel we are serious and ready for a *Day-Care Revolution*, there are good schools to go to and learn. Denmark is one of them.

Unfortunately, America does not like to learn. To *reinvent* is much easier. Dr. Paul Gagnon, in his unpublished article, *School Reform: Are We up to It?* (which I quoted already in essay *Training or Education?*) writes: "We could look abroad to see what school reform looks like. But [the]American educator's appetite for global consciousness falls off sharply when it comes to schooling. We cannot imitate, they say, 'cultures' unlike our own. They find it especially true of Western Europe, not wealthy as we but well ahead in matters un-American: health insurance, child care and parental leave, fair labor practices, slimmer income differences. Now they outdo us in public education, notably in early childhood, vital to close that learning gaps between social classes."

School

"Education—A debt from present to future generations."

—*George Peabody*

I have already talked (see the essay, "Training or Education?"*)* about what I see as the main problem of our educational system. We teach *skills*: reading skills, math skills, social skills, for example. In other words, we substitute training-like instruction for broad general education. In fact, it is rather difficult to discuss our education, for while doing this one inevitably runs into the situation of an old joke of a restaurant patron complaining to the manager: "Your food is firstly inedible, and then not enough."

Here I discuss not so much *what* our schools teach, rather I am going to focus on *how* they teach, although these two problems are tightly interwoven. In this essay I want to talk some more about how the wrong educational philosophy is destroying our schools. It is like destroying a city. Our children's future is buried under the ruins of shattered knowledge and culture.

It is not a secret that the teaching process in our public schools is lacking intensity, and a lot of discussion is focused these days on increasing the instruction time.. These strangers of mine in a scarlet convertible—they are idle, they have nothing to do. And this is in March, when youngsters of their age throughout Europe are studying hard before matriculation or end-of-year exams sometime in May or early June.

It is not a secret either that the senior year—the last year in our high schools—simply does not make sense. Think about it. Most colleges would accept students without any entrance examinations, based mainly on their SAT scores, an essay about why the student wants to go to *this* college, his or her average last year's grades and, well, perhaps their teachers' recommendations (which are not mandatory).

None of these factors will be significantly changed during the senior year. The youngsters know that. Therefore their attendance, during that idling year, is poor. They are just having fun and waiting for the spring proms and the culminating graduation ceremonies. Those who do not go to college could have been working full time already. Why do we need the senior year at all? Would it not be a tremendous saving—in terms of both funds and human resources—if the children graduated a year earlier? Some adjustments would be needed, but that is it.

This is an extreme example of wasting time. But the tremendous waste is going on every day, beginning with the preschool year. Of course, most of our teaching problems originate from the *Progressive* education ideological maxims that were discussed in the essay "Training or Education:" Learning must be easy, learning must be fun, and children should not learn what they do not like.

As I have already mentioned there, the principles of *Progressive* education were formulated over one hundred years ago in the era of intensive development of industrial capitalism in America. Not only have they survived the whole century of turbulent changes in economics and society, but they still are, in this high-tech era, the foundation of the teaching process in our schools. One does not have to be a PhD in psychology in order to see that the existential problems of our children that later develop into a full-fledged crisis of adolescence originate from the above *Progressive*'s maxims.

Perhaps younger children learn best when they play, although not always is this learning active. There is a limit, however, to what children can learn while playing. At some point, the play environment may be inadequate for learning. Very infrequently games teach tenaciousness and perseverance. A *stubborn* child's tenaciousness during a game is most probably a manifestation of that child's already developed personality, rather than the innate teaching quality of the game.

The ability to overcome obstacles can only be taught by challenging a child with an obstacle and insisting on its being overcome. This obviously contradicts the thesis that the learning process should not be difficult, but rather should be effortless, fun. On the contrary, it is always hard to learn something new and unknown and different. One of the ways to develop in the child the ability to overcome obstacles is by problem solving. No matter how much a teacher explains in class, the problem-solving activity should be given as homework. Besides, it is an intimate process, requiring individual concentration. Unfortunately, in our schools, homework, especially in the lower grades, is almost nonexistent. It is virtually nonexistent in high school also. A study at the University of California in San Diego has shown that the average American high school student does only about four hours of home work *a week*, compared with four hours *a day* in other post-industrial countries. There are even teaching experts who insist that homework is harmful because it prevents a child from spending time with family (watching TV?).

Children never play games that are difficult to play, that do not bring them satisfaction or pleasure. Why then should they like learning something that is difficult to learn? Of course they don't. But most of what they eventually have to learn and understand in order to become mature individuals *is* difficult. Most of our public schools do not have a well-established and strong *core* curriculum that is *absolutely* necessary for the normal development of a child at the beginning of 21st century. As a part of the educational reform that everybody is talking about, some states have developed (or are in the process of developing of) *recommendations*. But they are not mandatory, and thus a school district educational "expert" (or even a single teacher) may decide what to teach and what not. Now, in high schools, in fact, children themselves decide on the scope of this "core."

Here is a view of an American who cares: "A major factor in developing 'the sense of connectedness that the society needs' is a common cultural experience of its members provided by national curriculum for all. Young Americans, unlike their overseas counterparts, are left unattended to wander freely in the world's consumerism-driven jungle. Their souls are not firmly anchored in the rich universal cultural heritage..."[10]

The worst anathema in our schools—from preschool class through grade 12—is *mathematics*. Why? The answer is obvious. Since mastering math requires developing abstract thinking, this is not easy. It takes perhaps hours of instruction, discussion, and problem solving. It is rather like climbing a high mountain. If you, panting and out of breath, have succeeded, you see a wide and beautiful country at your feet. Instead of being an "unwanted child," math should have the status of a "prince."

---

[10] A letter to the Editor, *US News & World Report*, Oct. 2, 1995.

I am not sure that our teaching experts comprehend the simple truth: When the difficulty of understanding math (serious pre-college math, not the basic arithmetic) has been overcome, the learning process will accelerate, and not only in math. This is because of the intensive brain development that the creative learning of mathematics brings about. No matter how difficult, but this learning *must* take place. It is necessary not only because then all the *science* courses can be taught on much higher levels, but mainly because this will bring our children to the level of knowledge and intellectual development of our time.

Of course, attaining this level is impossible without violating the above pedagogical maxims. Here, math is just an example for me. What I mean is that our schools do not teach children to work *hard*, to meet challenges, to cope with difficulties and to overcome obstacles. Every grade has a level of knowledge that will be unattainable unless the children are encouraged, pushed, and even forced to work hard. It does not mean that in every grade the battle begins anew. The ability to concentrate—both physically and mentally—develops gradually. But once children already know how to do it when they are six, seven or eight years old, they will be able to learn actively and intensely at higher grades too. Possibly, then Ritalin will not be necessary.

A funny and surely, "insignificant" problem: Ours is the culture of pencils. Children, as well as college students, write exclusively with pencils. Every pencil has an eraser that makes it the easiest to use as a writing instrument. If you do not like what you just wrote—erase it. Result: children first write, then think. Then erase—or do not erase— it has been written already, why bother? Out of sight, out of mind. Besides, if it is a multiple-choice test, a chance is that the answer is right (even if one is not sure). If one is persistent enough to *think* after having written, then the eraser is used. Then, perhaps, the eraser will be used again, and again. Any teacher knows what a mess a typical student's written work is. However, this mess is not just something unattractive esthetically. It is the obvious result of lack of mental discipline. What if an *inerasable* pen, rather than a pencil were the writing instrument? Then one would have to use a scrap of paper or a scratch page to think and write on for as long as time allowed, putting the result into neat writing on the test or homework sheet when the thinking process was over. However, I do not even dare suggest that pencils be abolished. It would be absolutely *un-American.*

I should like to return again to the problem of homework. Of course, in order for the homework to be effective, there must be proper conditions at home. Not every home has them. Therefore the children must be able to stay at school for as long as it is necessary for them to finish their work. This would require a teacher's assistance, but it is a necessity. If the school requirements are firm, a child will not watch TV and, perhaps, will even encourage the parents to abstain from TV until the homework is finished.

Just one example: Asian-American immigrant families have strong traditions of doing homework together. In many families, doing homework is a ritual that involves both the children and the parents. Older children help their younger siblings. Statistically, the more children who are in the family, the higher the academic achievements of a child. (Typically, in America, the trend is just the opposite.) William Bennett, in his book, *Devaluing of America: The Fight for Our Culture and Our Children*[11] tells an amazing anecdote. In the Asian-American community in Riverdale, New York, the school authorities were puzzled that the number of textbooks being sold exceeded the number of children registered in classes. The explanation was that in most of the Asian-American families they used to buy two sets of books: one for the student, and one for the mother, who could better help and control her children, and sometimes would study together with them.

Having increased the teaching load both at school and at home, the time structure of the child's life will have completely changed. Everybody knows that boredom is a child of idleness. When children are busy learning—and this may be a fascinating and challenging process that, in spite of its difficulty, will bring deep satisfaction—their life is full. There is already a meaning in it. Even for those who hate to study, but must, there will be no other option. They will simply not have too much time for going out, hanging around and causing trouble.

Of course, it would be wrong if the homework load were so heavy that a child had no free time at all. There should be free time. But the school should take an active role in organizing that time. What I mean is an extracurricular activity at school.

America does have a form of extracurricular activity that may become a powerful tool of enriching our children's lives. What I mean is school clubs. I was unable to find the numbers—the percentage of American schools that have interest clubs. Perhaps the majority of schools have them. You may find in the Internet home pages of over 1000 school clubs. The programs and objectives of some of

---

[11] William Bennett, in his book, *Devaluing of America: The Fight for Our Culture and Our Children.* Simon & Schuster, New York, 1992.

the clubs are so mature, thoughtful, and "anti-*Progressive*" that they may serve as role models for the club movement in America.

The club activity has to be so magnetizing and vibrant that no one, even the less successful student, would be left behind. This kind of extracurricular activity must become a part of an *additional* curriculum—directed at the development of our children beyond the rigid frameworks of school programs. Below (the essay "Science and Society") I will discuss a possible way of achieving this goal. In order for the clubs to achieve their important role, they must be regarded as an *indispensable supplement* to formal education rather than just another nice activity. And they must target children of all ages, not only high-schoolers. An extremely important, if you wish, *existential* function of the clubs is helping children to find their *vocation*—to find the area of interests that would become *the task,* even *the mission*—the vector of the whole life. This search for meaning should be initiated as early in our children's lives as possible.

Let me stress again my main point: Only by increasing the intensity of education at our schools, increasing the homework load as an essential part of teaching, and organizing a vibrant extracurricular activity centered around our schools, can a difference be made. Then, not only will we have dramatically raised the educational level of our schools and removed our children from the streets (thus virtually getting rid of juvenile crime), but also—and this is the most important consequence of that measure—we will bring *meaning* to our children's lives, helping them begin the long and gratifying process of developing maturity.

Readers might have noticed that the school reform I am talking about is quite different from what is broadly discussed these days. Yes, it is important that the quality of instruction be improved. Yes, it is important that parents work together with school. And yet, again and again, it is about improving the *skills* that we are talking about, rather than giving *knowledge*, developing the *spiritual* in our children. And nobody today suggests getting rid of those vicious pedagogical ideas, the tenets that actually are the main cause of our education's deterioration to the level unacceptable at the beginning of the 21st century in the greatest country of the world. That would allow solving a host of other problems of a fundamental existential character that plague our society today.

Meanwhile, a few years ago, the best educational TV channel—PBS—advertising the new "Store of Knowledge" in Pennsylvania, put forward a call: "Entertain Your Brain." So, here is a new definition of education: *the entertainment of the brain.* I am afraid the struggle against these ideas and principles will be difficult and long.

Books

"We do not need to burn all the books to destroy our Western civilization. All we need to do is leave them unread for one generation"

—*Dr. Robert Maynard Hutchins, former President of the University of Chicago.*

To an optimist this warning would sound ridiculous. But one need not be too pessimistic in order to see in our society today the dangerous signs confirming that doomsday forecast.

Due to the deterioration of our educational system, the transfer of intellectual and moral values from the older to the younger generation is just short of being virtually nonexistent. The conflict of generations, which I have already discussed above, is more acute now than ever before. The young generation, being abandoned by the society of adults, creates from scratch its own culture based on its own perception of life—both the individual's and the life of the society as a whole. This perception is nihilistic, confrontational, and fundamentally wrong; hence the ugly "culture" that every day is being created by our children and which they later carry on as immature adults.

Forget the "culture" of inner-city ghettos, which, in its level of social organization, is far from the lowest forms of civilized society, being closer to that of the Stone Age or even animal hordes.[12] Everybody knows it is ugly. But what about the "culture" of our middle-class suburban youths? Who are their idols? Michael Jackson, Madonna, the host of MTV's stars, and the like. These are the people who blatantly and cynically exploit the urge of youngsters to some "truths," some ideas, some role models, giving them inedible and poisonous surrogates instead.

Erich Fromm, in *The Art of Loving*[13] (p. 98) wrote: "In previous epochs of our own culture, or in China and India, the man most highly valued was the person with outstanding spiritual qualities. Even the teacher was not only, or even primarily, a source of information, but his function was to convey certain human attitudes. In contemporary capitalistic society—and the same holds true for

---

[12] For someone who, like me, cares for what is going on in our "home," I recommend an extremely good article on inner-city culture. To me it was a shocking revelation. It is also a *guilty verdict* for our society. This is Alija Anderson's "The Code of the Street," *The Atlantic Monthly*, May 1994.

[13] Erich Fromm, *The Art of Loving*. Bantam, 1963.

Russian communism—the men suggested for admiration and emulation are everything but bearers of significant spiritual qualities."

These lines, written fifty years ago, are true today perhaps more than at the time they were written. However, you cannot blame the *idols* for being chosen and raised to a pedestal. There is always somebody to fill the vacuum. For the children, the choice is too restricted. Books are out of the question and only what the TV and movies can offer is left. And they do offer, but only what the children think they want or are able to easily consume. Again a vicious cycle.

Throughout millennia, before this high-tech era, society's values were transferred from generation to generation via the written word. We know the history of our civilization and those ancestors on whose shoulders we stand from books written on stone, clay, animal skins, papyrus and paper. Being able to read and understand was always a high virtue in societies as far back as humankind could trace.

It is not so now. A huge percentage of our population is functionally illiterate. Although they can read, they do not use this skill in their lives, and virtually cannot understand a written text even of moderate complexity, such as a manual for an appliance, a car, or a machine they work on, to say nothing of an insurance policy or a financial contract. Actually, they are not *illiterate*; they are *a-literate*. Books and reading simply are not playing any significant role in their lives. Less than 0.1 percent of Americans spend 15 minutes or more a day reading.

The late distinguished educator and popularizer of science, Carl Sagan, wrote:[14]

"What passes for literacy in America in late twentieth century is a very rudimentary knowledge of the English language, and television in particular tends to seduce the mass population away from reading. In pursuit of the profit motive, it has dumbed itself down to lowest-common-denominator programming—instead of rising to teach and inspire."

Reading and understanding are the two sides of the same coin. These days more and more people firmly believe that understanding can be achieved by some means other than reading: by TV, or a computer, for instance. This may be true in obtaining special knowledge (training.) or entertainment. But one cannot

---

[14] Carl Sagan, *Billions & Billion:. Thoughts on Life and Death at the Brink of the Millennium* (Random House, 1997 (p.206).

build up one's personality, with high self-esteem and a mature approach to life, without reading, and reading *a lot*. Extinction of books will eventually bring about the extinction of Western civilization.

People working at the forefront of computer technology do understand this. A research project at MIT is directed at developing a *high-tech* book. It will have the look of an ordinary book, with a number of pages in it. You insert a diskette (or a CD) with the book you want to read, or download it through your computer from a library, and turn the switch. A text appears on your pages, you can turn them, you can make notes on page margins; you can return to the page you want to reread. In this book of the future, all the advantages of unlimited access to the intellectual treasures of the world will be combined with the *old* intimate way of interaction of a human being with a written word.

Not many parents understand the danger of disappearance of books from our lives.. We may be unable to significantly improve our children's reading skills unless the children are encouraged to read a lot, unless reading a lot is a part of our school curricula. Unless reading becomes a mode, a necessity of our children's life all our efforts are in vain. Unfortunately, those who initiate the school reform do not understand this.

Reading is difficult. To read and understand is even more so. To read fast, to grasp quickly, and to develop an urge, a passion for reading is the destiny of the few.

I believe the situation would have completely changed if, at school, from the moment the children learn to read, a systematic process of improving their reading ability began. This process is impossible without a teacher spending hours patiently helping children to accept books and reading as a necessary part of their lives. It is impossible without every-day homework assignments of reading, gradually increasing the load, and arriving, say, at a permanent requirement of an hour of reading every day (it might be just 40 minutes, but it has to be a must) for all the years at school. Children have to write short compositions every time a book is finished. Special discussion sessions should be a part of the curriculum. Even weekends should have special reading assignments. Summer reading with written compositions must be mandatory. "Not a Day without a Line Read" must be the motto of our schools.

This seems to be a pipe dream. But thoughtful and dedicated teachers do make it a reality today even for remedial reading class students. Just to mention

Dr. Janet Allen—in her inspiring book[15] *It's Never Too Late: Leading Adolescents to Lifelong Literacy* (Heinemann, 1995), she told the dramatic story of her tireless work helping children to discover the hidden world of books. It is not just reading and writing *skills* that her children had acquired; they had fallen in love with reading, and it had made a crucial difference in their lives.

Imagine how many interesting books a child may be able to digest during just one year. Almost every subject—history and geography among them—may be taught through reading fascinating fiction books. Virtually no textbooks may be needed. Again, to develop a desire, a passion for reading is a difficult process, like climbing a high mountain. It goes without saying, the rights of children to learn what they want and not to learn what they don't want, will be violated. But later, at the top of that mountain, with the breathtaking view of the world before them, the children will be grateful to those "pitiless" torturers—the teachers and parents.

Books have an important advantage over the *video* tools of education and child development. Books develop imagination—the quality that is, perhaps, the most important component of creative activity of the human race. Albert Einstein even said that imagination is more important that knowledge. Maturity and, in fact, human happiness are virtually impossible without that quality.

Reading, unlike watching TV, is an intimate process, when the reader is one-on-one with the books' characters and events. Reading a lot, children gradually learn how to identify themselves with the book's characters and events, how to empathize with them. Book characters become alive. A child learns how to laugh, suffer, lose, and win together with the book's characters. They become a part of the child's personality. Reading, actually, builds the personality.

Mary Rommely, an illiterate elderly immigrant from Austria, at the beginning of this century, knew all these simple truths. We have forgotten.

Another important function of books in education is that they improve speech, build vocabulary, and make speech rich.

It is not a secret that the English language in this country is deteriorating. Our teenagers' speech is poor; they can hardly express themselves without interjections or mimicking what they want to say. Their speech is contaminated with slang and indecencies. No wonder. The words that for centuries could not be heard because they were firmly believed to be insulting and degrading to the moral values of people, are now widely used not only in everyday life but on radio programs, TV shows and in movies that millions of people watch.

---

[15] Dr. Janet Allen, *It's Never Too Late: Leading Adolescents to Lifelong Literacy.* Heinemann, Portsmouth, NH, 1995

Today, even a written exam, when a student is to explain something in words, rather than select a multiple choice, is a problem. When teaching materials science (almost twenty years ago) at Boston University—one of the America's best schools—I often encountered a situation when I could not grade an examination paper because I was unable to understand the explanation. Sometimes I did understand every single word, but could not grasp the meaning—so helpless were my students in expressing their thoughts. In such situations I had to set an appointment with the student, in order to understand what he or she knew or did not know—to give actually a kind of oral exam.

The language our youngsters speak reflects not only their intellectual underdevelopment, but also their social status—the permanent conflict and confrontation with the family and society. That is why it is so important that children read a lot of books written in good English, and be encouraged to discuss them both orally and in written form. In this respect, a more systematic use of oral exams should be a part of the educational reform I am talking about.

The word "cool" has conquered our language. Just a few years ago only teenagers used it. Now it is a part of the English language that not only "people in the street," but also the media, TV, and newspaper widely use.

Now it has a positive connotation of something or somebody good, excellent. People worth admiring are always *cool*. And nobody remembers that the origin of this word is the confrontation: with parents, authorities, the police, or whoever dares to infringe on teenagers' freedom. One has to be *cool* in conflicts with parents, school teachers, the police, etc.

Another word that competes tooth and nail with the "cool" in conquering our language is "sexy." Tony Perkins, a popular ABC weather man has said a while ago: "We are all cool and dead sexy!"

Recent (1999) poor results in writing tests in Massachusetts's public schools were to be expected. It is impossible to develop *writing skills* without first being able to express one's thoughts in any form. But our children are virtually unable to express themselves—even *orally*—because of their poor and inadequate English. How then can one hope they will be able to express themselves in writing? And again, there is only one tool that develops the ability to express oneself, both orally and in writing—reading good literature, and reading a lot of it.

Letters to Dr. Allen (whose inspiring and encouraging book I mentioned above) by her students are a convincing proof of the urgency of our efforts to bring the world of books to our children. Here are the excerpts from just two letters: "When I think about how I feel about reading now and not reading as a child, I feel cheated. I really was cheated....There are so many books to read, and I've got to make up for all the years I've missed..." "What you gave me, there is no way I can pay you back or tell you how much I thank you. You gave me the gift of reading. Reading is not just a gift; it is a power within itself. I owe you my life and my mind. You've opened so many doors for me. May God bless you." (pp. 144-148). President Ronald Reagan who used to read a lot often recalled his mother's "commandment:" "If you learn to love reading you will never be alone."

Please believe me, what I am discussing is not the nostalgia of an elderly man. The wisdom of my 68 years and my passionate urge to understand life tell me that returning to that almost lost treasure of books is one of the most important means of returning intellectual and spiritual health to our children—helping them in their search for meaning and direction. That, in due time, will change the whole society, for today's children's children will be different.

We have everything needed for that change. What is necessary is that our educators, and, perhaps, what is much more crucial, *we the people*, ourselves, understand the importance of the more responsible approach to our children's education and upbringing.

Love

"What you need is love..."

—*The Beatles*

A contemporary author once said: "We are sending our children to barricades of sexual revolution." Sending children to barricades to fight for a cause they do not understand is perhaps the worst crime that parents can commit. Contemporary society has let the sex genie out of the bottle, and allowed him to enslave the children. We, the adults, should not fool ourselves. This has been and is our responsibility.

Was it inevitable? In the age of freedom—unrestricted freedom—why should any taboo be left undestroyed? It is OK. But even the concept of *unrestricted freedom* is the sign of a deep societal crisis. For *unrestricted* means first of all that people have lost the feeling of *responsibility*.

I am not going to discuss here the history of the sexual revolution. Yes, it is our American baby. But, as is usually the case with abandoned children, the baby simply went out of control.

Although "sexual emancipation" began in the '20s, the real revolution burst out in the early '60s with the advent of the Pill. What, at the beginning, seemed to be a blessing—liberating woman from the fear of unwanted pregnancy, getting rid of the seemingly meaningless taboos of the previous centuries—turned out to be a curse for society only 25 to 30 years later. Great thinkers of the time, Mahatma Gandhi among them, did warn about the possible adverse affect of a reliable contraceptive on the stability of the family, and human relations. But it is never possible to stop a revolution.[16]

The sexual revolution did not begin with Sigmund Freud, although he was doubtlessly one of its prophets. "According to Freud, the full and uninhibited satisfaction of all instinctual desires would create mental health and happiness. But the obvious clinical facts demonstrate that men—and women—who devote their lives to unrestricted sexual satisfaction, do not attain happiness, and very often suffer from severe neurotic conflicts or symptoms. The complete satisfaction of all instinctual needs is not only a basis for happiness, it does not even guarantee sanity." Erich Fromm (*The Art of Loving*) wrote these lines over fifty years ago. The *sexual revolution* at that time had not yet burst out. It is only during the four recent decades that it has called to its barricades millions of innocent people, and has been ruthlessly killing them with its new weapon—AIDS.

One of the chapters of Eric Fromm's *The Art of Loving* has a title, "Love and Its Disintegration in the Contemporary Western Society." Sex is a surrogate of love now. Viktor Frankl also reminds us of an important truth we seem to forget: "Sex is justified, even sanctified, as soon as, but only as long as, it is a vehicle of love. Thus love is not...a mere side-effect of sex; rather, sex is a way of expressing the experience of that ultimate togetherness which is called love" (*Man's Search for Meaning*, p. 134).

Adults have their choice: if they are incapable of love, they just *enjoy* sex. But our teenagers do not have any choice. We have deprived them of the means of maturing, building-up personalities, by refusing to give them adequate education, necessary for

---

[16] For a condensed comprehensive account of the '60s with their ups and downs, see, for example,. *The Incredible Sixties: The Stormy Years That Changed America*, by Jules Archer; Harcourt Brace Jovanovich, Pub.., San Diego, 1986.

the soul to become strong. They drift. They desperately want love, but only sex is available.

"What you need is love," a famous line by the Beatles of over thirty years ago is still a desperate call for help. But our ears are deaf. Teenagers are struggling for intimacy, and cannot achieve it. They need intimacy as an ecological niche in this hostile world in order to start believing in themselves, to understand themselves, to find the direction. And they mislabel sex for this much-needed intimacy. If they were helped, if though for a moment, the cacophony of sex on all the wavelengths would stop, or at least be muted. They would attempt to achieve healthy and strong relationships outside of sex. And they are in fact trying to achieve such relationships, but it is very difficult.

Lilian B. Rubin, in her book on the consequences of the sexual revolution (*Erotic Wars: What Happened to the Sexual Revolution?*), from which I have already quoted, presents the data from a 1986 Harris poll (p. 61): 57 percent of the nation's 17-year-olds, 46 percent of the 16-year-olds and 29 percent of 15-year olds had had sexual intercourse; 66 to 75 percent are sexually experienced by the time they turn nineteen; a survey of 14-year-olds from three rural counties in Maryland revealed that 58 percent of the boys and 47 percent of the girls had been involved in sex activity.

We the people have no control of the media. We cannot fight the *First Amendment*—besides, it is one of the greatest achievements of our democracy. What can we do?

The answer is again in changing the way our children are taught at school. If the educational process is directed at developing children's personalities; if the curriculum is strong; if the children, from preschool age on are gradually taught how to concentrate, work hard, and get satisfaction from their studies; if they are taught *how* to read, and are given good books to read; then they will have eventually developed love for reading and knowledge in general, and the problem would be much easier.

Here I would like to touch on one aspect of abstinence that, as far as I know, has so far not been mentioned, at least in the literature for "pedestrians" like me. One of the important concepts of Freudian theory is so-called *sublimation*. Freud defines it as "a process of deflecting libido or sexual-motive activity from human objects to new objects of non-sexual, socially valuable nature." Although sublimation has an intimate and fundamentally personal character, it is an important social factor. Freud points out that this process "has furnished powerful components for all cultural accomplishments." Through sublimation "the excessive excitations from individual

sexual sources are discharged and utilized in other spheres, so that no small enhancement of mental capacity results from a predisposition which is dangerous as such.
This form is one of the sources of artistic activity,"[17] And I would add: "as well as any
other creative activity." I am sure Freud would agree with me, as would probably
many psychologists and psychiatrists.

In our society today, sublimation has been almost completely annihilated. One
feels an urge in one's loins—one copulates. If there is no partner, masturbation, "the
safest kind of sex," is at one's disposal 24 hours a day. The lack of abstinence is especially harmful for adolescents. It is also possible that the disappearance of sublimation can be one of the causes of the drop in our society's creativity—the quality we
were famous for among the nations just a few decades ago.

In my view, the disappearance of sublimation from our adolescents' life is also
a very powerful factor interfering with the process of developing intellectual and
emotional maturity, especially against the background of poor education.
Preaching abstinence as a *virtue* or *necessity* is naïve and may even be counterproductive. But the high load of studying, reading, other extracurricular activity, and
sports would inevitably deflect teenagers' attention from sex, and thus the so
important sublimation will be switched on again.

Then the youngsters would have to spend less time in conformist entertainment. They will learn to treasure their free time. The dates will be filled with
desire to share new experiences and knowledge, new discoveries in themselves and
in the world around, rather than just having fun together. Peer pressure will not
push teenagers into unwanted but *required* sex. Even sex against that background
will be different. And surely the children will not need sex at the age of fourteen,
and even fifteen. They would need *romance*.

> Lilian Rubin, after having interviewed hundreds of young people,
> reveals a sad truth: teenagers, the overwhelming majority of them, do
> not need sex, are afraid of it, and are deeply distressed, even depressed
> when it happens "for the first time." It is the world of adults, and their
> peers' community, as that ugly world's ugly reflection, that forces them
> to submit to the conformism (pp. 41-59).

In my view, one of the worst crimes our society has committed against our
youngsters is that it took *romanticism* out of their lives. Nobody explicitly meant to
do that. But when you stop (or have never even loved) reading books, how can you

---

[17] Freud quoted from: *The Basic Writings of Sigmund Freud.* The Modern Library,
Random House Inc. New York, 1938.

know that love, through the millennia, was the strongest, the most noble, and the purest feeling that men and women ever felt for each other? Even if Romeo and Juliet, Dante and Beatrice or Antony and Cleopatra are too far in time from us, there is other great romantic literature in the world the adolescent should read, even if for no other reason than to develop an ideal of the beloved to come.

Again, please do not accuse me of nostalgia. I want to recall my youth in the totalitarian state, one of the most inhumane in history, probably sharing first and second place with the Nazis. It is not that the Communists encouraged romantic literature. It smacked of "idealism"—the worst enemy of the official and harshly enforced materialistic philosophy, the only philosophy allowed. And yet, perhaps they understood the importance of this kind of literature—even if only to deflect the young people from sex.

The classic Russian literature of the 19th century is rich in romanticism—the list of authors is long and impressive. The beginning of the 20th century brought a great romantic, Alexander Grin.

He died in 1932, poor and abandoned. But he left the legacy that made his name, for a Russian language reader, a symbol of a bright and pure Dream. "If the ability to dream is taken away from a man, then one of the most powerful stimuli will die, that gives birth to culture, art, science, and the urge to fight for the brighter future," writes Konstantin Paustovsky, another great Russian romantic author of the next generation, in his preface to a book by Alexander Grin. On the same page he also writes: "Many people do not know how to dream, and, probably because of that, they cannot grow up to match their time."

As for Grin, in his dreams, he created a land—Grinlandia, as literary critics called it—with its palm trees, colorful flowers, and never-ceasing surf of the warm sea. Seashore towns with mysterious names like Zoorbogan, Lisse, Gel-Gju, Dagon, Doobel were the world where Grin's characters lived.

Here I want to share with you a story,[18] perhaps Grin's best:

---

[18] There is an English translation of this novel: Alexander Green, *Scarlet Sails*, Charles Scribner's Sons, New York, 1967. Some passages in the following narration are my translation from the original Russian text: Alexander Grin, *Selected Stories*, Moscow, 1956. To those interested to learn more about Alexander Grin, I recommend a very informative book, containing both Grin's biography and a thoughtful analysis of most of his works: N. J. L. Luker, *Alexander Grin, the Forgotten Visionary*, Oriental Research Partners, Newtonville, MA, 1980. (In most of the literature published in English, the spelling *Grin* rather than *Green* is used; therefore I am following this tradition.)

The Scarlet Sails

Longren, a sailor from the three-hundred-ton brig *Orion* was returning home to a small seashore village, Caperna, some four miles from Lisse, for a short visit. He was expecting to see his wife Mary waiting for him, at their small home. Instead, a sobbing neighbor widow led him to the cradle of his eight-month-old daughter, whom he had never seen. Mary had died just three months before of pneumonia that she caught when she was walking in a storm to Lisse to sell her wedding ring. The local shopkeeper, Menners, refused to give her credit, unless she agreed to sleep with him.

Longren left his ship, and devoted his entire life to bringing up his little daughter, Assole. To earn their living, Longren began making wooden models of ships, boats, and yachts. His toys were a work of art: the details of the ships' rigging and even tiny figures of sailors were precise and beautiful. He brought his toys to the town stores, and soon people began to buy them.

Assole grew up a lonely and thoughtful child. They were isolated in their poor old house. People of the village did not like them, partly because Longren refused to give as much time as the village's men did to drinking and other rough entertainment, but mainly because of a stigma that had singled him out. When Assole was five years old, in the early spring, Menners, the storekeeper, was overtaken by a storm while in a boat. Longren, who witnessed the beginning of the ordeal refused to help him. Eventually, Menners was saved, but he caught a severe cold and soon died, leaving his curse on Longren as his murderer.

All his free time Longren used to spend with Assole. He taught her to read and write, and on long winter evenings, while working on his ships, he told her endless stories about the sea, the mysterious lands, and his own sails. Assole helped her father as much as she could, both in their household and in his work. Often she even brought the toys to be sold to Lisse, to the town's stores.

She was eight or ten, when one day, while walking with a basketful of ship toys to Lisse, she got lost in the wood. This is how that happened: Instead of walking along a road, she used a path in the wood, which was weaving along a stream. Four miles is a long walk. She decided to take a little rest. Munching on a piece of pie that her father had given her, she was playing with a beautiful tiny yacht with scarlet sails. "Why not let her make her first sail? She will not get wet through if she sails for just a few minutes."

And she carefully placed the yacht in the water at her feet, and let her float along the stream for a few yards. She was talking with an imaginary captain, asking him where he came from, where he was sailing to, and what his load was, when a burst of wind filled the tiny scarlet sails, and the little yacht turned off shore and started floating along the main stream. The girl ran after the boat, but soon got tired and lost sight of the toy. The stream was flowing to the sea. When, eventually, Assole reached a clearing, she saw a strange-looking man sitting on a rock right where the stream was flowing into the sea. The tiny yacht was in his hands, and he was carefully studying it, turning it from side to side.

That was Egl, a wandering poet, and gatherer of folk songs and fairy-tales. He liked the girl, and she also felt a kind of trust talking to him. The man, smiling, told her that he was a magician, and that he could tell her exactly what she was doing: "You were sent to the town to sell your toys, then you decided to play with this yacht, but lost her. That is how you came here."

She was astonished that he knew all that. And then he said: "I do not know in how many years this will happen. But in your village, Caperna, a fairytale will have blossomed that the people will remember for many, many years. You will be a grown-up girl. One day, on the horizon, a scar-let sail will sparkle in the morning sun. Slowly, getting bigger and bigger every minute, the ship will enter the harbor, sailing toward you. All the people will gather on the beach waiting in astonishment. You will hear beautiful music, and a fast boat will float toward the beach. 'Why have you come? Who are you looking for?' the people of the village will ask.

"And then you will see a strong, handsome prince standing in the approaching boat. Reaching for you he will say: 'Good morning, Assole. Far, far away I saw you in my dreams, and I came to take you for good to my kingdom. There, among flowers and music, we will live, and we will be so happy, that your Soul will never know tears and sorrow.'

"And he will take you in his arms, and bring you to the ship, and you will leave for a beautiful and brilliant country, where the sun will rise and the stars will shine greeting you on your arrival." The man finished his prophecy.

"And all that is for me?" asked the girl softly. "But is it possible that it has already arrived—that ship?"

"No, you will have to wait, you will have to grow up first."

When, that evening, the girl told her father about that strange man and his prophecy, a village man overheard her, and a new stigma was born: "The Scarlet Sails Princess."

The story then continues in a different place, miles away from Caperna. Arthur Grey was born to a wealthy aristocratic family, their only son. They lived in the gloomy ancient home of their ancestors, in fact, a castle. Both his father and mother were the captives of their wealth and their social circle of the rich, the snobbish, and the arrogant. Arthur was different. He had a lively and passionate soul, rebelling against the rules set by his ancestors centuries ago. This liveliness, his complete "perverseness," showed itself already very early. He was becoming a knight of whimsical susceptibility, explorer and wonder-worker—that is a man who has chosen from the wide variety of roles in life, the most dangerous and touching one—the role of providence. When he was just eight years old, he climbed a chair and removed the nails from the bleeding wrists of Jesus Christ on the masterpiece of a famous painter—one of the family treasures—by simply painting blue over the nails. He befriended servants of the house, and became their defender and advisor. Once, when he was fourteen, he broke his moneybox and gave all his savings to a kitchen girl who could not get married because she did not have any dowry.

At the age of twelve, Grey discovered the castle's library. Its door was usually locked. But after days of thinking it over and numerous attempts, Grey managed to open the door, and enter a New World of leather-bound books, dust-covered manuscripts, and old paintings. Suddenly, the stuffy torpidity of this forgotten room vanished when Grey saw a big painting hanging right above the door entrance. It was a ship on the ridge of a huge wave—in her last moment before she would launch herself into flight. The sails were hardly seen behind the mist and foam of streaming water. Grey could feel the wild rage of the storm. There was the lonely figure of a man on the deck. Grey could see only his back, but the dynamic stress of the figure, his outstretched arms, and his frozen movement showed that he was in command, that his will was dominating the ship's destiny. Grey knew the man was a captain. His jacket, his white braid, and his black sword betrayed his high status. After that he spent hours every day in the library leafing through old books, passionately swallowing hundreds of pages, deciphering old diagrams—everything to do with the *sea*. And, of course, again and again, he returned to that magic painting. He knew he would become a *captain*.

One fall, when Grey was almost fifteen, he ran away from home and enlisted as a cabin boy on the ship *Ancelm* about to leave Doobel for Marseilles. The years that followed were difficult. Gop, the *Ancelm*'s captain, immediately singled out his cabin boy. He felt something unusual in him. After a long trial period, when Grey was gradually developing from a child into a mature man, the captain decided to make Grey his spiritual heir. He taught him all he himself knew and, at some moment, he felt that he could not give Grey anything that the boy did not already know. His education was over.

When, taking advantage of a short stop of *Ancelm* in Doobel, twenty-year-old Grey decided to visit his home, nobody could recognize the delicate boy in the seasoned strong man. A week passed, and Grey returned to Doobel with a large sum of money. He told Gop that he was going to buy a ship of his own. Some more time elapsed, and the Doobel port greeted the new ship—a three-mast two-hundred-sixty-ton galiot *Secret*.

Grey sailed for four more years till his destiny brought him to Lisse. For ten days heavy boxes of spices, tea, coffee and oriental fragrances were unloaded from *Secret* that was docked at a pier close to the lighthouse. On the eleventh day Grey decided to give his men and himself a day off. He took his fishing gear, and with one of his sailors, jumped into a rowboat and sailed northward along the shore looking for a good place to fish.

They found a place where a tiny stream was flowing into the sea. They were fishing all afternoon, then set a fire, and had a dinner of grilled trout and wine. Grey decided not to return to the ship that night.

He woke up next morning with the first rays of sun. His companion had gone fishing. It was quiet. The sun was already up and everywhere, and Grey felt a strange joy overflowing all his being. Thoughtfully he walked along a path leading off shore to the woods, when, stepping into a small clearing, he saw a girl sleeping in the grass.

It was Assole. She could not sleep the previous night, and early in the morning, before sunrise, she had run to that place where years before she had spoken with the wizard. She got tired, and unwillingly, fell fast asleep among the beautiful flowers. Her hair was in disorder; the upper button of her old homemade blouse was unbuttoned, showing a white small hollow on her neck. Her skirt was pulled up, exposing her knees. Her eyelashes slept peacefully on her cheeks in the shadow of her tender temple half covered by hair. Her head was resting on her right hand, with the little finger half hidden in the hair on her neck. She was fast asleep, and everything that belonged to her was sleeping: her dark hair, her dress and the folds of her dress; and even the grass and flowers close to her seemed to doze, so as not to disturb the harmony.

Grey dropped to his knees in order to see the girl better. Perhaps, in some other circumstances, he would have noticed this girl only with his eyes, but now he saw her in a different way. All was bursting with joy inside him. He did not know who she was, and why she was sleeping there, but that joy was with him. He then did something that he knew he must do no matter how this might change his life: he took off his finger the old expensive ancestral ring and carefully put it on the girl's little finger resting on her neck.

His companion was already looking for him, calling his name. Briskly, Grey walked along the path leading to Caperna, his sailor following him without asking any questions. They easily found the village pub. And there, by offering free drinks to the pub frequenters, Grey learned everything about that strange girl, about that unanimously despised *Scarlet Sails Princess*. Only one elderly man, all black with the dust of coal he used to deliver in his old horse-driven cart, rebelled against the gossips. He told Grey how kind and conscientious the girl was, how hard she worked, and how devoted to each other she and her father were. Grey left his companion in the pub to gather some more information and hurried to his ship. He knew what he had to do now.

The next day was spent in Lisse's fabric stores: dozens of rolls of red, rose and scarlet silk were inspected and rejected, until, finally, Grey found what he thought was the color the girl had expected to see. Then his ship was moved to a remote harbor and, in total secrecy, for the whole week the new scarlet sails were sewn and installed. The crew was mystified. Everybody believed that Grey was preparing his ship for a daring smuggling operation. On the eve of the final day Grey hired a band of musicians who, he believed, would fit right in with his plans.

When everything was ready, he gathered his crew and announced that he was going to get married, that his bride had already been waiting for him, and that they were to sail right away.

Assole discovered the ring the moment she awoke just a few moments after Grey and his companion left. She could not find an explanation to that miracle, but she knew that something was about to happen, and would happen soon. All that day, and the days that followed were like a dream, filled with anxious expectation of the unknown. On the eighth day, and seven years after a stranger on the seashore had told Assole the fairytale about the scarlet sails, the miracle happened.

As usual, Assole woke up early, and having finished her breakfast, sat at a window with a book. Their business could not feed them any more—the stores in Lisse recently refused to buy their toys: models of trains, automobiles, and airplanes were in high demand now. Therefore Longren, Assole's father, decided to return to the sea, and he found a job on a post steamer. He was to return home the next weekend. Assole was reading a book when something distracted her attention. First she thought it was a tiny red beetle on the window glass. But then she saw that it was not a beetle. It was a ship. It just appeared on the horizon, the morning sun burning in its *scarlet* sails. The *scarlet sails!*

Assole did not remember how she left her house. She was running toward the shore, her heart about to jump out of her breast. The crowd had already gathered near the pier. Never before had a big ship ever come so close to the village, but that one had *scarlet sails*—the one that that crazy girl has been waiting for all those years. People were whispering and crying, and their voices sounded like the hisses of snakes. Assole ran into that unfriendly crowd and through it right into the waves.

The ship was already quite close. Sweet music was heard from the ship. A small boat was lowered and sunburned sailors were rowing it toward the shore. A smiling handsome man was standing in the boat. "I am here, I am here, It is I." cried Assole, her waist in warm waves, stretching her arms toward the boat.

Laughing, the man in the boat lowered himself, and carefully took Assole by her waist and lifted her out of water. She closed her eyes for a moment, and then opened them, smiled and said. "You are exactly *you*."

"You are also exactly *you*, my child. Here I came. Have you recognized me?"

She nodded, smiled, and again closed her eyes. New happiness was deep within her.

The ship's deck was decorated with expensive rugs, all in scarlet flares. The crew was congratulating the new Queen, and a keg of three-hundred-year-old wine from the cellars of Grey's castle was opened. "Grey will drink it in paradise" said the old inscription. And this was the proper occasion.

This is, more or less, the end of the story. The *Scarlet Sails* has been treasured by at least four generations of reading people back in Russia. But why is this story so breathtakingly attractive, magnetizing? I believe that is most of all due to its simple idea: *miracles do not happen by themselves.* People create them. You and I can make them. We only have to be willing, passionately willing, to bring miracles to life.

A young and talented Russian Jewish poet Pavel Kogan was killed in 1941 at the Moscow front. In his breast pocket they found a notebook with an unfinished poem. It had the lines (in my translation):

"And again young moon hangs like a yatagan.
Chilling waves of the morning breeze.
Early, early, with sunrise, from Zoorbogan
Ships are sailing to Lisse."

As a matter of fact, the urge for the *ideal* is an innate quality of human beings. It is one of the fundamentally humane dimensions of our nature, and it has an enormous existential value. But the idealism is a delicate and short-lived flower—especially in a cynical and pragmatic society. Happy is he or she who, against all odds, has preserved the urge for the ideal in his or her soul. And even those who have lost it, from time to time, do feel the necessity of even a brief touch of something shining, bright, pure, that of which our everyday life is devoid.

We must help our children to restore that ability: to see "beyond the visible," to dream. We, adults also need it.

Music

"Music is a higher revelation than all wisdom and philosophy."

—*Ludwig van Beethoven*

At the beginning of the 21st century this thought of Beethoven's sounds like a prophecy come true, at least for our young generation. It is virtually impossible to see a teenager without ear plugs in his or her ears. It is virtually impossible to see a car with a youngster at the wheel that does not emit through its open windows thunder-like high decibel sounds. The extra loud presence of this music is a kind of manifestation of the right of our youngsters to live in their own world, different from the reality around them.

Allan Bloom, in his seminal book, *The Closing of the American Mind*,[19] wrote (p. 68): "Today, a very large proportion of young people between ages of ten and twenty live for music. It is their passion; nothing else excites them as it does; they cannot take seriously anything alien to music."

However, the music that completely absorbs our young generation is different from the one Beethoven had meant. This music is *rock*, the music of *body* and *sex*. It is devoid of any intellectual or spiritual content. And, not coincidentally, it does fit into the empty and meaningless existence of our children.

The mass nihilism of the '60s has left the rock culture as its legacy. Elvis Presley, who, when he had just appeared in the mid-fifties and was considered

---

[19] Allan Bloom, *The Closing of the American Mind: How Higher Education Has Failed Democracy and Impoverished the Soul of Today's Students.* Simon & Schuster, New York, 1987.

"indecent" by the media, seems now as innocent as the Beatles. Elvis Presley never proclaimed violence, and the moral harm he inflicted on the children in those days (and he was a *forerunner* of the sexual revolution) cannot be compared to the crimes against the moral health of our children being committed by the numerous *punk-rocks*, *heavy metals*, groups, for example.

Watching a rock concert, one cannot but freeze in fear for the thousands of teenagers jumping and screaming in agitation, with a horde of "animal bums" on the stage, in rags, in ecstasy, hysterically spewing indecencies, abuse and hatred, and exerting disharmonious sounds at the level of hundreds of decibels.

The following quote from Alan Blum is the quintessence of the music culture that has enslaved our children (pp. 74-75): "Picture a thirteen-year old boy sitting in the living room of his family home doing his math assignment while wearing his Walkman headphones or watching MTV. He enjoys the liberties hard won over centuries by the alliance of philosophic genius and political heroism, consecrated by the blood of martyrs; he is provided with comfort and leisure by the most productive economy ever known to mankind; science has penetrated the secrets of nature in order to provide him with the marvelous, lifelike electronic sound and image reproduction he is enjoying. And in what does progress culminate? A pubescent child whose body throbs with orgiastic rhythms; whose feelings are made articulate in hymns to the joy of onanism or the killing of parents; whose ambition is to win fame and wealth in imitating the drag-queen who makes the music. In short, life is made into a nonstop, commercially prepackaged masturbation fantasy."

The great German poet Heinrich Heine once noted that "when words leave off, music begins." But the music that thirteen-year old boy and our youngsters listen to virtually does not make sense without words. Separate pieces of music are called *songs*. And what are those "songs" about? Again I quote Alan Blum: "The words implicitly and explicitly describe bodily acts that satisfy sexual desire and treat them as its natural and routine culmination for children who do not yet have the slightest imagination of love, marriage or family."

But it is not only the sex that makes those songs so poisonous, they are filled with macho-male-chauvinistic disrespect to women, and violence: sexual violence, just violence for the sake of it, and political violence ("Kill the cop!").

The emergence of *rap* has completely liberated "songs" from tunes: only a bit is left. But the lyrics—originally the reflection of black inner city hatred toward the rest of society—are gradually shifting to include and express the general nihilism and hatred of the young empty souls irrespective of affluence or race.

Rock has become a multibillion dollar business, and our children bring in a good chunk of those billions. "The rock business is perfect capitalism, supplying to demand and helping to create it. It has the moral dignity of drug trafficking...Rock is very big business, bigger than movies, bigger than professional sports, bigger than television, and this accounts for much of respectability of the music business" (p.77).

Of course, any attempts to stop the spreading of rock and its soul-poisoning epidemic would be anti-constitutional. The *First Amendment* and the cohorts of the Left guarantee the impunity of the intellectual drugs. What is worse, however, is that our educators, and those who are responsible for supplying the children with knowledge, have agreed that rock and its consequences are not only inevitable, but also *acceptable*—not undesirable. Rap, for example, has been accepted as a manifestation of *African heritage*, and thus an important component of *diversity*. Recently, in the *PBS Kids* program's segment on library cards, in the cartoon the children sing about how good and how much fun it is to read books, but sing it as a rap.

I agree with Alan Blum that perhaps the most devastating is not the moral effect of rock music and its glorification of sex, violence and drugs, but its general anti-intellectual effect that ruins children's imagination, thus making it very diffi-cult—if not impossible—for them to accept art and literature as the most funda-mental sources of spiritual development. Allan Blum's experience as a university professor shows that addiction to rock music is virtually irreversible. "...as long as they have the Walkman on, they cannot hear what the great tradition has to say. And after its prolonged use, when they take it off, they find they are deaf" (p. 81).

Today's situation does not leave much hope. Often we hear that classical music is dead. It *is* dead in exactly the same sense as the book is dead. We do have thou-sands of excellent symphony orchestras, with classical music concerts—to which it is difficult to buy a ticket—as well as the thousands of book stores, with over-crowded parking lots, to say nothing of the thousands upon thousands libraries—in large cities and small towns—the true *temples of the book*. And we do have the most vibrant cultural elite, having absorbed the best achievements of at least two millennia of Western civilization. However the majority of Americans are getting more and more estranged from the intellectual and emotional nourishing spring of that culture.

And yet, the educational revolution I have been talking about would also return to our children the treasures of Western humanitarian culture, and with it, the treasures of classical music—the music of the soul.

Recently, quite by chance, I happened to watch a Russian TV program rebroadcast for American viewers over a special "Russian" channel. It was an evening program for children. This time it was a cartoon, quite an unusual one. The characters seemed to be welded from pieces of metal—abstract, slightly elon-gated forms, but very impressive.

The place: a fairytale kingdom, most probably in Norway. The King is about to get married. We see preparations for the wedding ceremony. Elves are painting everything they can paint, either in black—for the King, or in white—for the Bride. The King gives orders: "Do not forget music by Edward Grieg," he says. In fact, Grieg's music—his beautiful piano concerto—is heard in the background.

Then we see Edward Grieg himself in his remote mountain home playing a grand piano. He has a huge head with a wild mustache and a lion's head of hair. The elves are about to finish their preparations when the music suddenly stops. "Something must have happened!" roars the king, and he sends the elves to find out why he music stopped. The wedding cannot go on without Grieg's music!

We are in Grieg's home again. He is sick, sitting in his armchair, head fallen on his chest, exhausted, seemingly tired of life. A doctor is trying to reason with him. "Maestro, you should not work so hard; you should not play so much music."

It happens that Death has learned about Grieg's sickness. He penetrates his home disguised as a nurse. The doctor asks the nurse to care for Grieg while he fetches some medicine for him. The moment the doctor leaves, Death produces a sand-hour glass from his garment and sets it. The sand begins to stream, counting down the seconds of Grieg's life. Meanwhile, Death begins to destroy Grieg's work, throwing his sheet music into the fire. It burns convulsively desperately resisting the ruthless fire. The elves, who see this through tiny peepholes thawed by their breaths on the frozen window, rush into the house attempting to save the music. Death kicks them out. The elves sob piteously.

The sand stream gets thinner and thinner. The last grain of sand falls. Death is triumphant. Then, something miraculous happens. The fire in the hearth bursts forth, explodes with a magic force, and the burned music—now in the form of pure notes—streams out of the hearth, transforming the bare frozen earth around the house into blooming flowers. The sun throws its powerful rays at Grieg, waking him from his death-like sleep. He is back at his grand piano, and the powerful chords of his piano concerto again fill the universe.

Death is desperate. He does not understand. This has never happened to his victims before. The doctor, who has just returned with the now useless medicine, triumphantly explains. "This is beyond your nature. Grieg is an Artist, and Artists are immortal."

Back in the King's castle, the wedding begins. The King and his beautiful Bride raise their wine glasses. "To the immortal Edward Grieg," exclaims the King.

I do not claim that all children in crime- and corruption- infested, post-Communist Russia, where the elderly beg for a piece of bread, and even a university professor collapses of malnutrition, know who Edward Grieg was, or even love classical music. However, those who created this program wanted to give children something that would later become a solid foundation in their lives. They wanted the children to have their first *taste* of eternal, immortal beauty. Their objective was to help children open their souls to *the beautiful*, to help them take their first steps toward maturity and happiness.

Yurii Bashmet, a brilliant musician and, probably, the best violist in the world, said recently in an interview, "I would not speculate that classical music will someday become mass culture. This will never happen....But the more people listen to classical music the higher the spirituality in people. Because classical music is, practically, both a faith and a religion. It is the expression of the highest level of spirituality in human beings."

Much evidence is now being accumulated by researchers who claim that classical music is instrumental in developing children's brains and minds, in curbing their hyperactivity and promoting their concentration. Will we, parents, and grandparents in America today, live to see our children eagerly listening to the music of Grieg, Mozart, and Chopin?

Violence

"They have sown the wind, and they shall reap the whirlwind."

—Hosea 8:7

By the time our children reach high school, they will have seen on TV 33,000 murders and 200,000 other acts of violence; of course, mostly because they watch adult programs. However, the culture of violence is also our children's culture from very early childhood. Most of the cartoons are violent. Animals behave like hoodlums—cheating, degrading, beating, and mutilating each other.

Of course, everything is funny. Also, in most cases, vice is punished and virtue is rewarded, but quite often the *vice* and *virtue* have nothing to do with the concepts of *Good* and *Evil*. Fairytales, both in books and in cartoons, are also stuffed with violence. Sometimes the violence is alien to the plot and the spirit of the film or the book, but it is there.

Just one example, but it is very regrettable, the Disney film *Beauty and the Beast*. The fairytale itself is of international character. It exists in many languages. In Russian, it is known as *Scarlet Flower*, and was retold by the great Russian author of the 19th century Grigorii Aksakov. The story's universal popularity is obviously due to the high-pitched humanistic idea: *Love Creates Beauty*. As for the Disney film, it is filled with violence (among the *bad guys*, of course). But why? Why should the miracle of love be accompanied by evil? Is it to make the film more marketable?

Of course, the children do not take the world of cartoon characters as real. Besides, *Good* overtakes *Evil* in most cases. But what is important, in my view, is that from very early childhood children accept violence as a *normal* way of resolving conflicts.

Later, the *real life* characters take over, with shooting, killing, verbal, and physical abuse, and, of course, suspense, and adventure. This is already the world of adults. Why we, the adults, like and want to watch this kind of movies and TV programs is a different story. I do believe the reason is exactly the same as that, which, two millennia ago made the Roman mobs pack the Coliseums where gladiator slaves killed each other, or were thrown to wild animals. This reason was and is *boredom*.

The same reason applies to our children also. Everyday life is boring and meaningless. Watching action or crime movies enables them (probably even to a higher degree than in adults) to live a different life, that of daring, bravery, and even insolence, shrewdness, ruthlessness and *Superman-ness*. The whole cohort of movie stars has emerged, arrogant and cold-eyed, and not only on the movie or TV screens, but also in real life (drug abuse, bashing, and sex scandals). They readily fill the vacuum and climb the pedestals as role models for our children.

Does the violence on TV screens and in media affect children's lives? Some children do not believe the violence is for real, some do. Even if most of the children do not become violent as a result of the exposure, violence drags children from real life, and in this capacity, is equivalent to drugs. Twenty-six to 28 hours of TV per week (mostly off prime time) could have been spent in something fascinating, and developing imagination, enhancing the urge to do good. In fact, 25 percent of the children's free time during the day has been stolen from them.

Actually, it is again a chicken-egg problem: Is the high level of violence in society increased by the media and film-making industry, or (as in the case of supply of drugs) they are supplying violence in response to the demand of *the intellectual and emotional market*? I am sure that, yes, they do supply the violence-drug to society because we want it. On the other hand, the violent programs do create an atmosphere facilitating the proliferation of crime and violence. At least in some cases teenagers, having committed violent crimes, acknowledged the influence and even stimulation by a movie or a TV program.

Some psychologists insist that the link between violence and media is unproved; moreover, it may even be beneficially, because children are learning that the forces of *Good* eventually do overcome *Evil*. But then one should somehow explain why so many l students in our schools carry weapons. Juvenile crime will double by the year 2010 if the present situation does not change. There are also greater chances that youngsters will be victims of their peers. (Just recall the recent Columbine high school massacre.)

> In this essay I do not even touch the, at present unsolvable, problem of juvenile crime. It is growing from organized gangs to just isolated (and more and more often seemingly unmotivated) murders, thefts, vandalism—both in affluent suburbs and in inner cities. So far the only solution has been putting more and more children behind bars. And nobody talks of *why* children resort to violence. Viktor Frankl quotes Robert J. Lifton from his book *History and Human Survival*: "Men are most apt to kill or wish to kill when they feel overcome by meaninglessness."[20]

Even if the question of whether the media stimulate crime by teenagers or not is still controversial, it is obvious that the exposure of our children to crime and violence does not bring them any good. Even if in most cases they do not copycat the crimes, psychologically, it would be much better for a developing personality if the examples shown by the media were *good* examples, not *bad*, especially, if the characters glorifying violence are the candidates to become *role models*.

The video ad by Michael Jackson: He jumps on a car roof, his face grimaced with hatred. He crushes everything around, and every couple of minutes grips his crotch (very attractive from the marketing point of view— Madonna also used to do that). Just imagine if people would refuse to buy this video, or even boycott Michael Jackson's concerts, or boycott the TV channel that airs that ad or shows movies filled with murder, violence and flooded with blood? Do you think the Michael Jacksons, as a social phenomenon, would survive? Do you think

---

[20] Derek L.T.Gill, *Conversation with Viktor Frankl*, in *Finding Meaning in Life: Logotherapy*, Ed. by J.B.Fabry, R.P.Bulka and W.S.Saharian, Jason Aronson, Inc., Northvale, NJ, 1979. I am quoting from the 1995 soft cover edition, p. 23.

Hollywood—the studios that shoot films like that—would survive? There are precedents. In 1991, ABC lost over $14 million from commercials canceled because of viewer protests. And, for the same reason, Pepsi canceled a $10 million advertising campaign featuring Madonna. But would this be possible now, a decade later, at the dawn of new century?

Everybody talks about the V-chip today. Parents may be able to turn off the channels they believe are harmful for their children's spiritual health. But there are already signs that one can expect libertarians to rebel against that as a violation of children's rights (I discuss the problem of our children's rights in essay *Beware of the Indifferent*).

Any restrictions of the right of TV, movies, authors, artists and actors prohibiting airing, showing, exposing or performing what can be coined as "violent" or "indecent" or "offensive," would definitely violate the *First Amendment*—one of the most important clauses of our Constitution (also see *Beware of the Indifferent*). Therefore, when the White House says to Hollywood: "Look, guys, you'd better think twice before you start shooting a new violent film, or else..." it is mostly an empty threat.

A natural way out of this controversy is *self-restraint*. In fact, what we call *responsibility* is always a voluntary restriction of our rights. However, our society is still too far from sacrificing dollars for the sake of "abstract" moral concepts, although, what the majority of those *to whom it may concern* believe to be abstract morals is, in fact, the spiritual, emotional and physical health of our children.

If Hollywood and the major TV producers agree to comply with the President's request to impose a voluntary self-restraint, it will be an enormous step forward in our social culture.

And yet, this would only be equivalent to a (highly hypothetical and unlikely) agreement of a drug-manufacturing country to stop smuggling drugs into the US. In the case of drugs, internal manufacturing of even more efficient drugs, possibly of a non-chemical character, would most probably take over, if the popular demand is high, and the foreign supply has been stopped (see essay *Just Say No*).

In the case of proliferation of violence in the media, one does not have to look for a substitute for the "self-conscious" Hollywood. The Internet is already there. And this is something nobody can control, no matter how sophisticated a means is tried. One can already find in the Internet detailed instruction of how to make a bomb and use it. The so-called *virtual reality* may turn out to be a virtually unlimited possibility to *rehearse* violence, the arena of *working out* various scenarios of violent actions, for example. A good many computer and video games are already a first step in that direction (*Grand Theft Auto* among them—see essay *Beware of the Indifferent*). In fact, as in the case of high-tech drugs, here is a wide-open field for imagination and creativity.

Here I should mention a kind of violence that is pandemic in our society—sex violence. Not unexpectedly, our teenagers have also been infected. Is it the influence of rock music, movies, computer and video games, aiming directly at children, or the chicken-egg collision with the adult world? A survey of high school students has shown that "56 percent of the girls and 76 percent of the boys believed that forced sex was acceptable under some circumstances" (for example, if the boy spent a lot of money on the girl). Even among 11- to-14-year-old children, 79 percent of the girls and 87 percent of the boys justified sexual assault if the man and woman were married, and 47 percent of the girls and 65 percent of the boys believed "it was acceptable for a boy to rape a girl if they had been dating for more than six months" (see the website, www.infoplease.com).

Although some relatively mild forms of sexual harassment are present even in middle school, the sex violence among high schoolers is probably more of an *abstract* character—a part of their *world outlook,* so to speak. It, however, becomes an actuality among college students. Here, 54 percent of the surveyed women had been victims of some kind of sexual abuse (57 percent of assaults occurred on dates); more than one-in-four college-age women had been the victim of rape or attempted rape, but 84 percent of men who committed rape did not label it a rape (*ibid.*).

During 1997-1999 the violence among our children rose dramatically. According to the National School Safety Center (NSSC), in 1997, comparing it to 1996, "the number of violent deaths in schools rose 60 percent…to a total of 41, nearly half of which are multiple shootings…The rate of death as a result of firearms among American children 15 years and younger is 12 times higher than it is in 25 other developed countries combined…"[21]

"All of a sudden" our children have become aggressive and violent. The media, on all wavelengths, discuss the problem of our children's emotional instability and, in panic, again and again ask *why?*

In my view, the problem of children's violence has two aspects. First of all, children have always been aggressive. Boys have always played war. In the urge to feel strong and more secure, perhaps for millennia, children have brandished toy daggers, swords, and later rifles and handguns. It was a part of the painful process of growing up. But now real guns are available everywhere, virtually in every household, and our children learn how to use them. Unlike their toy counterparts this weapon kills for real…

In England, only one massacre of sixteen school children and their teacher in Dunblane, Scotland, in 1996, was enough. The protest of the nation has resulted in the confiscation of virtually all firearms in England. Now the English police do

---

[21] The quotes are from *Scientific American*, Sept. 1998, p. 15.

not carry arms any more, nor do they need them. How many more massacres followed by analyses of children's emotional instability and aggressiveness does America need before we understand that "a law-abiding citizen" *must not* carry arms in order to defend his or her home? For this purpose we have the police and the army.

Another question is, of course, our children's so-called *emotional instability*. Yes, our kids are more and more emotionally unstable. The "fuse" preventing a teenager from violent actions is getting shorter and shorter. *Why?* The media is correct in looking for the answers in the adults' violent culture—TV, computer games, the Internet, for example. The April 1999 massacre of thirteen school children and a teacher by two outcasts in Columbine High, Littleton, Colorado, has shown that "America confronts the alienation that grips so many teenagers" (*US News and World Report*).

As I stressed in the *Preface*, unfortunately, it is not just "alienation." It is *To Be or Not To Be* asked in earnest. One third of American teenagers contemplate, attempt, or commit suicide. If one thinks about suicide, why not homicide? In both cases there is a common cause—life is *unbearable*. In many interviews teenagers complain that their lives are *boring*, that is why they need *fun*. But do our child psychologists discuss *why* our children's lives are boring and unbearable? This is just exactly what my book is about. This is what should be at the core of our discussion of the future (or, for that matter, the present) educational reform.

I see only one solution to the problem of violence in our culture. Not accidentally, it is also the solution to the problems of drugs in our society. If the demand disappears, the supply will stop right away. The demand, in turn, will disappear only if *boredom* in human lives disappears. The latter will happen if *meaning* is restored to people's lives—if lives are again full and fulfilling.

And the way to achieve that—the only way I see—is in the dramatic improvement of general education in this country. Let us begin with the children. The next generation will already be healthy.

The Working Class

"We are millions, we are millions, We are the young working class"

—*Communist song (c. 1965-85)*

Now I am attempting to threaten one of the American culture's "sacred cows." We encourage and, often, even send our children to earn money at the earliest possible age. We believe it is *good* for their future. I am going to argue that not only is it *bad*, but it serves as one of the foundations of their future crises. To some of my readers, what I am going to say may seem to be un-American, an insult, disrespectful to what they believe is a cornerstone of American life. But I just want you, my reader, to listen to what I am saying. Perhaps, at least some of you, upon reflection, will agree with me.

The law does not prohibit the employment of *minors* altogether. There are some restrictions, but basically, kids may work. Here is the law: Anyone under the age of 14 is prohibited from working by federal law. Exceptions are made for some agricultural jobs. At any age, however, children may deliver newspapers. Minors ages 14 and 15, during normal school sessions may work up to 3 hours per day (and up to 18 hours per week). During school recessions a full 40-hour working week is allowed. There are some restrictions to the jobs 14- and 15-years-old may be engaged in. But such occupations as cashiers, food servers, custodians, car washing and delivery work are typical and permitted. Teens ages 16 to 18 do not have restrictions on the work duration, but are not permitted to be engaged in the jobs deemed "hazardous." In 1991, about 5 million teenagers worked in the US.

Twelve-year-old children *legally* deliver newspapers. They have to get up very early in the morning, in order to finish their work by the time a school bus takes them to school. I doubt that their parents can force them to abandon TV and go to bed as early as 9 p.m. It means that they do not sleep enough. I once heard the objection that even without the early-morning job, they would sit at the TV for as long as their parents do—so, it would not make any difference anyway. That may be true, but two wrongs do not make a right.

Returning from school, since there is virtually no homework, children—this time it is mostly the junior high and high school gang—stream to supermarkets and department stores. Here they work as cashiers or clerks for a few hours. Evenings are spent in all kinds of entertainment. They earned it, for they *worked hard*.

Psychologists have found that 80 percent of teenagers have a part-time job sometime during high school. An average working high school senior works 20 or more hours a week, half of a full-time load.

Summer jobs are typically full time. Some chores around the house, like lawn mowing, are also paid jobs, but this time paid by parents.

Not all children follow this scenario. Some jobs, especially in rural areas, are necessary and must be done so the family can make ends meet. But what I am talking about is this: we believe that the children *must* learn how to earn their own money *as early as possible*.

There are so many negative aspects to this belief that I do not even know where to begin. Let me begin with the money. The adults earn money in order to sustain their families and meet other responsibilities. This is the main objective. Of course, then follow expenses that have to do with hobbies, entertainment, for example. But in the main, the most decisive component of adult life is *responsibility*. Children do not have any. Typically, they do not have to sustain families or pay for health insurance. In fact, the main reason they need the money is entertainment. Buying all kinds of paraphernalia, such as fancy sneakers, T-shirts, chains, rings, earrings, for example, is a part of the necessary attributes helping to have really good *fun*.

According to the International Mass Retail Association, youngsters of ages 8 through 17 on average make 12.7 shopping trips a month, spending per trip: ages 8-12: $18.50; ages 13-17: $31.20. Teenagers spent in 2002 $170 billion, which is roughly $400 per teenager per month—the amount of money rarely spent by an adult on personal needs.

I kind of shy away from saying that a good amount of money is spent on alcohol, drugs, and entertainment, which even the most liberal-minded parents would not classify as *innocent*. Unfortunately, it is true. A huge industry has grown up around these millions of dollars ready to be spent by pleasure and fun seeking teenagers. Most of the goods the children want to buy are not cheap. Even among inner city gangs, the chains are of real gold, and the sneakers are real Nikes.

Almost every *working* teenager has at least a few hundred dollars ready to be spent right away. And they spend it, apart from clothes and jewelry, on the Madonnas, Michael Jacksons, and other "idols." A new, high-tech entertainment—computer and video games—is also at their disposal now.

So far I have mostly talked about teenagers. Younger children—the newspaper delivery gang—do not have that much money. But they have enough to occasionally buy a fancy T-shirt, baseball cap, or a chain, or to spend hours in the nearby mall's game room. A very small percentage of children care to put the earned money aside for their future education.

So much for the money. Let us put aside, for the moment, the moral aspects and the fact that working for 20 or more hours a week during school year definitely hurts the children's academic performance. Is the situation with the millions of school-age teenagers in the work force good for the country economically? I do not think so. First of all, using the Marxist terms (please excuse me), the children are being pitilessly exploited by the employers. The latter prefer to hire children, because they do not need any benefits. However, everybody who does have benefits as a part of their wage package knows that the benefits often comprise over 50 percent of the salary. Imagine that one day the children, say, go on strike. What would the employers have to do? Hire adult workers (perhaps, even with preliminary training), with the whole package of benefits: health and life insurance, pension plan, for example.

I should also say that some of the jobs our teenagers take are rather *superficial*. We could do without those jobs. Europe does not have that supermarket service—putting purchases into plastic bags—and for two reasons. First, the buyers pay for this extra service through a *hidden surcharge* on any purchased item, and second, Europeans believe that their children's study at school is already *a full time job*—and it is. Here, in America, we the parents and grandparents, have agreed to pay from our pockets (through that hidden surcharge) the salaries to our children—and it is now over $5.50 an hour—spending hours doing meaningless jobs. Just think of it. Doing meaningless jobs in order to what? To earn the money to be spent on what? On something that is not good either for their present or their future—thoughtless and often not quite innocent entertainment, and all kinds of paraphernalia having to do with having fun. And this is while their studies, and the process of learning and maturing is being sacrificed.

As I mentioned in the *Preface*, encouraging children to work when it is not a necessity makes them take the first step toward their existential misery in the future. Too early they learn that a job, whose only meaning is money, is boring, adding to the general boredom of meaninglessness of their life. They agree to any job that pays. But the thesis that any job is good that brings in the money (and the more, the better) is profoundly wrong. For only that job is good that brings satisfaction. It also brings happiness. And both are impossible unless a person is intellectually and emotionally mature.

The children do not know that important piece of wisdom. Unfortunately, the majority of adults today do not know it either. And, as I have already stressed many times, education is the only means of achieving the level of maturity necessary to meet the challenges of a high-tech society and achieve internal harmony and happiness. However, in this respect our education fails miserably.

If King Solomon were in today's America, he would add to his immortal wisdom on time (Ecclesiastes 3) the new wisdom: "A time to work and a time to learn."

Time is the most mysterious concept of our life. Sometimes it runs slow, sometimes it runs fast. But the most fateful quality of time is that, if lost, it cannot be returned. That is why the above wisdom is so profound. Children do not think too much about their future. Future life seems to be an eternity away. It is not. In fact, a very short period—only some ten or twelve years—is at our teenagers' disposal for their preparation for adult life. Children do not understand that. The adults *must* understand. Whenever children waste this precious time—it is our responsibility as their parents and grandparents.

These ten or twelve years are not a long time. In order to prepare a child intellectually, emotionally, and morally for life in the 21st century, not a single day should be wasted. The hours spent delivering newspapers are the hours lost for reading interesting books. The hours spent at supermarket counters, in restaurants as waiters, at gas stations as assistants, and so forth, are the precious hours lost for learning—exciting reading and learning that could give children both pleasure and satisfaction they would never get in any other way. Of course, children are not to blame. It is our educators who bear most of the responsibility. We the parents and grandparents do share it.

Having understood our responsibility, we must realize that our attitude toward the ugly educational system that makes our children intellectually and emotionally handicapped is the most important factor that can make a difference.

Of course, if and when the teaching curriculum at our schools—from preschool through the last day of high school—becomes strong, and the teaching switches from drilling *skills* to giving *knowledge*, the problem will be solved automatically. The children simply will not have time to earn money. As a side effect, the so much needed *sublimation* will also start working, deflecting our children from unnecessary sex.

But teenagers do need at least some pocket money. There are quite a few ways of resolving this problem. One of them is a parent's allowance. A good majority of American families can afford a modest allowance of pocket money for their children. Europe, which is much less affluent than we are, does that. Let me repeat: the children are not encouraged to work during school years there because people believe that school itself is a *full-time job*

There is, however, a more revolutionary approach. (Please, do not throw rotten tomatoes at me.) You have probably agreed with me, that it is we, buyers in supermarkets and department stores, who pay for most of the jobs our children do there. I would not mind putting my purchases into plastic bags myself; neither would probably most of my readers. Why not to ask the store owners to donate the money they would pay to the children at those jobs to schools (and we would probably agree to pay even a few pennies more for milk and bread). The money, as an obvious charity, would be tax-deductible so that a system of stipends could be established.

Just imagine that beginning with high school, every student received a check every other week (or every month), and the amount of money paid as a stipend depended on the student's academic progress during the pay period. In short, since for a youngster (at least at the present time) it does not matter what the job is, so long as it pays, why not create a material stimulus for study? There is nothing immoral in that. Besides, it will take off or ease the burden of families to support their children in their pocket money needs. Then the job of intensive study and reading will compete with jobs of washing cars or sweeping floors. And I do believe that education will win that economic competition. But what is much more important, the children will gradually understand that studying, learning, and reading are *fun*. The vicious cycle will be broken.

The problem of meaningless and degrading jobs is not only the problem of school-age children. Most of the jobs of college students are as meaningless. There, however, the jobs are necessary to share the parents' expenses on tuition, room and board, as well as to sustain a definite standard of living as a young adult. Most of the jobs around the campus are low paying, and sometimes even superficial. At the same time they are a shameful example of the waste of the intellectual potential of the students. A girl majoring in physics washing dishes at a restaurant, or serving pizza, a young male history major as a receptionist in a dry-cleaning business. And mind you, these people do have to sacrifice their studies in order to earn that money they really need.

> My close friend (now deceased), a distinguished nephrologist, and one of the pioneers of kidney transplants in Russia, used to joke, in response to his wife's request to wash dishes after dinner: "One would not plough fields with an Arabian charger, one would not nail nails with a microscope." But he always washed the dishes anyway.

It is ugly that our society cannot afford to support our college students through their years of education. And they are our future. Their expertise (or lack of it) can make a difference in the years to come. Again, "a time to work, and a time to learn." But I do not want to excite the rage of *anti-socialists* by suggesting this kind of sweeping reform (although, establishing free higher education is much more a matter of common sense and society's responsibility for its future, than socialism). However, something thoughtful can be done about the problem of college jobs.

In another essay (*Science and Society*), I suggest that one of the ways of significantly improving the teaching process at our public schools could be by using university students as *teaching assistants*. This should not be restricted only to science. A few pages prior, I also discussed the necessity of dramatically expanding the extracurricular activities at our schools that would extend the hours of instruction, but on a voluntary basis. Children interested in history could spend a couple of hours—say, twice a month—talking, reading and discussing history with the help of a history major of a nearby university. Just imagine a girl from a nearby university majoring in music coming to the homeroom of a class, and spending an hour with kids telling them about the life of Beethoven and playing, say the *Moonlight Sonata*.

The university student string quartet and symphony orchestra could give regular concerts at the school this university sponsors. Thousands upon thousands of physics, chemistry, biology, psychology, history, literature, and music majors could lead the clubs of extracurricular studies in our schools. In fact, that would be one of the best versions of the *national service*.

It is not only that it would be nice to have something like that, our society needs—and needs very badly, I should say needs *desperately*—such a service. One does not have to be a PhD in any area to see how many of the problems our education faces today would be solved if the system *Kids Teaching Kids* were to be initiated.

Apart from the important educational effect—increasing the level of knowledge (both by children and their young "teachers")—a much more important result would have been achieved. A student-teacher is a strong candidate for being a role model for a dozen children sitting around and discussing the drift of continents, the orbit of the newly discovered comet or the life of Sir Winston Churchill. The children will *believe* these enthusiastic young teachers much more than they believe the adults. They will want to follow them, be like them. With the trust (and even admiration) of a person who brings fascinating knowledge, the urge for knowledge will inevitably follow.

To conclude this essay, let me repeat what I have already said before. The American educational system deprives our children of intellectual and emotional nourishment that could make their lives meaningful and interesting. It prevents them from acquiring *maturity*. While immersed in having fun and idling, children attempt to make sense of both their present and their future. The present is meaningless, the future is in darkness—with a good chance to being even worse than the present.

So often we ask our little ones: "What do you want to be when you grow up?" But this is just a game on our part. We do not actually mean to help our children to look into the future and understand what is there for them. At the same time, serious discussions on the individual and group level of people's professions, their impacts on society and the world, their attractiveness and drawbacks, could make a difference. This could help our children to gradually enter the future, first with their dreams, then with learning more about and even preparing for the future profession. Nobody expects a ten- or even seventeen-year-old to take a *final* decision to become a business manager, a computer engineer, or an astronomer.

However, our children must be helped and encouraged to dream, to think, and to listen to their souls. Although this strategy could be successfully employed even today, within our sick educational system, the real success that would have completely transformed our children's lives requires the educational revolution I have been discussing.

The year 1999 brought the deadliest school massacre that the United States has known in its history. Crime among our children is on the rise. No propaganda, no *Just Say No* pleading stops our children from using drugs. The whole society is alarmed. The media, again and again, asks the same question: *Why? US News and World Report* in its August 9, 1999, issue even carried a sensational article: *Inside the Teen Brain: The Reason for Your Kid's Quirky Behavior Is in His Head.* There, the authors attempted to explain our children's emotional instability- and, by implication, its social consequences, referring to the most recent developments in child physiology and biochemistry of the teenage brain.

And not a single word is heard from our educators, doctors, child psychologists or sociologists that the major cause of our children's "problems" is the misery of their empty, boring and meaningless existence. Their bodies are just the ground on which the *existential drama* of blind and wandering souls is unfolding, with the unfriendly, and even hostile adult world of violence, sex and entertainment in the background. Nobody asks a simple question: "Wait a minute, are the brain biology and physiology of French, German, Japanese or Chinese children different?" It is so convenient for us not to ask this simple question? How many generations of children are we going to sacrifice before the irresponsibility of our educators and politicians has been overcome?

Our society has abandoned its children. When *we the people* fully understand the scope of disaster that our indifference wreaks on our children, then and only then meaningful reforms in day care and education will be possible. And then we will win our children's souls back. Children who know who they want to resemble, who know what they are going to live for, will become a strong foundation of the *New America*. And that America will be the light unto the nations, a site eliciting deep respect and emulation. These children will also be the first generation of a new civilization, in which anti-intellectualism and meaninglessness in human lives will disappear.

This is my dream. Will it come true? This will depend only on *us, the people*.

SCIENCE AND SOCIETY: OUR SCIENTIFIC IGNORANCE

"I want to know how God created this world."

—*Albert Einstein*

These days are marked by quiet revolutions—the ones the man in the street does not even suspect. New fundamental discoveries are being made in almost all branches of science and technology. Most visible—because they are immediately transformed into products we buy right away—are those in computers, electronics, telecommunications, medicine, and new materials. Our space exploration programs bring spectacular, breathtaking discoveries about the universe. Literally, not a week passes without announcement of a new drug, a new life-saving surgical procedure, or a discovery in molecular biology. Genetic engineering gradually has become a profitable business. And a huge and unprecedented project has been recently concluded—the project of identifying the whole set of human genes, the so-called *Human Genome Project*.

What used to be a science-fiction pipe dream is now a reality. We are used to driving our cars—they are an important and indispensable part of our life. When we are planning a trip, we just call a travel agent who, by a few magical strokes on a computer keyboard, reserves for us an airline seat, a hotel room, and a rented car. Telephones and computers are household items now. An idling teenager carries a beeper or a cellular phone. Only a few years ago these devices were used only in cases of emergency by medical doctors or trouble-shooters. And, within just a few recent years, a worldwide communication network has emerged, and is now also an indispensable part of our lives. Those who may have tried to connect to the Internet know how web-like the Worldwide Web is. Its newborn child, the *dot com* economy—especially Internet shopping—is now an every day reality.

All these miracles are now commonplace. But only a very few of us feel a deep sense of awe, astonishment and, if you prefer, pride in "us the people,"—*humankind*. What about the others—the people in the street? Most of them just accept these miracles as things *taken for granted*, and simply do not care. This

135

stuff is just a convenient part of life. We pay for those conveniences, and we have them.

The world has just stepped into the new high-tech century. However, more and more people neither understand those wonders nor can work them, and more and more people just use them and do not care about the *why* and *how* of those miracles. American society today is the most conspicuous example of that social phenomenon. This is simply because of the disintegration of the only social device that could make a difference—our educational system.

The scientific ignorance in our society is absolutely unprecedented. The prevalence of so-called *soft knowledge*, which does not require intellectual concentration (and a definite level of intellectual development in the first place), makes scientific ignorance quite a natural and normal phenomenon, especially if making money, entertainment and having fun are the main objectives of people's lives.

As usual, superstitions come with ignorance. Millions of Americans passionately believe in the supernatural—from devil worshipping to UFOs and "aliens." Fifty-two percent of teenagers believe in astrology. And not only teenagers. More than half of the American population today believes that astrology has scientific foundations—and this is because people do not understand at all what the scientific method is. More than half also believes in miracles that appear in everyday life. A new branch of popular culture has emerged, and symptomatically its name was coined as the *New Age*—everything occult, supernatural, parapsychological is there. People believe in everything that is exciting, which gives something to their empty and wondering souls. And this is against the background of diminished faith in God—a faith that makes one morally strong and helps one to live a fulfilling life.

An old friend of mine, a professor at a Moscow medical school and a practicing psychiatrist, told me of an interesting experience. A few years ago in Russia (particularly in Moscow) all kind of psychics, magicians, astrologers and other "occult specialists" became popular. They were even given prime time on TV. At that time, my friend came across a few cases of psychoses that he had never before encountered in his practice as a psychiatrist. At the same time, seeing those patients he could not help feeling that those symptoms were somehow familiar to him. He eventually recalled that he had read about such psychoses in a book by the great French psychiatrist of the 19th century Jean-Martin Charcot. Those psychoses had to do with obsession of the patients with "evil power." My friend was shocked to encounter a mental disorder that had been quite typical in the 19th century, had completely disappeared in the 20th century, and had reappeared in our time with the recurrence, in a time of societal crisis, of old superstitions.

I am sure American psychiatrists have also observed cases like those inherited from medieval superstitions. But perhaps much more widely spread today are the psychoses having to do with science-fiction scenarios. Among them, of course, is the *alien abduction* craze. Is it possible that people's obsession with UFOs and aliens have a powerful existential drive? Being unable to find meaning in their lives, people sub-consciously hope that the arrival of some "aliens" will solve their problems, will give their lives direction, and will make their lives meaningful. Or is it just a primitive urge for excitement caused by boredom? It seems—at least to me as a "man in the street"—that there is no attempt on the part of psychiatrists or psychologists to explain to the public the origin of these phenomena. On the contrary, sometimes it is representatives of these professions who are involved in reinforcing the beliefs in the alien interference in our lives and who give these beliefs professional credence.[1]

While magic is something that people understand well, science becomes more and more estranged from their intellectual life. Even worse, it is not being trusted any more. Freeman Dyson, one of the renowned theoretical physicists of our time, wrote: "The image of noble and virtuous dedication to truth, the image that scientists have traditionally presented to the public, is no longer credible. The public, having found out that the traditional image of the scientist as a secular saint is false, has gone to the opposite extreme and imagines us to be irresponsible devils playing with human lives."[2]

Negative attitude toward science, in our society, is not restricted to just mistrust. The intellectual Left, as a part of their general philosophy of *post-modernism*, rejecting any *absolute* attitude toward the world, has been attempting to strip science of its *objectivity*. Since, according to this philosophy, "all facts are socially constructed rather than being deduced from evidence…scientific knowledge is merely a system of beliefs" and as such is…a subjective human construction, like art or music." This harmful perception of science has been gradually taking over our education, both in schools and colleges.[3] The detrimental situation in teaching science in our schools, which I briefly touch on below, is mostly the result of the *Progressiv*ist educational philosophy.

Mistrust or no mistrust, for the man in the street, as well as even for many people highly educated in the humanities, science is yet a kind of *magic*. This belief can be easily understood in those people who have never seriously studied science. Yet, it is astonishing (at least to me, a scientist, who has devoted over 40 years of life to scientific research) that people are simply indifferent to the physical world we live in—to its miracles and mysteries.

---

[1] See, for example, a book by Harvard psychologist: John E. Mack, MD, *Abduction: Human Encounters with Aliens*, 1994.

[2] *Nature's Imagination. The Frontiers of Scientific Vision* (Edited by John Cornwell), Oxford University press, Oxford, 1995, p. 9.

[3] For scientists' critique of these principles see, for example, K. Gottfried and K.G.Wilson, *Nature*, April 1997, p.545, and D. O. Morrison, *Scientific American*, Nov. 1997, p. 114 (the above quotations are from this article).

Just a few anecdotes from my own life.

A nurse, attaching electrodes to my head, asked, "What do you do for living?"

"I am a physicist."

"What is that?"

"Well, I am doing research in physics. Did you study physics in high school?"

"No".

"Did you ever hear of the laws of Newton?"

The nurse said, "Have they something to do with a falling apple?"

She did hear somewhere the legend that a fallen apple had prompted Isaac Newton, the great English physicist, to formulate his law of gravity, but that was all she knew. The conversation was over. She was beginning a sophisticated test on my head, involving state-of-the-art devices that had been developed by physicists. She knew how to attach the electrodes. But she did not care about how our world was made. Very unlikely did she know anything about the brain waves she was going to measure, and the electric processes behind those measurements. To me it was a shock.

The same question about the Laws of Newton I had also put a few years before to an attractive young woman, a mother of four, who had parked her SUV, "stuffed" with little ones, next to my car in a supermarket parking lot. Neither the children nor she were buckled up. When the car stopped, the children were everywhere, even in the space between the front passenger and driver's seats. I first decided that there were more than four of them. That woman said that she had never heard the name of Newton. I explored further.

"You know, Newton was a great scientist. He lived in England almost 250 years ago. He discovered that if you abruptly brake your car or collide with another car or an obstacle, your body goes on moving and strikes the windshield with the force proportional to your deceleration and your body's weight. If you brake abruptly enough, then you surely will smash your head against the windshield."

"But this is a matter of luck, if I strike the windshield or not, isn't?"

"Well, it is a matter of luck if you are severely hurt or not, but the law of inertia will work on you all the same, unless you buckle up. That is, it will not stop working if you buckle up, but the belts will prevent you from smashing the windshield."

"But what kind of a car did that guy have? Mine is very safe."

I gave up. I apologized and left. She was very friendly and patient with me; besides, I was a foreigner, with a funny accent.

One more anecdote having to do with "popular mechanics." Just a few months ago the extension of the speed limit above 55 mph was being discussed on a talk show. The host, a journalist who I highly respect, was discussing the pros and cons of the new law with someone competent in safety on highways.

The interviewee said, "Don't forget that increasing speed from 55 mph to 75 mph would double the energy released in case of an accident."

The host was astonished. Perhaps, he expected that with the double energy increase the speed should have also doubled. Obviously he did not know a simple fact (fundamental for our physical world) that the kinetic energy of a moving body is proportional to the *square* of its velocity rather than proportional to it. Then, in order to double the energy, the velocity has to be increased by just a factor of 1.4 (1.4 times 1.4 is approximately 2).

The formula is: the energy of a moving object, $E = 1/2 \ \mathbf{m} \ \mathbf{v}^2$ (pronounced: "E equals one half m-v squared") where $\mathbf{m}$ is the mass (weight) and $\mathbf{v}$ is the velocity.

I recall the joke very popular among us, sixth-graders (13-year-olds), back in Russia, when we were taught mechanics as a part of a Physics-I course. A guy is falling from a roof of a skyscraper and cries out, when flying by another guy in the seventh floor window,

"Thanks to God it's one-half!"

"What one-half?"

"m v squared!"

Finally an anecdote having to do with "global warming." I had a discussion with a woman in her mid-forties, a receptionist at a New Hampshire ski resort hotel. Because there had been no snow in December, we discuss how the climate has obviously changed during the recent decade. "You know," says the woman, "my mother—she is an avid reader—has a theory of this warming. Our earth's axis is tilted a bit, and because of that, from time to time we get more sun energy. We are now in one of these periods."

I was stunned. "Well," I said, "actually, because of this axis tilt we have *seasons* on this earth. Scientists believe that the warming up of the climate has to do with the so-called "greenhouse effect" caused by accumulation of carbon dioxide in the atmosphere. We burn too much fossil fuel, and thus produce too much of this gas."

The woman smiles condescendingly. "Oh, that theory of my mother's—it may be wrong. You know, she is almost seventy years old."

There is nothing mysterious about such ignorance. If a teenager is allowed to choose what to study and what not, the outcome is quite obvious. I am not going into details here of the flaws in our educational system. I have already discussed them elsewhere. If you really want to learn the sad truth ("I'll tell you truth that is worse than any lie"—W. Shakespeare)—look up the excellent book by William Bennett,[4] a former Secretary of Education. "If you give the average fifteen-year-old the choice of trigonometry or, say, 'Rock and Roll as Poetry' and 'Baja Whale Watch,' many will opt to take the latter—not because they're stupid or bad kids, but simply because they're teenagers" (p. 53). I would add, "because they're teenagers who had not been taught to work hard and to get satisfaction and even pleasure from the process of learning—teenagers, who are not *stupid* but, most probably, are already severely emotionally and intellectually underdeveloped."

I wonder what percentage of high school graduates can explain how an internal combustion (or a diesel) engine works (and that is the heart of our cars.); or what electric current is (a clerk in a Radio Shack store who sells electric appliances could not answer my elementary question about the electric parameters of a relay I was going to buy); to say nothing of why the sky is blue, and the grass is green. And to say nothing of basic facts from atomic and nuclear physics or astronomy. Just ask why we have seasons on Earth, or name the planets in the solar system. Forget about other planets. Ninety four million Americans (52 percent) do not know that their own planet orbits the sun once every year. It is even worse: 20 percent of Americans think the sun goes around the Earth. And only 11 percent can define a molecule. Our little ones are obsessed with dinosaurs, but half of their parents believe that humans and dinosaurs had once been contemporaries.

Paul Davis, in his excellent book[5] writes: "The neurotic fear of mathematics experienced by most ordinary people is chiefly responsible for their estrangement with physical science. It is a barrier that efficiently cuts them off from a full appreciation of scientific discoveries, and prevents them from enjoying vast areas of nature that have been revealed through painstaking research."

No wonder that our ignorance in science originates from our pathological ignorance in even elementary math. Millions of people presumably do not understand what a *percentage* means. Otherwise how could advertisers have the guts to claim that a cereal is "20 percent more crunchy"? Or a trailer is "25 percent easier to tow?" Even more people do not understand such important

---

4　W. Bennett, *The Devaluing of America: The Fight for our Culture and Our Children*, Simon & Schuster, New York, 1992.
5　Paul Davis, *God & the New Physics*, Touchstone Books, New York, 1984 (p. 221).

concepts in everybody's life as *probability* or *statistics*. If you really want to learn how disastrous our illiteracy in math is, I recommend the book by John Allan Paulos[6].

Our ignorance in understanding the concept of statistics and probability is already taking its toll. The number of parents who have chosen not to vaccinate their children is growing. Virtually all drugs have side effects—vaccines are no exception. In 1997, about 100 million vaccinations were given, and only 92 deaths in children (that might or might not have been caused by the vaccination) occurred. However the information that vaccines "are not safe" is deep in our psyche. As a result, parents, deliberately, refuse to vaccinate their children. According to the Center for Disease Control, the chance of *contracting* encephalitis from the vaccine is 1 in a million, whereas an unvaccinated child has a 1 in 2000 chance of suffering encephalitis as a complication of measles. Fortunately, in our relatively healthy environment, the chances of contracting a deadly disease for an unprotected child are rather low. It is regretful, however, that many parents do not understand what the concept of *chance* is.

Another example. After the 9/11 terrorist acts, the number of people using airlines as the main mode of long distance (i.e., interstate) transportation has significantly dropped. Instead, people now use alternative ways, but mostly cars. As a result, the number of cars on our highways—especially during holidays when most non-business travel happen—increased, with the increase of automobile accident related deaths. People did not understand, and nobody cared to explain them, that the probability to be in a plane that becomes a victim of a future terrorist attack is thousands of times less that to be killed in a car accident. More over, even officials—especially immediately after the terrorist acts—explicitly warned the public about the dangers of flying.

Over the last 15 years, the number of students receiving a bachelor degree in engineering dropped 50 percent. Fewer and fewer college students major in science. Within the last decade, the number dropped by almost 40 percent. John

---

6   J. A. Paulos, *Innumeracy: Mathematical Illiteracy and Its Consequences*, 1988

Chancellor[7] writes: "From 1950 to 1970, the number of degrees awarded in the basic sciences increased fourfold. In those decades, carrying a slide rule or working in a laboratory was a mark of prestige on American campuses. And those young scientists created the American dominance in technology. Today, the image of the student scientist or engineer seems to be that of a nerd" (p.46). And further: "Half the doctorates in physics awarded by American universities in 1986 went to foreign students. In American graduate schools of engineering, half the assistant professors, under thirty-five, are foreign" (p.47).

These professors, having been hired as talented or even distinguished experts in their fields (and the competition in academia is pitilessly severe), many of them do not master fluent English. As a result, the quality of teaching suffers (to say nothing of the fact that teaching is often entrusted to graduate students, also mostly from other countries). Should our universities lower their standards and begin hiring professors based on their mastering English rather than being high-quality scientists?

And where are the smart American boys and girls? The really smart go to medical and law schools—for the training promises a lot of money in the future—while the less talented prefer business administration. A bit less money, but much easier studies—just *soft knowledge,* and no *boring* math and science whatsoever. Dr. Chancellor also gives an excerpt from the 1983 report of the National Commission on Excellence in Education, "A Nation at Risk," which disclosed the shameful state of our education: "If an unfriendly foreign power had attempted to impose on America the mediocre educational performance that exists today, we might well have viewed it as an act of war" (p.49).

This trend of almost twenty years ago not unexpectedly had our society pay a toll. During the economy boom of the late 90s, and the explosion-like development of computer and communication industries, the lack of qualified specialists in computer and engineering in general, was felt very acutely. The only way out that many companies had was to import the specialists from overseas, mostly from Eastern Europe and Southeast Asia. The number of working visas issued by the US Naturalization and Immigration Office (before the post 9/11 economic crisis) increased every year, but it was not enough. Typically, all the quotas were gone within just a few months of the new fiscal year, leaving American businesses in limbo for the rest of the year.

During the recent recession and the avalanche of "outsourcing"—moving high-tech jobs oversees—we lost close to a million high-tech jobs. But when our economy is back on track, we will feel the shortage of qualified people again.

---

[7]   John Chancellor, *Peril and Promise: A Commentary on America.* Harper Perennial, New York, 1991.

Unfortunately, the consequences of our illiteracy in math and science are not just a state of *ignorance*—the inability of ordinary people to understand the important issues that have to do with our physical world. The social consequences are much more serious. Among them: inability to control politicians who manipulate scientific issues for their political purposes (or special groups who back them), and inability to make a judgment that would enable to actively support this or that program involving scientific issues.

In fact, some of the consequences of this peril are already comparable to a devastation of war. Take nuclear energy. It occupies a special place in the psyche of many Americans. *Nuclear* inevitably means some kind of a *doom*. A very powerful medical method originally named after the physical phenomenon called the *Nuclear Magnetic Resonance* (NMR), has been renamed *Magnetic Resonance Imaging* (MRI)—to get rid of the word *nuclear* and thus enhance confidence in the method's safety, not only in patients but also in doctors. The method has absolutely nothing to do with nuclear energy or radioactive isotopes. It is about the response of the nuclei in our body's atoms to an external magnetic field. I wonder what the reaction of an "average American" would be if tomorrow Peter Jennings were to disclose that the human body consists of *nuclear matter*—exclusively nuclear matter, and nothing else. For every atom in our body (as well as everywhere else in the universe) does have a nucleus.

Here are some impressive statistics.[8] A poll of radiation health scientists shows that 82 percent of them believe the public's fear of radiation is "substantially" or "grossly" exaggerated. Another poll shows that 89 percent of all scientists, and 95 percent of all scientists involved in energy-related fields, favor proceeding with the development of nuclear power. However, 56 percent of the American public is opposed to having a nuclear power plant in their own community, while this opinion is shared by only 31 percent of all scientists, by only 20 percent of scientists specializing in fields related to energy, and by only two percent of scientists specializing in radiation or nuclear science.

Especially after the Chernobyl catastrophe, nuclear energy in this country has been an absolute *taboo*. A few insignificant accidents in American nuclear plants have sealed the verdict on the fate of our nuclear energy industry. If, again, you

---

8   Bernard L. Cohen: *Before It's Too Late: A Scientific Case for Nuclear Energy.* Plenum Press, New York, 1983.

ask a man in the street whether we should use nuclear plants for producing energy, the answer will almost unanimously be *no*. Why? "It is unsafe, it is hazardous." And nobody listens to the experts who are desperately trying to convince society that nuclear energy can be made (and, in fact, already is) as safe and "clean" as any other energy. Nuclear energetics, like most of the new and pioneering projects, has its own risks originating from our as yet insufficient knowledge. Activists burning symbols of nuclear energy at their demonstrations do not know how much effort and scientific ingenuity is being devoted to solving the problems that the development of nuclear energy poses.

Safety of reactors is one of the problems. But the most serious problem is not the reactor safety, as people believe, but nuclear waste disposal. And here, the projects that scientists discuss address the issues that may be important thousands of years from now. The integrity and responsibility of these scientists and engineers are unbelievable, and yet they are being condemned and castigated by the crowd of people who do not even understand the whole problem and therefore cannot see it in perspective.

It is very difficult to estimate the scope of negative effects on the many sectors of our life and on policies that have been inflicted by all kinds of lobbyists. Usually, a special group is behind a lobbying effort. I doubt that this is the case for the anti-nuclear lobby. Although the leading anti-nuclear activist organization in the United States is the Union of Concerned Scientists (UCS), its social support comes from the general scientific ignorance of the population and its acting force—activists who lack a basic educational background in physics.

Nuclear plants are not competitors to the conventional electrical energy plants. The demand for electrical energy exceeds, and will probably always exceed the existing power plant capacity. We are always encouraged to save electricity. In addition, the supply of oil on this earth—our main source of energy—is coming to an end. We may encounter serious problems already by the middle of this century, while coal is environmentally less safe and much less efficient. Owing to the efforts of the anti-nuclear lobby, we are absolutely unprepared for the challenges of the times to come.

Let us hear what an expert on nuclear energy, Dr. T. A. Heppenheimer says:[9] "Our 109 plants in operation are a legacy of decisions made in prior decades. Even before the 1979 accident at Three Mile Island, the utility industry had virtually ceased to order new reactors, and afterward it canceled nearly 100 plants that had been on order. Since 1974 no nuclear power plant has been ordered without later being canceled." (These words were written almost ten years ago but noting "positive has happened since".)

---

[9] T. A. Heppenheimer, *Innovation and Technology*, Summer 1995, p. 38.

On the other hand, most of the world's industrial countries have developed a strong nuclear energy base. In Britain and Germany 25 percent of electricity is produced by nuclear plants; in Japan, 30 percent; in Sweden, 50 percent. As for France, it has made a real commitment to nuclear energy. Its share in the country's electricity pool is as great as 80 percent.

Since *we the people* are unprepared to listen and understand serious discussions on the issues regarding the technological future of our country, these discussions simply do not take place. Meanwhile, such serious and important decisions are being made by the government and Congress, based on a shortsighted view, aiming at achieving immediate benefits, regardless of the consequences and insignificance of these benefits (on the scale of the total budget) in dollar savings.

I refer to such detrimental congressional decisions as scrapping, in the late '90s, the project of the superconducting supercollider—a device that would enable us to make a breakthrough in understanding the most fundamental nature of nuclear matter and, in fact, the origin of the universe; drastic cuts in funds for fundamental research (done mostly at universities); the plans to abolish the Department of Energy, for example. The voices of experts are not heard by politicians (who are themselves, in their majority, scientifically ignorant), and *we the people* are simply unable to help, since we do not understand what it is all about, and, above all, we do not care.

Let me add just a few more words regarding the future energy problems and the basic *philosophy* behind the scientific research. Whenever, in my discussions of scientific and technological problems of our civilization with non-scientists, I voice my concern about the diminishing supply of energy or the growing environmental problems, I hear a unanimous optimistic response: "Well, it is not for the first time that the earth is facing problems. Scientists are smart. When the time comes, they will come up with something."

Alas, science is not magic after all. What most of non-scientists do not understand is that our knowledge of nature and its laws is still far from being perfect or complete. Even though some phenomena (not only physical but social as well) may obey established and well-understood laws of nature, it does not mean that we can reliably forecast the outcomes of these phenomena or technological (societal) implementations of those laws.

Unfortunately, typically, we do not know the time that may be required to solve some of these important problems. We may pretend that they are unimportant, or that much time is still left, but too often this is just self-delusion. When attempts to attract society's attention to the pressing time problems are interpreted as an "assault on American values," it is tragic and, unfortunately is just a manifestation of ignorance, rather than of patriotism.

Returning to the energy problem. We are running out of oil. Gas will soon follow suit. Actually, the sooner we run out of fossil fuel, the better.

During the recent decade we managed to reduce air pollution due to fossil fuel burning. Carbon monoxide decreased by 37 percent; lead by 78 percent. But the best, the *ideal* burning process, inevitably produces two "natural" chemicals: water and carbon dioxide. The latter, like water, is an indispensable part of our physical world. We exhale carbon dioxide, but plants breathe with it, turning it back to oxygen. And yet, carbon dioxide is the main source of the so-called *greenhouse effect*, the accumulation of heat in our atmosphere.

Global warming is accelerating at such a pace that some unprecedented intergovernmental measures are needed to curb the deterioration of our climatic equilibrium and maintain it at least at its present level. According to the UN's Intergovernmental Panel on Climatic Change, such a curb requires *immediate* reduction of at least 60 percent of fossil-fuel use. Nobody knows whether tomorrow is too late. Some forecasts are quite gloomy.

Against this background, America, with its population of just four percent of the world population, contributes 22 percent of carbon dioxide into earth's atmosphere. In France I saw a tiny Ford automobile—only 11 feet long. In America, Ford manufactures and successfully sells huge SUVs. And SUVs are infamous for their low-energy efficiency, high-polluting power, and low safety. Of course, Ford is not an exception. Virtually all companies supplying Europe with economical and environmentally friendly small cars have jumped on the SUV bandwagon, and now have a big chunk of profit from rich and heedless America.

But what is the alternative? Nuclear energy is "bad," "unsafe," "hazardous," "dangerous." As a matter of fact, for decades, the United States was a leader in research and development of so-called *renewable energies*, among them solar and wind energy. This leadership since has been lost due to the shortsighted government policy I have already mentioned. Today the future of these energy sources in this country does not look bright.

Scientists throughout the world are working on developing non-conventional energy sources. Although not promising to solve the carbon dioxide problem, these energy sources would champion efficiency. Some of the devices have already been used in space technology, but they are not quite sufficiently economical to be used in everyday life. Will they be efficient enough by the time we cannot do without them?

Now I am coming to a dramatic moment. I am sure that very few non-scientists are aware that for almost fifty years a concerted effort by scientists of a dozen industrial nations has been launched, directed at the development of so-called *controlled thermo-nuclear fusion*.

Thermonuclear fusion is just the process that makes the H-bomb what it is. In the H-bomb, a chain reaction of the fusion of four hydrogen atoms into one atom of helium releases an enormous amount of energy within a millionth part of a second. Now, the problem is how to make this reaction proceed slowly, how to control it, to monitor the energy production. If and when this problem has been solved, the earth will have access to an unlimited source of energy. Our oceans are an inexhaustible reservoir of hydrogen that can be produced from water.

After almost fifty years, and hundreds upon hundreds of billions of dollars, and the full-time work of the thousands upon thousands of scientists, Nobel Prize laureates among them, we are still too far from a solution to the problem—a solution that could be satisfactory enough for any application. Nature has its secrets, and nobody knows how much time our science will need in order to crack those secrets.

Here is another example out how nature can keep its secrets. Fifty years ago, at the dawn of the computer era, the great mathematician John von Neuman, one of the fathers of computer science, believed that when computers became sufficiently powerful we would be able to forecast weather at any point on earth with needed precision. Weather is but a direct consequence of atmospheric phenomena that can be described by well-established, albeit very complex, equations and then solved by a powerful computer. Alas, von Neuman did not know then that when one deals with so-called "nonlinear" equations some of the solutions are fundamentally unpredictable, no matter how powerful the computer that attempts to crack them. These solutions are called "chaotic." A huge branch of mathematics has developed since then called "chaos." The weather forecasts become better and better every day, but they are inevitably short-ranged in time. When we better understand chaos, they may become even better, but, probably, never absolute.

Here I would like also to mention the tragedy of one of the greatest scientists of all times—Albert Einstein. Everybody knows that he was the one to formulate the *theory of relativity* that became a foundation of the 20th century physics, and that was, in particular, important for both the development of nuclear weapon and for cosmic research. However, non-scientists probably do not know that Einstein's great works—the so-called *special and general relativity theories*, as well as the theory of the so-called *photo-effect* (for which he was awarded the Nobel Prize)—were done at the very beginning of the 20th century, when Einstein was a young man. During the next almost-40 years of his life, Einstein feverishly worked on the *unified theory*—a theory that would explain within the same framework all the known interactions in matter: the electromagnetic, the "weak," the "strong," and the gravitational. And he failed. Not because he *was not smart* enough, but simply because, at that time, there was not enough experimental information that would have enabled him to put forward the *right* hypothesis and draw the *right* conclusions. The new experimental data were obtained, and the breakthrough in the unified theory was achieved only after his death.[10]

This is something important that activists lobbying for enhancing the speed of scientific research should understand. Too many people still believe that in order to get a breakthrough in physics, biology or medicine, all we need is just more funding—more and more and more. And those who refuse to give the money, or do not do it willingly enough, are morally responsible for not solving the burning problems in question.

Of course, I refer to the desperate attempts to speed up the anti-AIDS research. AIDS is a real threat to our civilization. It has already claimed hundreds of thousands of innocent victims, and nobody knows how many more people are doomed. The problem is exacerbated by the ignorance of the most endangered groups of people or their unwillingness to take elementary precautions against contracting the disease.

The recent development of a combination of drugs may be able to prevent the virus from killing people, but will not eliminate it altogether. Although the drugs will have saved lives, they will also dramatically increase the possibility of the spread of the disease. The latter will enormously increase the importance of our attention to the social aspects of the current AIDS epidemic. And yet, the development of an efficient anti-AIDS vaccine may be still many decades into the future—no matter how much money is injected into the research. The example with controlled thermonuclear fusion should be a warning to those who want a quick solution to difficult problems.

Let me return to our children's education. The non-humanity subjects in our school curricula are subdivided into "math," "science," and "biology." This kind of subdivision already invites abuses of the learning process.

I spent hours at my computer, scanning through the Internet home pages of dozens of high school math, science, and biology departments. Obviously, the departments that had resources, expertise, and enthusiasm to organize their own home pages (and some of them are state-of-the-art masterpieces) are well above the average. And yet, the picture I saw was rather depressing.

In our public schools, up to the tenth or eleventh grade, "math" inevitably means "a little bit of math"; "science" means "a little bit of this, and a little bit of that about nature." By this age, in all the developed countries I know of, children

---

[10] Abraham Pais, *Einstein Lived Here: Essays for Laymen*. Oxford University Press, New York, 1994.

have already explicitly studied a lot of arithmetic, algebra, geometry, and trigonometry and, perhaps, an introduction to calculus. In Europe the course called *nature* is taught in grammar school, while in middle and high school, a series of courses called *physics* is taught, and there are two separate courses on *chemistry*: inorganic and organic. And these courses are *mandatory*.

Biology, in my Moscow school was split into three separate courses: *botany* (sixth grade: 13 year-olds), *zoology* (seventh grade), and *anatomy and physiology of man* (eighth grade).

In American public schools, typically, only in high school, separate courses of algebra, geometry, and trigonometry (the latter not in all schools.) are taught. Physics, chemistry and biology courses are also put off until the last two years of high school (and mind you, the senior year is extremely unproductive). And, as much as I could understand from course descriptions on the Internet home pages, most of the courses are application-oriented. They do not give a real understanding of the fundamental scientific ideas and principles behind our today's knowledge of nature (for example, students do not have to prove theorems when studying geometry). And the serious *science* courses in high school are not mandatory.

An ad by a book-selling company: *Basic College Mathematics*, Third edition. by [...], et al. "Textbook covers the topics needed for success in a developmental math program, providing background and review in whole numbers, fractions, decimals, ratio and proportion, and measurement as well as an introduction to algebra and geometry, and a preview of statistics and consumer mathematics..." The subjects listed here are covered in grades 5 through 8 in most European schools, including Russian schools. In high school there it is no more "introduction to algebra and geometry," but serious algebra, geometry—both two-and three-dimensional—and trigonometry. The book would probably be a good textbook for a remedial course, but unfortunately, today *it is* "college mathematics."

Geography is also an elective course in many American public schools. As a result, the majority of American students cannot locate the United States on the map, to say nothing of other countries. But what is more serious, our kids are ignorant about the *outside* world and, in the future, will be indifferent to the world's problems. Back in Russia, in my time, there were at least four consecutive geography courses: *The physical geography of the world*, *the political geography of the world*, *the physical geography of the USSR*, and *the economic geography of the USSR*.

(As far as I know, public school education in the former Soviet Union, with the collapse of Communism, has also collapsed. However, the tradition of excellence in education has not died. A variety of semi-private and private schools has emerged.)

The above-mentioned report of the National Commission on Excellence in Education, "A Nation at Risk," among other things recommended that the high school curriculum require at least three years of math and three years of science. Comparing these requirements with the already existing curricula in most European countries (requiring four years of math and science[11]) one can see that our *projected* requirements are mockingly insufficient. And yet, we are still far from implementing them.

> Somewhere else, I have already quoted Dr. John Silber, an educator and former president of Boston University, writes. Let me quote again:[12] "At the present moment, I believe very few [American] college graduates could pass the A-Level examinations required in England of students who wish merely to enter the university."

Below I will make a suggestion on how the teaching of scientific subjects could be improved. But what do we do *now* to improve our children's knowledge of our physical world? Not much. A few years ago PBS, the Public Broadcasting System, had a few scientifically oriented programs for children. But, from my view, some of them were seriously flawed.

As I have already discussed elsewhere, the main idea of our educational establishment is that the learning should be easy, should be fun. I do firmly believe—and the grim consequences of this concept have proven that I am right—that this idea lies in the very core of the failure of our educational system. Only knowledge that has been obtained by hard work is firmly established and stays forever. Only overcoming difficulties brings about satisfaction—hundreds of seminars teach that to adults. But we deprive our children of the happiness that a victory—even an insignificant victory—brings.

Our educators believe that if the knowledge they want children to absorb is in an entertaining or, even better—amusing form—the children will learn it better and faster. Again, I believe this is fundamentally wrong. Meanwhile, PBS—the

---

[11] Across French middle and high school, six years in math and five years in science are required

[12] John Silber, *Straight Shooting. What Is Wrong With America And How To Fix It*, Harper & Row, New York, 1989.

only TV station that is really concerned with our children's education—unfortunately does espouse this philosophy in their programs for children.

A few years ago, children could watch the fascinating *Bill Nye the Science Guy* program. It should have been called *Clown Bill, the Funny Science Guy.* The host, "Bill," has all the attributes of a good circus clown. He grimaced, walked in a funny way, talked in a funny way. They even used state-of-the-art television tricks to make him even funnier by distorting his face or body, for instance.

In the program on energy, a teenage girl helps Bill. She comments on some experiments or animated illustrations of the physical ideas that Bill wants the children to learn. Of course, the girl uses *teenage* language. It is not a secret that, as a result of the functional illiteracy of our children, their language has become increasingly poor, the vocabulary restricted. In fact, the ability to express themselves has been severely hampered.

This deterioration is quite understandable. Both the vocabulary and ability to express oneself and to speak fluently develop only as a result of massive reading. No exception in the history of world pedagogical science is known. However, our children are no longer encouraged to read, They watch TV. The producers, who want the children to like their programs, do exactly what *the children* like. The characters of their programs look like the kids, talk like the kids and behave like the kids—the kids in conflict with the adult world—those very kids who watch these programs. And here is the vicious circle. How can children develop meaningful role models if they are being convinced that *they are OK*, when they *are not?*

Returning to *Bill Nye the Science Guy,* as I said, that girl, who helped Bill, spoke teenagers' language. One of the most important and most meaningful words in the children's (and more and more often not only the children's) vocabulary today is *cool*. Its meaning is virtually unlimited. It has mostly a positive connotation: great, fantastic, and fabulous. After Bill showed a very interesting experiment demonstrating the transformation of energy from the kinetic form to potential and back, the girl commented: "Isn't it *cool* how the energy transforms from one form to another?" But the culmination was at the very end of the program, which concluded with the girl's words: "Energy is *cool*."

To me, the person who values language as one of the greatest treasures of our civilization, this abuse of language does not make sense. But what is even worse, in the context of physics, it *does not make any sense at all*. Especially when it is used for *educational* purposes, and used deliberately in order to *score* with the children.

This is just one of the programs from the *Bill* series that were presented to our children a few years ago. The ideas were great. Their realizations, I am afraid, were counterproductive. The *Bill* program does not exist any more[13], but open a PBS web page, and you will see the invitation to click a promising link: "Computers are *cool*."

Another example is in geography. Of course it is *Carmen Sandiego*, which also used to be on PBS, and is now the multimillion source of revenue as a video game. The producers of this series and the whole *Carmen Sandiego* industry have decided that children will learn geography better if it is somehow connected with a criminal element. Besides, the kids just love to watch all kinds of *action* movies with violence and crime. Why not to make use of their interest and their love?

Accepted. Carmen Sandiego is a famous criminal—a woman (by the way, is this *politically correct?*) who escaped the cops and is hiding somewhere in the world. And we want to find and punish that villain. Like in the *Bill* program, the hosts wanted to be as funny as possible. Both the man and the woman (the *Boss*), who directed the story, looked, talked and behaved arrogantly.

The man wore a shabby suit, with a hat shifted either forward or back to the extent that either one almost could not see his face or that the hat might fall at any moment. He inevitably reminded one of Chicago mobsters of the Prohibition era. This was surely the image the producers wanted—to suit the criminal foundation of the show. As for the Boss, she made villainous and funny faces when she spoke

The show was a competition among a few whiz kids who had to guess the names of rivers, mountains, cities, for example, often obscure and unknown to anybody but geography fans. By their faces one could see that they did not very much like what they were doing—because they demonstrated not *knowledge* about our earth but a set of *labels* learned by heart by someone with a good memory. At the end of the show, the winner, upon a bell signal, had to locate several countries on a huge map on the floor. The poor kid rushed through continents and oceans, trying to place a red pole in the proper place before the pitiless bell interfered. This was also hard to comprehend. If I know where Brazil is, it is unimportant how long it will take me to find it on the map. And a crowd of cheering kids in the background demonstrating the recent fashion in their ugly garbs—which parents are unable to control, but PBS enthusiastically endorsed.

People may disagree with me as to whether learning should or should not be fun, or whether a criminal element can or cannot make teaching more successful. But there is no doubt that an educator should not be disguised as a clown or a Mafioso. In fact, something much more important is at stake and to be deplored, rather than just the producers' bad taste.

---

[13] Now the videos and books on these programs are widely available through *Amazon.com*.

Youngsters desperately need and are looking for *role models*. In so many cases I have observed during my life, it is a *teacher* who became the role model, having changed the whole life direction of a group of youngsters. As a matter of fact, subconsciously, children hope that somebody will win their hearts. This somebody must be *greater* than they are. That person must be somebody the youngsters want to emulate when they grow up. Do you remember that the rating of President Clinton dropped abruptly when, sometime during his first term, he showed up in a McDonald's? He wanted to show that he was *like everybody else*, whereas the people wanted the President to be different, special—to be *the President*.

When a teacher wants to win cheap popularity among children, not only does he or she lose but, what is much more important, the children lose. They lose the secret hope that "this is the one—the one I have been waiting for." The educational impact will most probably also be lost, for it is of secondary importance to the children, the primary being the teacher's personality. If they *love* the teacher, learning is successful. If they do not respect the teacher, there is *no* learning at all. And you cannot win children's love and admiration by being funny or arrogant. There is, however, a sure way to help youngsters to find the role models.

If you still want to follow me, let us try to see what can be done in order to bring us out of this state of scientific ignorance.

Of course, the earlier the education begins the better. As I already discussed elsewhere (see essay *Training or Education?*), the initial "natural" learning of a child, during first years of his or her life, is *intuitive*. The objective of education is to introduce the *true,* non-intuitive understanding of the world. This process has to begin as early as possible. The later it begins, the more difficult it is for a child to abandon the intuitive. It is quite obvious.

As a physicist, with the experience of explaining physics to very young pupils, I know that discussing fundamental phenomena of nature on a *scientific,* rather than an entertaining level, with parallel experiments performed by the children themselves, may be for them a source of deep satisfaction. It may also bring about to the children true knowledge, which apart from being an important fragment in their picture of the world, may also be a springboard to their future careers and meaningful lives.

Many years ago, as a high school student and a "leader" of the "physics circle," with a dozen 13-year-old boys (there was no coed education in the Soviet Union at that time), we recreated Thomas Edison's invention of an electric bulb. We made it of a few pieces of wire, graphite from a pencil, and a chemical retort. Slowly increasing the electric current with a rheostat, we made the graphite first glow and then shine brightly. I wish you could have seen the faces of my boys. They were also glowing with happiness at the achievement, by their own hands, of something that they knew was extremely important.

Another experiment I performed with my boys was the Volta arc: two graphite rods from an old battery and a water solution of regular salt as an electrolytic rheostat. We also played the game: "What would have been if…?" What would happen if there were no force of friction? Or, would balloons fly if the earth's gravitation were twice as strong? It was great.

The experiments to be reproduced with kids are in the thousands. As a result of only one year of this activity (two to three hours every other week, after classes), my boys not only knew, but also understood and could explain what the Newtonian laws were, why a rocket propelled, and what atoms were made of. Most of this material they would have to study in physics courses, two or three years later (although in the sixth grade they had already started their first Physics-I course, mechanics). In fact, their understanding of many physical phenomena at that time was already profound enough to save much time in the future.

This kind of activity in groups (they were called *circles*) was encouraged by Communists, simply because they understood that a teenager in a classroom is much better than a teenager in the street is. There were "circles" in physics, chemistry, mathematics, biology, geography, literature, theater, dance, photography— and this was at a quite ordinary Moscow public school, one of many.

Usually a teacher, or an older student was in charge (as in my case, when we were "inventing" the bulb, I was 17, in my senior—tenth—year, about to graduate from high school), but sometimes a university or a technical college sent its students to organize the activity. Moscow University, the best in the then Soviet Union, and, now recognized as one of the best schools in the world, had under its auspices a series of *circles* for high school students (grades 8 through 10). In fact, almost every department had its own *circle*. I attended the physics *circle* at the university and the astronomy *circle* at Moscow Planetarium. Every spring all-Moscow competitions of these *circles* (they were called *Olympiads*) were held. The *Olympians*, winners of, say the physics competition, were granted privileges upon entering the university.

The Moscow Planetarium deserves a few warm words. Apart from being the largest in Europe, it had on its staff true enthusiasts and devoted scientists. Attending lectures there was in the tenth grade astronomy curriculum of many Moscow schools. And those were times, when space travel was still just science fiction. Sitting in a comfortable leather chair, with the bottomless night sky high above, recognizing old friends—the constellations (which, I knew, would be blinking again through the smoggy Moscow sky on my way home after the lecture)—I felt happy and proud of *humankind* that some day would challenge the Universe.

At that time, the only tool to penetrate the mystery of space was the optical telescope. The Planetarium had a good 5-inch refractor telescope in a dome pavilion (it was used for "serious" research by more experienced "astronomers"—there were a few absolutely bright teenagers; I wonder, what has happened to them), and another one—a 3-inch instrument just under a sliding hood-like cover. In order to use it, one had first to pass an exam and get a special license. (I recently found that license among my old papers.) On cold Moscow winter nights, it usually took at least half an hour just to remove ice from the hood and open it, and then, perhaps another hour (rarely more) drawing the contours of the moon's oceans and craters, with the pencil almost slipping from one's numb fingers. I remember those enchanting nights of 50 years ago, as if they were yesterday.

It was at the Planetarium, in the eighth grade (I was 15 years old), that I decided to become a physicist. On the first floor, there were a few small lecture rooms where, for groups of 15-20 students, lectures on various subjects in physics and astronomy were given—mainly by the planetarium professors or Moscow University astronomy students. I do not remember what that important lecture was about—it was probably on low-temperature physics. As one of the experiments, the lecturer made a hammer out of mercury (frozen by immersing it into liquid nitrogen), and hammered a nail into the blackboard covered with drawings and formulas. I was stunned. A youngster needs just one event like that, and his or her life becomes meaningful, acquires direction—the star that will always shine, and will never fade away.

I met Zeya, my future wife, on a hiking trip in the Caucasus Mountains after our freshman year in college. But we could have met three years earlier at the planetarium astronomy circle. She, a PhD in electrical engineering, for twenty years had been one of the leading developers of new high intensity gas discharge lamps with OSRAM Sylvania. However, her life as a future engineer and scientist also began as an astounded fifteen-year-old youngster in the planetarium. Then, the lecture was on luminescence—the glowing of gases in electric field. After the lecture was over she knew, yes, she would be a *lamp scientist*. She would create new lamps that would be better and brighter.

This system of *circles* that I have described does have a counterpart in American education. What I mean are *school clubs*. Elsewhere I already discussed the importance of school clubs in organizing a vibrant after-school extracurricular activity. What I want to stress, however, is that the role of school clubs in our school's extracurricular activity would be enhanced manifold were they led by students of sponsoring universities rather than by school teachers. I also want to stress again that in order for the clubs to achieve their important role they must be regarded as an *indispensable supplement* to formal education—an *indispensable part* of children's lives, rather than just another nice activity.

Of course, in order to organize an extracurricular activity of this kind, huge resources are needed. Again, as in the problem of improving the quality of education in general, what we need is not so much money, but enthusiasts. These days we hear a lot about the necessity for college students to fulfill so-called *communal services.* What can be more useful, meaningful and noble than to send those young people into schools: to teach, to show miracles, to play with the *lost* (and abandoned.) teenagers, to bring light and meaning into their lives, to be their role-models. This work, the necessity and importance of which is simply impossible to overestimate, will also be important for the young "teachers," for their maturing into responsible adults.

There is no doubt that this movement—*Kids Teaching Kids*—will be a success, for, with the conflict of generations in full swing and at its worst, only people of the same or almost the same age group are able to help each other. This does not contradict what I said about the necessity for a teacher to be *above* the students. A young teacher is *above* simply because he or she is a *teacher,* someone who is knowledgeable and respected. Besides, he or she is a vivid example of what can be achieved by a student just in a few years. If this comes to pass, there will be deep understanding and trust between them, and our society will change fundamentally.

Of course, perhaps MTV, and the thousands of other businesses that produce all kinds of poisons for our children's consumption will disappear. I wish I could live to see our teenagers, who are truly happy, know how to dream, and how to fight for their dreams to come true.

Here I would like to say a few words about the relationship between science and religion in our society. I discuss somewhere else the difficult problem of religious education. There is no religious education in American public schools, and yet it is today the battlefield of an endless struggle between religion and science. Of course, I mean the renewed discussion of whether *creationism* as a literal interpretation of the Bible should be taught in public schools.

Unfortunately, in America, the discussion of world creation takes on an irrational and even ugly form. A scientific truth is becoming a matter of approval (or disapproval) of taxpayers. Katha Pollitt, a noted essayist and poet wrote:[14] "In France, where the curriculum is national and firmly in the hands of educational authorities, it does not matter how many ordinary citizens think the Earth is only 10,000 years old. In Kansas it matters." No doubt, the irrational and absurd discussion on *creationism* as a substitute or an alternative to the scientific theory is a reflection of our educational and cultural crisis.

And yet, in spite of the struggle between the extremes—the religious fundamentalists and the uncompromising atheists—the relationship between religion and science is now entering a new, more constructive and meaningful phase.

---

[14] *Free Inquiry,* Feb. 2000.

The substitution of *creationism* for the modern sciences in public school curricula, whether some tax payers like it or not, is *wrong*. It is wrong not because the story of creation as we know it from the Bible should not be taught as a substitution for the scientific facts, but because in the 21st century, one should expect a more profound understanding by our children of both religion and the physical world around them.

I do believe that *creationism* must be taught in our schools and colleges but, in the 21st century, that course would consist of, three parts: *Cosmology, Molecular Genetics*, and, without saying, *Evolution*, with the necessary prerequisites of a few years of advanced physics, biochemistry and general and molecular biology.

Let me explain what I mean. This is very important not only from the point of view of the unification of the school curriculum or improving the quality of science education but for the understanding of our goals as *human beings* in the 21st century.

The revolution in modern science, not only in physics (and especially in cosmology), but also in molecular biology and medicine, has had a dramatic impact on the world outlook of a category of people who were traditionally ardent and uncompromising materialists: the scientists. Not only is it the *Big Bang* theory of world creation that has influenced their thinking. The origin of this intellectual revolution lies much deeper.

The *reductionist* approach, that the understanding of a complex phenomenon can be attained through detailed understanding of the simple components of that complex object, as applied to science in general—to physics, biology, medicine, psychology—is under fire today. And it is under fire not by some mediocrities, but by leading world-famous experts in their fields. A less dogmatic, perhaps less *materialistic*, a so-called *holistic* approach to the world, which is against *reducing* the complex phenomena to the simpler and easy understandable ones, and which, instead, focuses on the properties of the complex object that do not follow from the analysis of its components, is in the minds of the pioneers of contemporary science.[15]

For the first time in the history of science, God is mentioned by scientists not in a negative, confrontational or ironical context, but as a constructive possibility, a synonym of something challenging but as yet *unreachable*.

The 1999 Templeton Prize for Progress in Religion, the largest world monetary award, was awarded to Dr. Ian Barbour, a theologian with a background in

---

[15] See the excellent book of essays *Nature's Imagination: The Frontiers of Scientific Vision* (edited by John Cornwell, with introduction by Freeman Dyson). Oxford University Press, New York, 1995.

nuclear physics. In 2000, this Prize was awarded to a man with no religious background—the Princeton's Institute for Advanced Studies professor emeritus Freeman Dyson, one of the most distinguished theoretical physicists of our time, whose name I have already mentioned. A book with the title *God & the New Physics*[5] would have been impossible, say, thirty years ago. The *Anthropic Principle* that was always in the realm of philosophers is now the object of a constructive discussion by physicists. One of its formulations reads: "The universe must have properties, which allow life to develop within it at some stage in its history." It means that a *Homo sapiens* might have been the ultimate objective of creation.

I address the interested reader to the excellent and fascinating book by John D. Barrow and Frank J. Tippler.[16] The authors, world-famous experts in cosmology and astrophysics, discuss the various aspects of the *Anthropic Principle*. The *Anthropic Principle* reveals this new (to the physicists) aspect of creation; the one that can be confirmed and verified by the contemporary science and, at the same time does not contradict the ideas of the Hebrew Testament. Half of the book, filled with formulas from advanced cosmology, is for specialists. The other half (in fact, the first half) is a thoughtful analysis of religious, philosophical and general scientific aspects of that quality of our world. It is well possible that it had been created in order that you and I could appear one day and could observe and witness that miracle with awe!

To physicists, the universe is not any more something meaningless and completely estranged. Roger Penrose, a famed mathematician and theoretical physicist, wrote:[17] "Some people take the view that the universe is simply there and it runs along—it's a bit as though it just sort of computes, and we happen by accident to find ourselves in this thing. I don't think that's a very fruitful or helpful way of looking at the universe. I think that there is something much deeper about its existence, which we have very little inkling of at the moment."

The same applies also to understanding the process of evolution of life on earth, the *natural selection*. Yes, "nearly every important bone in the human body can be traced back to the skeletons of the first fishes that left the water 350 million years ago. The modification in the bodies of the backboned animals runs in

---

[16] J.D.Barrow and F.J.Tippler, *The Anthropic Cosmological Principle.* Oxford University Press, New York, 1986.

[17] *Stephen Hawking's 'A Brief History of Time': A Reader Companion,* (Edited by Stephen Hawking). Bantam Books, New York, p. 142.

a clear line from the fishes to the amphibians, the reptiles, the mammals, and, finally to man." But, as Robert Jastrow, an acclaimed scientist and founder of NASA's Goddard Institute, from whose book *The Enchanted Loom: Mind in the Universe* this quote has been taken, adds on the same page: "Whether this long process, culminating in man, is the expression of a *plan* or *purpose* in the universe seems to me to be a question beyond the reach of human understanding, or at least beyond the reach of science" (emphasis added).

And yet, we are passionately willing to understand, to find out *why* we exist, and *how* we came to have being, together with the universe and (possibly) as its indispensable part. Stephen Hawking, who perhaps shares first and second places among the world's greatest physicists with his colleague and friend Roger Penrose, writes, in his famous book, *A Brief History of Time*: "There may be only one unified theory that allows for the existence of structures as complicated as human beings who can investigate the laws of the universe and ask about the nature of God." And a few pages over: "If we do discover a complete theory, it should in time be understandable in broad principle by everyone, not just a few scientists. Then we shall all, philosophers, scientists, and just ordinary people, be able to take part in the discussion of the question of why it is that we and the universe exist. If we find the answer to that, it would be the ultimate triumph of human reason—for then we would know the mind of God."

This is Hawking's dream. Understanding the great achievements of science must not be the intellectual privilege of just a few. Understanding the world we live in and our role and *mission* in it, is a must for *Homo sapiens* in the 21st century.

The foundation for this understanding, as a part of a broad general education, can be laid already in high school. A good teacher, even now, can easily enable the students to grasp the main ideas of the Big Bang—a sudden emergence of our physical world with its space, time, and matter some fifteen billion years ago—and the *Anthropic* aspects of the events of the "first two days" of creation. But that would require a strong scientific knowledge (and even a definite level of intellectual development) that our school does not give these days. Against the background of understanding the events of creation as seen by physics and biology, religious studies in public school (and this is just a pipe dream now) can also be made interesting and exciting.

However, with all these fascinating discoveries of science one should not forget that religion is not so much about how the world has been created, but rather about how we became *human*. That is why religion is so important, especially in the time of our crisis of meaning.

But let me return to what this essay is about: the role of science in our society and the importance of education. I want to answer the obvious objection that some of my readers may voice. "Why, on earth, should I study all this stuff about energy and atoms that I will never use in my life, and that will not help me earn my living?"

My response is also the gist of this book, and the gist of the fight, which Harvard University President Charles William Eliot and his Committee of Ten lost over one hundred years ago: *Education*—a profound academic general education—is necessary for everyone, and *not* in order to help one to make money. As a matter of fact, it may be *absolutely useless* for that purpose. Specialized *training* will do that. *Education*, as I understand it, and as it has been understood by thoughtful and responsible educators in this country for over one hundred years, is necessary for an individual to become a member of the family called *humankind* and, as such, have a share in its inheritance, and be responsible for its destiny.

Learning the world's history enables us to understand where we came from. Knowledge of literature and reading enable us to understand ourselves and envision the road ahead of us. Learning the arts teaches us to better see the beauty of the world, both within and without us. Learning science enables us to be the masters of our world. Having absorbed all these treasures we gradually learn how to *love*. And then we see that the world is *good*.

Stupid idealism? But the gist of my book is also that unless, through making mistakes and bruising ourselves, we start moving that way, our civilization, and our Democracy are doomed…

There is also a factor (I have already mentioned it above) that is far from any idealism, but rather is extremely important in our everyday life. That is what Dr. James C. Garland, a noted physicist writes:[18] "I fear we may have seriously underestimated the consequences for our culture of a scientifically illiterate population. Lacking an understanding of the physical world, we easily fall prey to hucksters, charlatans, and those who promise easy solutions to complex problems. We abrogate our social responsibility to self-styled experts. We waste our dollars—and sometimes our lives—on useless medicines. We allow our political leaders to embark on costly, ill-fated schemes cooked up by special interest groups. We ignore real dangers to our planet because we cannot understand the warnings." Gradually, *we, the people* are losing control of our own destiny. Where will it lead our society?

Everybody loved *Star Trek*. It was breathtaking. It was enchanting. It was entertaining. Among the host of entertaining programs that the TV industry has been feeding us with, that one was perhaps the most thought provoking.

---

[18] *The American Physical Society (APS) News*, Nov. 1996.

But have you ever thought what kind of society was on the planet Earth at that time? Those kind, brave, and intelligent people on board the *Enterprise*, although being probably among the most qualified and the smartest of the Earthians, and yet were they, in a broad sense, *representing* the human race on Earth? Was the Earth still their spiritual and cultural *home*—the home they loved, the home they wanted to return to? When they return, will they still be a part of the Earth's society?

If the answer is *yes*, then how can we envisage our ascent from scientific ignorance to the heights of scientifically enlightened society, challenging the universe in the endless quest for knowledge? If the answer is *no*, then is it not difficult to imagine the Earth as a huge GULAG, with the majority of population, ignorant and good for nothing, contained in Pleasure Cities? Supplied with unrestricted amounts of entertainment and drugs, they are allowed to intellectually and emotionally rot in their prison of pleasure. The minority of the population are those who were able to overcome the hedonistic spell of the majority, made use of hard work and intensive studies. They are *The Ruling Class*. They may be the guardians of the Earth's intellectual treasures, but the Democracy on the Earth is dead. Scenarios of this kind have already been explored by science fiction writers.

Think about it. Fewer and fewer people now understand (and, as a matter of fact, even care about) the fundamental scientific and technological basis of our civilization. Is that not awful? Is that not mind-boggling? And yet, not everything has been lost. *We the people*, can make a difference.

THE BELL TOLLS:
SOCIETY'S COGNITIVE INHOMOGENEITY

"...never send to know for whom the bell tolls: it tolls for thee."

—*John Donn, Devotions*

This line is a part of the epigraph to Ernest Hemingway's great novel *For Whom the Bell Tolls*. Hemingway's novel is about *responsibility*. "Any man's death diminishes me, because I am involved in Mankind..." These words just precede the stanza in the epigraph.

Remember, Cain asked God, "Am I my brother's keeper?" And the answer should be *yes*. When people forget this simple commandment, tragedies happen.

Our time is full of examples of irresponsibility on all possible levels. We have entered a new millennium unprepared for its challenges, and we seem not to hear the *bell*. Its tolling is warning us. For there is still some time left, although nobody knows how much.

That *bell* seems to have nothing to do with the bell of *The Bell Curve*[1] But publication of this book by Drs. Herrenstein and Murray has again raised the question of *responsibility* in our society.

The book produced the effect of an explosion. Dr. Earl Hunt writes:[2] "*The Bell Curve* made its authors' names household words, sometimes accompanied by four-letter words." The book enormously enhanced the ideological polarization of our society. Never before, perhaps, were the positions of the Left and the Right so diametrically opposed. Against the background of the fierce struggle between the Democratic President and the Republican Congress, over the role of government, and the responsibility of society over the have-nots, this book caused a head-to-head collision of the Left and the Right.

---

[1] Richard J. Herrenstein and Charles Murray *The Bell Curve: Intelligence and Class Structure in American Life*. The Free Press, New York, 1994

[2] *American Scientist*, Jul.–Aug., 1995

162

The liberals saw and still see in the book a diabolical assault on the whole ideology of *equality* and *humanity* (which the book does not contain). The conservatives brandish the book as a "scientific" weapon justifying cuts in social programs. And a significant section of American society sees in the book a "scientific" foundation for their (often subconscious) racist beliefs.

In short, both sides have found in the book what they wanted to find—a confirmation of their ideological stance. And both sides somehow refuse to recognize a very important fact: that the book is a piece of high-caliber scholarship; that the authors are honest and thoughtful scientists; that the book is an example of humanistic integrity; and that the book is a call for responsibility.

This essay is not a review of this book. It cannot be. Only scholars competent in the fields of social psychology, psychometrics, and education can provide a competent and objective critique of the book. No doubt there are already a host of professional articles responding it.

The objective of this essay is to show that the book *is not* what the liberals and conservatives claim it to be. I also believe that the book is very important, for it brings *out of the closet* something that should not and must not be hidden: a discussion of the *role of intellectual abilities in modern society.*

In fact, as Dr. Hunt writes, following the public outrage, as a second reaction, "some commentators suggested that Herrenstein and Murray were merely bringing up facts that were well known to the scientific community, but perhaps best not discussed in public"—a *mokita*, the New Guinea term meaning "truth that we all know but agree not to talk about."

No matter how *politically incorrect* and even insulting to some the book seems to be, it is first of all a scientific work. The war against the *politically incorrect* in our society today reminds me of the infamous ideological campaigns against academic research in Stalin's totalitarian Soviet Union. In the '30s and '40s, the best Soviet geneticists (who were then the leaders in world genetics) were physically exterminated, for they were, according to the political commissars and mediocre scientists, "enemies of the Soviet people." In the late '40s and '50s, the cybernetics and the relativity theory were disparaged as "idealistic and bourgeois." I do not see a fundamental difference between those labels and the infamous *political incorrectness*—the latter implies that there is an absolute, and *the only correct* point of view, and this is exactly what the Communists believed they possessed.

Scientific research may have a serious impact on society and social policies. No matter what the ideological beliefs of people are, the scientific results and their possible impact on society have to be discussed without stigmatization or insults. If the results are incorrect, then that is the job of scientists—experts in the field—to prove and to show where and why the results are incorrect. Political activists should have nothing to do with evaluation of scientific work, as much as the official Communist ideologues and volunteer activists should have had no business in interfering with the work of biologists, mathematicians and physicists and, in no way should they have had any say in whether mass can transform into energy and *vice versa*.

Conservative thinkers see in the *Bell* book a new justification for cutting many social programs directed at improving education, especially among minorities and the otherwise underprivileged. They believe the book has proven that *that* educational effort is meaningless; but they are mistaken. The book's authors do not believe and do not stress that the special educational efforts are meaningless.

As for the segment of American society, for which the *Bell* book is a confirmation of their *gut feeling* (if not firm belief) that blacks are inferior in all respects, not much can be done to change their view now. A campaign of training would not help. I discuss the origin of racism in the essay, *Harlem High, Year 2050*: Racism is a direct psychological consequence of lack of education, inherited by humans from their animal ancestors. But again, the book *does not claim that blacks are inferior*.

Returning to the contents of the *Bell* book, what is the book about? Having done enormous, *titanic* work in analyzing both new and old data, Drs. Herrenstein and Murray have shown that there are statistically reliable correlations between a parameter called *Intelligence Quotient*, or IQ, and a host of important quantities characteristic of dozens of spheres of human activity in society. Distributions of those quantities as a function of IQ have the *bell* (or as scientists call it, *Gaussian*) shape—hence the book's title.

The gist of the book is that, in today's America, a new class, which can be called a *cognitive elite*, has emerged. Its emergence is the result of a kind of *self-selection* process, in which high cognitive ability (or high IQ) is a leading factor. The opposite of this process is perpetuation of a class of people with relatively low IQ. These people are doomed to be in the lowest level of society, suffering from inadequate education and a lack of basic skills and, as a result, will have difficulty in finding a job, and the high probability of losing any job obtained, thus remaining unemployed. As a result, there is unavoidable poverty and welfare dependency. This low IQ group also contributes most to such social ills as out-of-wedlock births, crime, and many other social problems.

At the same time, the authors acknowledge that "…the identification of IQ with attractive human qualities in general is unfortunate and wrong. Statistically, there is often a modest correlation with such qualities. But modest correlations are of little use in sizing up other individuals one by one. For example, an individual can have a terrific sense of humor without giving you a clue about where he is within thirty points on the IQ scale. Or a plumber with a measured IQ of 100—only an average IQ—can know a great deal about the functioning of plumbing systems. He may be able to diagnose problems, discuss them articulately, make shrewd decisions about how to fix them and, while he is working, make some pithy remarks about the president's recent speech" (p. 21).

The authors also break another taboo. They have shown that the ethnic groups have different IQ levels. If the average IQ level for whites is 100, then that for African Americans it is 85, and for the Latinos it is 86.

Another important conclusion of the book is that the IQ differences mostly have an inherited character of between 40 and 80 percent. Therefore the IQ is very tenacious. It is extremely difficult (although not impossible) to change. That is where the doubt regarding the efficiency of some educational programs comes from.

The results are absolutely reliable statistically. The authors meticulously check every possibility of a bias, or an inconsistency, or interference with other uncontrollable factors. What then is the criticism of their opponents?

The main objection of social psychologists is that a single parameter, the IQ, is simply not enough to describe such a complex phenomenon as human intelligence. Nature is more complex. However the authors do discuss some of the objections to their methodology at the very beginning of the book (pp. 13-15). Whenever an ambiguity arises, they honestly address it.

When and if books of Drs. Herrenstein and Murray's scientific opponents are published, with the fundamentally different conclusions regarding the role of cognitive abilities in our society, that will be a new and different story. But now, supposing that Herrenstein and Murray are right in their interpretation of the statistical data—that a low IQ is the main cause of many social ills (even if IQ does not completely determine cognitive ability)—what are the possible measures to be taken in order for our society to meet the challenge of *inherent* inequality of its members?

Most of the answers are given in the book. The chapter "Living Together"— dealing exclusively with the social problems of a society where there is significant cognitive inequality—is the longest among the four book chapters. Let me stress again that the authors are extremely conscientious. They understand what kind of a Pandora's box they have opened. One can feel their concern when they discuss their results.

They are, however, quite optimistic: "…the evidence presented here should give everyone who writes and talks about ethnic inequalities reason to avoid flamboyant rhetoric about ethnic oppression. Racial and ethnic differences in this country are seen in a new light when cognitive ability is added to the picture. *Awareness of these relationships is an essential first step in trying to construct an equitable America*" (p. 340; italics is added).

The main problem is, of course, whether IQ can be significantly enhanced. It looks as though there is not much hope (at least for now) for a dramatic rise in

IQ. But, the data reported in the book show that the enhancement by eliminating some environmental factors can be achieved. Even the better nutrition of children improves their IQ. However, there are other, more important environmental factors that can and should be eliminated.

According to the data presented in the book, the probability that an individual will commit a crime is strongly correlated with a low IQ. And yet, obviously, there are some other environmental factors that are important. Otherwise, how could one explain the great increase in crime during recent years? Another example: Out-of-wedlock births are also strongly correlated with the mother's low IQ; their number out-of-wedlock births underwent a tremendous increase in the recent years, as well. The third example has to do with the *civility* level in our society. Low civility—lack of social activity and, in particular, indifference regarding one's duties as a citizen, such as voting—is also correlated with low IQ. At the same time, in this country less than 50 percent of people of voting age care to vote—significantly more people than those with low IQ. Why? The authors are aware of all these facts, and honestly acknowledge that they do not have an explanation.

Obviously, education is among the most important environmental factors. However the authors are somewhat skeptical that education can significantly improve IQ.

Against the background of failure to dramatically increase IQ by improving the education of preschoolers, adoption at birth away from a bad family environment to a good one increases the child's IQ on an average of six points. This is almost half of the disparity between blacks and whites. What is the secret of that success? What are the environmental obstacles that are being overcome when a child is removed at birth from the biological family of low IQ? Why is the effect not so dramatic when a child changes environment at the age of six? Have a few important years been already lost?

These are the extremely important questions to which we have to find answers. Is it possible that the teaching techniques used in the special programs for preschoolers are not the optimal ones? Is it possible that if a child is simply read a story at bedtime *every day* from the age of one, his or her IQ will increase? What about listening to Mozart or Chopin?

I again recall the dialogue between the elderly mother and her young daughter who has just become a mother (Betty Smith, *A Tree Grows in Brooklyn*; see the essay "Abandoned…")—about reading to children at bedtime. There are at least two *great* books to be read: Shakespeare and the Bible…

However, as writes Dr. Hunt, "even if we do not know how to improve intelligence, as indicated by the test scores, the economic issue is what skills people possess, not what their IQ scores are. We may not be able to destroy the linkage between IQ scores and the relative possession of cognitive skills (and it is not clear why we would want to), but improved education and training can raise the average achievement of all students."

In fact, Herrenstein and Murray *do* understand and stress that an individual has his or her unique value regardless of the *bell curve*: "Measures of intelligence have reliable statistical relationship with important social phenomena, but they are a limited tool for deciding what to make of any given individual" (p. 21).

In the quote from Dr. Hunt's article above, two aspects of possible influence on the individual's cognitive ability are mentioned: education and training. As I have already discussed elsewhere, they are fundamentally different in their nature. That directed training can and in fact does improve one's skills—and thus improves one's standing *vis-à-vis* society's economic forces—is obvious and has been confirmed by sociological studies.

One of such studies is mentioned in Dr. Hunt's article. A group of high school students took a yearlong course in elementary physics that focused on active problem solving. It was discovered that "IQ may not have been changed, but cognitive competence, in the sense of the problem that student could solve, was increased"

The other factor, education, is actually of much greater importance. Its impact on an individual is inevitably an enhanced maturity, resulting in adding to (or even simply developing) the *meaning* in one's life. That is what Viktor Frankl says: "In fact meaning is available to each and every person—regardless of sex and age, IQ or educational background, environment or character structure, or—last but not least—whether or not he is religious, and if he is, the denomination to which he may belong."

As I have already stressed elsewhere, meaning is a fundamentally individual concept. It does not make sense to talk about *the* meaning of life in general or on average. No matter how high or low the IQ, an individual can live a full and fulfilling life provided that this hidden treasure has been found. Thus, a multimillionaire or a Hollywood star or a successful medical doctor may resort to drugs or commit suicide, while a modest janitor or even a jail inmate may be happy (see diagram on page 46). Heredity itself also does not uniquely determine the moral standing of an individual in society.

Viktor Frankl writes,[3] "As for inheritance, research on heredity has shown how high is the degree of human freedom in the face of predisposition. For example, twins may build different lives on the basis of identical predispositions. Of a pair of identical twins, one became a cunning criminal, while his brother became an equally cunning criminologist. Both were born cunning, but this trait in itself implies no values, neither vice nor virtue"

I do believe that human life is the realization of a *task*, of a *mission*. As such, it is unique and important. Its importance is unrelated to the contents of the mission. Although different missions may have different impacts on society (a university professor and a humble janitor seem to be incomparable in their roles in society), but to the individual, his or her mission is unique. Having realized it as such—which may take years to do—it becomes the ultimate meaning in one's life.

We still do not know what is it that IQ measures, or what factor could be called the *true Intelligence Quotient*. But realization of *the* mission does not take an IQ, it takes *heart*—the human ability to *respond* and to *love*. With respect to their unique missions, the high-IQ- and the low-IQ-individuals have equal existential values. According to the Talmud, in the world to come, one will not be asked why one has not been somebody else. One will be asked why one *has not been* what one had to be according to the one's own unique *mission*.

Finding this unique treasure—meaning—would be significantly facilitated if people had access to the treasures of culture that our civilization has been creating and accumulating for millennia.

Today the doors to the treasury of our civilization are locked for millions. However, everyone should be able to enter and take from it without limits. It is the challenge to our society to give everyone a key. IQ has nothing to do with the ability of an individual to enter and take as much of the treasures as one is able carry into one's life.

I believe that an individual with a *below average IQ* is able to feel the heroic might of Beethoven's 5th or 9th symphonies, or the overflowing tenderness of Mendelssohn's piano trios and Chopin's nocturnes, or may be stunned by the tragic power of Botticelli's *Pieta*, and enchanted by the virgin beauty of Claude Monet's *Water Lilies*. It is a great tragedy that for millions of people, the treasures of music, literature, art and science do not exist.

---

[3] Viktor E. Frankl, *The Unheard Cry for Meaning: Psychotherapy and Humanism.* Washington Square Press, New York, 1985, p. 44.

The dreams of idealistic philosophers of the past for an *equitable* society in the sense of equal distribution of wealth, or equality in the workplace will never come true. Attempts of Communists to build such a society cost humankind close to one hundred million lives, and even threatened its very existence. Yet it is quite meaningful to speak of *constructing an equitable society*. Though people are not equal in their cognitive abilities, and perhaps not in hundreds of other qualities, they, as *human beings*, have an equal share in life on this earth. "The differences in talents, intelligence, knowledge are negligible in comparison with the identity of the human core common to all men," as Erich Fromm in his *The Art of Loving* puts it. Life, being the main existential objective, can be made *meaningful* regardless of the differences.

That is why the *Bell* book is so important. Now that we know that our society is cognitively not homogeneous, a serious effort must be undertaken in order to make society more equitable in arriving at a fulfilling life: Thanks to the fundamental works by Viktor Frankl we know what that means.

To conclude, let me again return to the *Bell that Tolls*. Yes, it tolls for us. It is everybody's responsibility, in the beginning of the 21st century, to help our children—as well as ourselves—to find place in this world. Our *mission* is to make our lives meaningful, irrespective of race, ethnicity, and IQ. We know what must be done—I do believe we will succeed.

JUST SAY NO: AMERICA'S DRUG CULTURE

> "I think of those youngsters who, on a worldwide scale, refer to
> themselves as the 'no future' generation. To be sure, it is not just
> a cigarette to which they resort; it is drugs."
>
> —*Viktor E. Frankl, Man's Search for Meaning*

The problem of illicit drugs is one of the most pressing problems of America today. President George H. W. Bush, in 1989, called drugs "the gravest domestic threat facing our nation." Later, President Clinton termed drugs as America's "constant curse." In 2002, the percentages of high school seniors who had ever used drugs were: alcohol—78.4; marijuana—47.8; cocaine—7.8; hallucinogens—12.0.[1] The street cocaine market in the United States has been stable for years and totals $6 billion a year. Approximately 1.5 to 2 million people are regular cocaine or crack cocaine users. The total number of people using drugs either regularly or casually is ten times greater than this, comprising a significant percentage of our population. Our children are an inherent part of the drug culture. The use of drugs and alcohol among high school students is extremely high, and is currently showing the tendency to rise again, after a relative drop from 1988.

Here are some very impressive statistics:[2] "We are losing perhaps $100 billion per year…in drug-related crime, medical costs, and lost productivity. Another $60 to $100 billion is spent every year by consumers to purchase the illicit drugs themselves. The total annual cost of the 'drug problem' in dollars, therefore, may be as much as $200 billion, more that the entire annual deficit only a few years ago"

---

[1] *National Institute of Drug Abuse* (NIDA), www.nida.nih.gov/Infofax/ HSYouthtrends.htm.

[2] Steven B. Duke and Albert C. Gross, *America's Longest War: Rethinking Our Tragic Crusade against Drugs*, 1993, p. xvi.

Not only does the "drug culture" cost our society enormously economically, it is also the main cause of the steadily growing crime rate.

The dynamics of drug use in this country have not been well understood. Nobody can explain (at least, a layman like me has not been informed by the media) why drug use declines and then increases again. Of course, the reaction of our government to proliferation of drugs was instrumental and important. Since March 1989, when the *Office of National Drug Control Policy* was established, its directors—*drug czars*—played an important role in formulating and executing anti-drug government policy.

The dramatic story of his tenure as a drug czar for twenty months (1989-91) was told by William Bennett in his book, *The Devaluing of America: The Fight for Our Culture and Our Children.* No doubt the actions the agency took under his leadership were successful. The overall drug use by 1992 decreased by almost 50 percent from its peak in the seventies. And yet, we are still too far from not only the *final* solution to the problem, but from any meaningful solution at all.

In this essay, I will try to analyze the *why* of our drug problem. Addiction to drugs is a very complex problem, combining in itself physiological, psychological, and sociological causes. And yet, I hope to convince my reader that its *why* is, to a large extent, a direct consequence of our crisis, and that the drug problem will never be solved unless *meaning* in people's lives is restored, and *boredom* has disappeared. I am afraid this will be impossible unless our educational philosophy and the whole educational system have been radically changed.

As with almost any important issue in our life today, the anti-drug strategy and policy are a matter of political partisan approach. The Right believes that drug use is a vice. The Left insists that drug use is an illness and, *as such,* should have the highest government priority. The Left also claims that drug use is a social illness—that the main cause of drug proliferation in the inner-city ghettoes is poverty, whereas the Right argues that, on the contrary, inner-city poverty *is* the direct consequence of drug use. Both sides, however, agree that both the supply of drugs into this country and its being dealt on streets have to be stopped, although the level of priority in law enforcement changes from government to government.

Among the many drug problem's facets, of utmost importance are its two aspects: *supply* and *demand.* For years, the anti-drug efforts of our government have been focused on the supply side. Since 1981, well over $100 billion has been spent trying to stop the flow of drugs into the United States. Seventy cents of each dollar appropriated for anti-drug effort is absorbed by law enforcement. William Bennett, during his tenure, insisted on army assistance and, in fact, succeeded in involving the

Pentagon in the drug war. In fact, the *drug czar* appointed in 1996 was a retired four-star general (Barry McCaffrey).

It goes without saying that active and pitiless law enforcement is needed. One cannot but agree with William Bennett that when a child playing with matches starts a fire, the first thing to do is to extinguish the fire. However, it is of extreme importance to understand *why* the child was playing with matches in the first place, in other words, to understand the *demand* side of our drug problem. Unfortunately, here not only don't we have a clear-cut government policy, but even a basic understanding of the problem seems to be lacking.

In one of his interviews, not long before he was killed, the Colombian drug cartel leader Pablo Escabar said (not a direct quote): "Why do you accuse us in your drug problems? It is a free economic system. You have demand, we provide supply. If and when the Americans do not need drugs any more, we will go broke and go out of business." A bitter truth.

Why do millions of people use illicit drugs anyway? Perhaps unemployment and poverty have something to do with the drug use? Perhaps, those unfortunates just fell into drug use *accidentally* and do not realize that it is bad and harmful? As for youngsters, don't they just experiment out of curiosity, or just follow bad examples? Since people do not understand that drugs are harmful and dangerous, we should *educate*—both adults and children—*about* the harmfulness of that bad habit. As for those who are already addicted, we should provide them with adequate medical help. (Alas, we do not have enough funds to treat all who would like to be treated.)

This is, more or less, how we understand the supply part of the problem. It was against that ideological background that the campaign *Just Say No* was launched in 1985, and the anti-drug campaign was launched by the then First Lady Nancy Reagan. Ten years later, as a part of the 1996 presidential election campaign, the Republican candidate Robert Dole put forward, with the endorsement of Mrs. Reagan, a similar slogan *Just Don't Do It.*

With all my respects to Mrs. Reagan and the President, who completely endorsed that campaign (and, for that matter, to their ideological successor, Robert Dole), I do believe that the campaign's foundations were and are extremely naïve. The scope of the problem, its adverse effects on both the individuals involved and the society as a whole are so enormous, so devastating, that one has to look for some more fundamental causes, rather than *ignorance, bad examples,* or *lack of character or will power.*

First of all, America still believes in the myth that the main realm of drug abuse is the inner-city ghetto. However, ghetto dwellers are unable to spend $60 to $100 billion per year on drugs. According to the National Institute on Drug Abuse, among the *current* drug users are a little over two million blacks, one million Hispanics, and *nine million* whites. Although, in percentages, the numbers of minority users are higher, the market itself—and that is what is important even if one only wants to stop the spread of drugs—is sustained mainly by whites.

William Bennett writes in his book (p. 106): "In fact, significant numbers of inner-city residents do not commit themselves to the drug world. Most blacks in our inner city are law-abiding citizens who live decent lives and disdain drugs; they are victims, not perpetrators of drug crimes."

At the same time, as a witness of an undercover operation in Detroit, he "…was struck by how many people who drove into that almost exclusively black neighborhood were whites (probably from the suburbs)…" (p. 109). No wonder, most of the law-enforcement operations are directed at the inner cities, which are the main source of drugs both for blacks and whites. The reason is obvious. No matter how many whites use drugs (in percentages, not many), they would not tolerate a drug dealer in their own neighborhood.

One should distinguish between those who use drugs on a more or less permanent basis—once a week or a month—and the so-called *casual* users, who use drugs as recreation or entertainment. However, the overall picture is obvious: millions upon millions of Americans—both adults and adolescents, blacks and whites—use drugs. But why?

Is William Bennett right claiming (p. 95): "It was the collapse of institutional government authority, essentially giving permission to take drugs, that was largely responsible for the epidemic that eventually hit us for almost two decades—and with catastrophic consequences—many forgot how to answer the question, 'Why not drugs?'" Very unlikely. The question is why the mere idea *of getting high* is so infective that a free man, without pressure of whatever authority, so often succumbs to it?

This is something we should have understood years ago—before billions of dollars had been spent on the war on drugs, the war that, as we see now, is far from being won. Alas, we have *not* understood, and I, a man in the street, cannot comprehend why.

In this essay I just want to remind my reader of a point of view that in no way is new or revolutionary. Almost fifty years ago, in 1956, even before the onset of the sixties with their explosion of drugs and sex, Erich Fromm, had perceived the main problem of our society to be in the "separateness" of people. He wrote in *The Art of Loving*, "Alcoholism and drug addiction are the forms which the individual chooses" to escape one's separateness. "While they try to escape from separateness by taking refuge in alcohol or drugs, they feel all the more separate after the orgiastic experience is over, and thus are driven to take recourse to it with increasing frequency and intensity."

What Fromm calls *separateness*—the emotional and spiritual isolation of an individual, the feeling of being lost—Viktor Frankl would call an *existential vacuum:* "What threatens contemporary man is the alleged meaninglessness of his life, or as I call it, the existential vacuum within him. And when does this vacuum open up, when does this so often latent vacuum become manifest? In the state of boredom" (*Psychotherapy and Existentialism*, p.122). Elsewhere (*Man's Search for Meaning*, p. 145) Frankl writes: "Just consider the mass neurotic syndrome so pervasive in young generation: there is ample empirical evidence that the three facets of this syndrome—depression, aggression, addiction—are due to what is called 'the existential vacuum,' a feeling of emptiness and meaninglessness."

And what is the best way to get rid of boredom? To try to *escape* the real life that has caused this unbearable state of meaninglessness. To achieve that end, all means are good. The overwhelming desire to have fun, in all its endless varieties, is one of them. Of course, TV is the best and the first attempt to fight the all-penetrating boredom.

Psychologists describe three stages of *entertainment addictions*. What in the following quote is called *hobby* can be a hobby, sports or, more widely spread today, the electronic media, i.e., TV, computers, video games, and the Internet. Here are these three stages:

"1. Interest: Participants enjoy engaging in the hobby when time, work and family responsibility allow. When they finish with hobby activity, they move smoothly back into normal daily routine. They may speak about the hobby outside the hobby setting but mostly in a casual manner for a limited amount of time.

2. Preoccupation: Participants spend an inordinate amount of time thinking about or seeking out hobby-related information. They may talk for an extended time about the hobby if there are like-minded individuals around. If they sense others to not share their enthusiasm, they may become less social and explore new ways of enjoying their hobby. Work and family responsibilities are not ignored but may suffer slightly.

3. Addiction: Participants spend all their time thinking about the hobby and when they can do something related to it. They may either talk about their hobby incessantly or become immersed in their own thoughts if there are no willing listeners. Any compliance with work or family responsibilities is done so they can hurry up and start engaging in their hobby. It becomes obvious to

co-workers and family that their priorities are not with them." In its social consequences, this form of addiction is only slightly different from the addiction to chemical drugs.[3]

Once this point of view has been accepted—that the drug culture in this country (and, as a matter of fact, everywhere in the world)is an instinctual attempt by helpless frustrated people to avoid the unbearable boredom of meaningless life—some important conclusions as to both the strategy and tactics of the drug war may be drawn.

The most important conclusion is that it is the *demand* for drugs that is the origin of the problem, rather than the drug *supply*. Return meaning to people's lives, make their lives full, interesting and fulfilling, and the drugs will disappear. And, in my view, only through education can this goal be achieved.

The fundamental difference between Frankl and Freud is that the latter placed one's animal, instinctual, subconscious behavior in the center of one's life, while the former insisted—and in fact proved—that it is the *human* component, based on meaning and responsibility that makes us what we are. All our great deeds result from our unending and fierce fight with and rejection of those animal instincts implanted in us by evolution. Meaning is one, perhaps the most important, component of one's personality that makes life worth living. Dr. Frankl's experience as a Nazi death camp prisoner showed that people could die not because of the unbearable hardships of everyday life, but because the meaning in their lives had been lost.

In the state of existential vacuum the animal takes over the human. Among those *animal* qualities discovered and crowned by Freud is *the will to pleasure*. According to Freud, pleasure is one of the most powerful stimuli of human life. On the contrary, Frankl argues that "Pleasure is, and must remain, a side effect or by-product, and is destroyed and spoiled to the degree to which it is made a goal in itself" (*Man's Search for Meaning*, p. 145). That is why pleasure is so easily devalued. In fact, one quickly becomes addicted to it, and needs more and more of it, and is never satisfied.

We *are* animals in this respect. In the early 1950s, American biologist James Olds and his colleagues, in a series of experiments on rats, discovered (almost by accident, by the way) the existence of a "pleasure center" in a rat's brain located in a narrow bundle of fibers known as the *medial forebrain bundle*. An electrode

---

3   Quoted from the paper by Kirk Findley presented at the Eleventh World Congress on Logotherapy, Dallas, TX, June 25-29, 1997; to the best of my knowledge, unpublished.

sends an electrical stimulus to that spot and, instead of trying to avoid a second stimulus, the rat is waiting for it. The researchers then found that in order to receive the desired stimulus, the rat would climb heights, run through mazes, and even cross electrified gates—which they had found impossible to go through when they were hungry and looking for food. Eventually, a device was built allowing the rats to stimulate themselves, and the results were breathtaking. Left to themselves, the rats stayed in the device days and nights, pressing the stimulating lever at the frequency of 10,000 times an hour. If not removed from the machine, the animals would die of exhaustion, hunger, and thirst. Even sex did not interest them any more.

The experiments of James Olds' group generated enormous interest in the scientific world. During the following decades, thousands of experiments were performed on many animals: rabbits, dogs, cats, goldfish, birds, several species of monkeys, dolphins and even man.

The reader interested in more details on that dramatic and sensational discovery may find them in a fascinating book by Lewis Thomas[4], biologist, physician, and one of the greatest science popularizers of our time.

He writes: "The range of animals possessing a pleasure center is already broad enough to allow for the generalization that it is a property built into all vertebrate brains…" Eventually, the term *pleasure center* was dropped from scientific publications, for obvious reasons—to somehow distract attention from possible biological and social implications for humans. Now this research has quite a low profile.

But what surprised me was Dr. Thomas's notion: "Meanwhile, it seems to me that the phenomenon has been laid in front of us as a free gift, taken as far as it can be taken by skilled, reductionist research, resting there for the mind's eye, free game for speculation by any interested party, including me" (p. 33). If this discovery is a gift, it is a gift of a very specific nature. It is a warning that there is something in us which, conditions being appropriate, may destroy our civilization and return man to the animal kingdom.

From a philosophical point of view, this evolutionarily acquired (rudimentary?) quality of our brain is a trap, set by God. Nay, perhaps it is better to say a *test* administered to us in order for *us* to see whether we are really *human*, or we have the potential to become as "animal-ish" as rats.

Long, long before, another crucial test had been administered by God—back in the Garden of Eden. And we passed it with distinction.

---

[4]   Lewis Thomas, *The Fragile Species.* Macmillan Publishing Co., New York, 1992, pp. 28-37.

Both Eve and Adam proved that the quest for knowledge for them was more important than the complete security of life in Paradise. At that moment, perhaps for the first time, God saw that what He had made of humans was *good,* for He had really created humans in His own image. That was also the beginning of human civilization on earth. One disclaimer, though: Adam refused to take responsibility for their *sin*: He voluntarily *reported* on Eve. *Responsibility* is still our weakest point…

What fascinated Dr. Thomas about that discovery was that evolution had supplied us, the animals, with a mechanism to experience *pure pleasure*, uncontaminated by any emotions or thoughts—the mechanism that, in his view, is a way to permit "an organism to know, to be sure that it is alive" (p. 36). In one paragraph further on we read: "And don't talk to me about cocaine or amphetamine or the other pharmacological tricks that may have come into fashion for artificially switching on the pleasure mechanism. I doubt that they, or any other artificial devices, can really switch on something as fundamental as this."

However we must turn on all our imagination, no matter how hard and unpleasant it may be, and see what a desperate man can do, if that lever were available.

Science-fiction writers do have such imagination. I want to share with you a story told by the great Russian science fiction writers, the Strugatsky Brothers. This story was, in fact, inspired by those Olds's experiments.

Back in Communist times, science fiction in the Soviet Union was a form of literature that was allowed (if the authors were smart enough to cheat the literary censors). Of course, there *was* science-fiction literature directed solely to entertain. But the most talented authors—among them, perhaps the best, Arkadii and Boris Strugatsky—created worlds in the not very remote future, that allowed them to discuss and frequently analyze the Soviet society, as if they were hostile alien civilizations on remote planets. The destiny of the Western civilization was also of deep concern to the Strugatsky brothers.

The story I want to share with you is the gist of their novel *The Last Circle of Paradise*[5]. The original Russian title, *The Predatory Stuff of Our Time*, however, seems to suit better to the novel's content. Quite a few other novels by the Strugatskys have also been translated into English.

The time is quite close to our time. The place is somewhere in Europe. Humankind has managed to avoid nuclear war, and now the world is a

---

5   A.&B. Strugatsky, *The Last Circle of Paradise*. D. Dobson, London, 1979.

more-or-less harmonious "peaceful coexistence" of Communist and capitalist worlds. The UN Security Council plays an important role in observing, supervising and, if necessary, interfering with everyday life, in order to sustain stability. One of the functions of the Security Council is to watch the use of illicit drugs throughout the world, and to take the necessary measures if something dangerous begins to evolve.

The Council has undercover agents in all countries under suspicion. From one of the countries alarming reports begin to reach the Council. A new and very powerful drug seems to have appeared. A growing number of deaths are reported. Then, somehow the agent accredited to that country becomes silent. All reports cease. Something dangerous is going on there.

Therefore, the Council sends its agent, a Russian named Ivan Zhilin, to that country in order to find out what is going on. Ivan is an extremely intelligent and experienced agent, who, before that assignment, participated in suppressing a couple of Fascist revolts throughout the world as well as in a few interplanetary expeditions.

That small republic is an interesting place. The technology is so developed that people are virtually unnecessary for producing both food and most of the other commodities. Almost all food and services are free, the exception being some imported items, hotels and some entertainment. People work primarily in offices, and only for just a very short period during the day. The rest of time they are free. All life is an endless entertainment: orgies, some nerve-tickling adventures (like fighting a "mad" old interplanetary robot or a huge spider from another planet in tunnels of an old subway).

There are sects and cults—hippies, punks, sophisticated drunkards. There is a society dedicated to hunting down and destroying pieces of "ancient" art. Ivan observed how a painting by Cezanne was being ripped into pieces by a roaring mob. Every night psychogenic collective orgies attract thousands of people to the city squares ("Drozh-ka. Drozh-ka." roar loudspeakers and people in a convulsive trance join them: "Drozh-ka. Drozh-ka.").

There is a tiny group of people who everybody else hates. They are called the *Intels*—intellectuals and university students who are trying to somehow fight the system. They have their underground organization that attempts, from time to time, to interfere with those orgies, by blowing makeshift bombs.

What Ivan sees is more or less normal—an obvious degeneration of a culture of overfed, oversexed, and ignorant people. An *intel* with whom

Ivan tries to have a conversation, from the very outset, becomes hysterical. "Spirit! There is no spirit any more! It is dead! It choked in fat! Oh, dear God, dear God. To think of what we are doing. But tell me—somebody does fly to the stars. Somewhere they build meson reactors. New learning systems are being devised. We are not even a backwater. We are a preserve. In the eyes of the whole world we are a sanctuary of stupidity, ignorance and pornocracy. But you do not care...Nobody cares...Nobody damned cares..."[6]

Of course, alcoholism is thriving. But for awhile, Ivan cannot discover any traces of that new and dangerous drug. He finds the agent who has stopped sending reports. The man is permanently drunk and is virtually impossible to communicate with. His hotel room is but a dirty storage place of empty liquor bottles and detergent containers. In order to get rid of Ivan, the man sends him to the old subway, where Ivan survives the encounter with a mad robot by mere chance, only because he used to work with exactly this kind of robots on one of his interplanetary missions.

Gradually, Ivan learns that there is something called *slug*, presumably a very powerful drug. People do not like mentioning this word. It is a kind of taboo. Sniffing around, bribing barmen and saloonkeepers, Ivan tries to find traces of the new drug manufacturers or dealers. For awhile he suspects a university chemical lab, but then he learns that *intels* manufacture their makeshift bombs there. Eventually he is given the address of a den keeper named Booba.

He is astounded to recognize in Booba his old friend, Peck, with whom just a few years before he had parachuted into fascist territory, and who had saved his life by destroying, with a rocket propelled grenade, a tank that was about to crush him. But this is not the Peck who he used to know. This is a bum with red eyes, swollen face, and trembling hands. Booba does not want to recognize Ivan, especially after the latter directly asks him about the *slug*. Finally Booba yields, and tells Ivan the story which is hard to believe, but which is true.

Let me retell it in terms of today's America. There are no drug manufacturers, no drug dealers. You want a *slug*? OK. You buy a Sony walkman (the cheapest—$19.99 would do). You open it (just unscrew four

---

6 This quote is a mixture of the original translation (p. 116), and my own translation that seems to make the text more adequate. The same applies to the other quotes below.

tiny screws). There is a part there, rather like a capacitor, sitting in slots. You remove it. Now you need a part to substitute. Originally people had to buy a GE hair dryer, open it—and there it was—a part, the same size, also in slots. You take it out and insert it into your walkman. Later it was discovered that the same part could be purchased in a nearby Radio Shack for just $1.99 (plus tax). So far so good. Now you fill your bathtub with hot water (over 90 degrees), pour in a capful of laundry detergent: "Dash" or "All" ("Tide" is no good), have a shot or two of something strong, lie down in the water, put on earphones, and tune your walkman to music, any music. That is all.

When Ivan asked Booba: "And then *what*?" The latter giggled. "You try it, man, and then tell me." Ivan borrowed the *slug* and left for his hotel. He tried it that very night. He followed the instructions exactly, then he turned the walkman on, and…he regained consciousness, when the water became cold. It took him a while to get himself together. "Think, think hard," he ordered himself. A storm of thoughts invaded him. Ivan recalled the experiments of James Olds—he had gotten an A on his PhD exam on psychodynamics two decades before.

"The imagination allows man to be both a rational being and a sensual animal, but…the psychic subject matter evoked by uneducated man for his illusory life of splendor derives from the darkest, most primitive reflexes…" And Ivan saw very clearly that just a short while ago he had been nothing but a rat—that rat turning a lever. "The *slug* is invading the world," he thought. "It is about to conquer it, and the world will be more than happy to surrender….No, this is not a narcotic—a narcotic has a long way to go to approach *slug*. In a way, a narcotic is exactly appropriate. Here. Now. To each time its own. Poppy seeds and hemp—the kingdom of sweet blurred shadows and peace—for the beggar, the worn-out, the downtrodden. But here no one wants peace, here no one is dying of hunger, here life is simply a bore. A well-fed, well-heated, drunken bore. It is not that the world is bad. It's just plain dreary. World without prospects, world without promise."

And all of a sudden Ivan felt that it was the end for him. It was so cozy and pleasant to be destroyed. At that moment, he forced himself into a rage—and he succeeded. He got mad—mad at himself. He jumped out of the bathtub, splashing water, hastily got dressed, called a cab, and rushed to Booba's place. Booba was dead. They had found him in his bathtub just an hour before.

This is, more or less, the end of the story. Ivan had a clash with his boss who flew from Geneva the next morning. The boss immediately suggested radical measures like military occupation, or a blockade, for example. Ivan passionately objected. He knew there was only one way. And that way had nothing to do with calling the troops.

That way is long and difficult. "Restore to men a spiritual content, spiritual concerns," as Antoine de Saint Exupery, the author of immortal *Little Prince*, has put it. This quote has become the epigraph to the Strugatskys' novel. It is also the epigraph to this book.

Returning to our time, if people need drugs, no force in the world can stop them from getting them. Seal all the borders. Bomb and burn all marijuana and cocaine fields everywhere in the world. And then? A new drug will be developed here, at home. I hate to be a prophet of doom, but I am afraid that a new era of non-chemical, high-tech drugs is about to dawn. The talented graduates of the best American universities will be developing them in their basements and garages—so that we could use our PCs and Macintoshes to get a *high-tech high*. Or, without any whiz kids, Strugatskys' scenario will be realized—with walkmans or cellular phones—and, perhaps with extra-strength Tylenol instead of detergent. Impossible science fiction? Nothing of the kind.

Underground labs within the US produce synthetic drugs without any help from the Colombian drug cartel. Experimentation with new *homemade* drugs is going on in America, and has been going on for a long time.

The use of amphetamine—a synthetic, domestic drug—is spreading in America. President Clinton, in one of his election campaign speeches in October 1996, said that the amphetamine spread must be stopped before it turns into an epidemic, like that of crack cocaine. In the same speech President Clinton announced that he had just signed a bill stiffening the penalty for dealing drugs. And not a single word about the origins and sources of the drug epidemic.

The use of another dangerous synthetic drug has been spreading, especially among teenagers and college students. It is *ecstasy* (or GHB). Believed by many youngsters to be harmless, the drug has a very narrow margin between the "safe" dose and the one that may be a killer. Together with another drug, *Rohypnol*, *ecstasy* is called "the date rape drug." As in the science-fiction story I just retold, *ecstasy* can be made from easily accessible substances—like stripper, drain cleaner and caustic soda. Today ecstasy is mainly manufactured in Europe, but at least one underground lab on university grounds has been discovered in the US.

Our children are in the forefront of drug experimentation. Getting high on *Robitussen*—an over-the-counter cough medicine—was discovered by fifth-graders a few years ago, and quickly became popular. Sniffing glue and aerosol sprays is also a good way to get high. Five to six million children experiment with inhalers. In Vermont, a 24-year-old woman recently died after inhaling fumes from three cans of air freshener. Five teenagers killed in a car crash in Boston were found to have high concentrations of an inhaler in their blood. The use of *ecstasy* among high school seniors has recently skyrocketed.

The use of illicit drugs (marijuana, by the way, is often grown by youngsters in their parents' gardens or even in pots on windowsills) and alcohol among young people is increasing. Many children, especially teenagers, are just experimenting with drugs. It is not a "creative" exploring. It is exploring ways of killing boredom.

Binge drinking among college students is an epidemic today. In a letter to the editor of *US News & World Report* (Feb. 16, 1998), a reader wrote: "We have succeeded in creating an open, anything-goes society at our universities. We have created a life for our students so bereft of direction and true passion for life and meaning, so empty of any meaningful experience, that they take to spending their evenings and often days in a drunken stupor, and celebrate what life they have by quickly entering a state where awareness of life itself leaves them as rapidly as possible."

It goes on, and on, and on. It is simply because our younger generation feels the meaninglessness of life more desperately, more acutely than the adults do. The life ahead of them is a complete darkness, with no sparks of light: *getting high* seems to be a kind of way out.

And yet, we still believe that in order to stop the drug epidemic we should mobilize the army, navy (and possibly the national guard) to seal our borders and, of course, *educate* people *about* the harm of using drugs. I addressed the problem of *educating about* somewhere else. But if the money—over $100 billion—that we have spent on trying to stop the drug supply (and who knows how much more will be spent in the future) were directed at improving our education—not *about drugs*, but our *general education*—that would open a window on the world to our youngsters and make their lives interesting and fulfilling, we would not need the army and the navy anymore as our defense against drugs.

There is a point of view that most illicit drugs, which are illegal today, should be legalized and allowed to be used. Here I refer my reader to the book from which I have already quoted (Ref.[2]). The authors compare the drug situation today with that of *the Prohibition* of the '30s, when alcohol production, sale, and consumption were illegal. The book discusses in detail all the possible aspects of the suggested solution to the drug problem—all but one. If the arguments I have presented so far are valid—and I, together with Erich Fromm, Viktor Frankl, and many psychologists and physicians who use Dr.

Frankl's *Logotherapy* in their profession,[7] believe they are—then legalizing drugs will be a first step toward giving a man that fateful lever that was so popular among Dr. Olds' rats. It would make sense, were our society healthy—but then the drug problem would have not arisen in the first place.

This is something to think about. But please remember: You and I, and our children—we all on this planet—have in our brains those tiny cells, a time bomb, that one day can turn us into animals. If we do not acquire *something* that will enable us to resist the temptation of unlimited pleasure—if we are not strong enough to resist that animal in us—then, inevitably, either a scientific development or an irresponsible mob will let the genie out. This "something" is *meaning, direction,* and *fulfillment* in our lives. Let us begin with our children The next generation will be different.

7 I address the interested reader to a collection of papers and essays sponsored by *The Institute of Logotherapy* (Hardin Simmons University, Abilene, TX): *Finding Meaning in Life: Logotherapy*, edited by J.B.Fabry, R.P.Bulka, and W.S.Sahakian. Jason Aronson, Inc. 1979 (soft cover edition 1995).

MEN ARE FROM MARS,
WOMEN ARE FROM VENUS

"What are little boys are made of, made of?
What are little boys made of?
"Snips and snails and puppy-dogs' tails;
And that's what little boys are made of, made of.

"What are little girls are made of, made of?
What are little girls made of?
"Sugar, and spice and everything nice;
And that's what little girls are made of, made of"

—*Mother Goose Rhymes*

Increasingly more people—even those who have never studied genetics—are becoming aware of the important role heredity plays in our lives. The media is in the forefront of disseminating all kinds of information having to do with all kinds of *predispositions*. These efforts to bring *new information* result in stressing the idea of diversity. "People are so much unlike each other. And what can we do about it? People are different *by nature*." We also learn that human qualities are predisposed, if not through genetics, then through *evolution*.

The so-called *social Darwinism* is flourishing. Conferences are held, and dozens of university professors are doing research trying to prove that some of the conspicuous features of our social behavior are the result of *natural social selection*. As such, they are *positive*, for they improve the chances of society's survival. We learn that love and romance are directed by rules originating from the Stone Age, which since have been enforced by natural selection. Even an addiction to adultery is the result of the evolutionary process. "Lifelong monogamous devotion just isn't natural, and the modern environment makes it harder than ever."[1] No

---

[1] Robert Wright, *The Moral Animal: Evolutionary Psychology and Everyday Life* (1994).

question that the "inherent" difference between men and women is also the object of scrupulous attention in our society.

And now, here is an important new revelation: *Men Are from Mars, Women Are from Venus.*[2] This is not the very first book (to say nothing of the numerous articles in popular magazines) devoted to explaining problems in relationships between men and women by focusing on and stressing their *inherent* differences.

After the first book: *Man Are from Mars, Women Are From Venus* (1992) and its tremendous success, the avalanche of Dr. Gray's cosmological theories followed. Here is the impressive chronology:

- *Mars and Venus Together Forever: Relationship Skills for Lasting Love* (1996). An extended 1998 edition had a new subtitle: *A Practical Guide to Create Lasting Intimacy.*

- *Mars and Venus in Love: Inspiring and Heartfelt Stories of Relationships That Work* (1996)

- *Mars and Venus in Bedroom: A Guide to Lasting Romance and Passion* (1997)

- *Mars and Venus on a Date: A Guide to Navigating the 5 Stages of Dating to Create a Loving and Lasting Relationship* (1998)

- *Mars and Venus Starting Over: Finding Love Again after a Painful Breakup, Divorce, or a Loss of a Loved One* (1999)

- *Practical Miracles for Mars and Venus: Nine Principles for Lasting Love, Increasing Success, and Vibrant Health in 21st Century* (2000)

- *Mars and Venus in the Workplace: A Practical Guide for Improving Communications and Getting Results at Work* (2001)

- And a new book published in 2002: *Mars and Venus in Touch*

As one can see, Dr. Gray also believes (based on his "astronomy" model) that stable relationships can be achieved by appropriate *training* and developing the adequate love *skills* (see *Training or Education?*).

Of course, the book's objective is to help people somehow overcome this difference in their everyday relationships. The subtitle of the book reads: *A Practical*

---

2 John Gray, PhD, *Men Are from Mars, Women Are From Venus.* Harper Collins Publishers, 1992

Guide for Improving Communications and Getting What You Want in Your Relationships. A couple of more quotes on the dust jacket (presumably from the book reviews) suggest that the book is "a superb guide for understanding male-female relationships," and "a valuable, much-needed book. A contribution to the understanding of the communication styles of men and women." Moreover, the book "replaces worn-out theories with fresh awareness appropriate of our time." In the above quote, I would like to emphasize the words *our time,* for what Dr. Gray believes is the fundamental and inherent difference between men and women is but the ugly reality of our time and our current existential crisis.

In the introduction (p. 5) Dr. Gray explains the main idea of the book: "*Men Are from Mars, Women Are from Venus* is a manual for loving relationships in the 1990s. It reveals how men and women differ in all areas of their lives. Not only do men and women communicate differently but they think, feel, perceive, react, respond, love, need, and appreciate differently. They almost seem to be from different planets, speaking different languages and needing different nourishments." Dr. Gray recognizes (p. 5) that the question *why* "is a complex question to which there are many answers, ranging from biological differences, parental influence, education and birth order to cultural conditioning by society, the media, and history." However, he takes for granted that if what he believes should be changed in male-female relationships, the situation will be sort of *normal.* There will be nothing ugly, nothing unhealthy, and nothing crying for change—if men and women behave according to the profound differences he has discovered.

Hundreds of people attended Dr. Gray's seminars where "they were amazed to learn that their differences were not only normal but were to be expected" (p. 3). Dr. Gray refers to many letters of gratitude from couples whose love and relations had been restored and salvaged after attending the seminar. It well may be true. But if the book's picture of the man-woman relationship is true, and the recipes suggested by the author do work, then Dr. Gray's book is a *guilty verdict* against our present society.

What I am going to discuss is an inherent part of our crisis. In my view, it is a direct consequence of the extremely low educational and intellectual standards of our society today that has exacerbated the grave societal illness—the loss of meaning in the lives of millions of people, a significant segment of the population. The *meaninglessness* of life finds its direct manifestation in gender relations and stereotypes.

I am going to use Dr. Gray's book for *textbook* examples of gender relations today. I strongly recommend that you, my reader, read the book, and decide for yourself whether what I am going to say is right or wrong.

The book is easy to read, because, as in a magazine or newspaper article, the most important thoughts are singled out and printed as *bullets.*

Let us look first at the most important men's qualities:

"A man's sense of self is defined through his ability to achieve results" (p. 16).

"To offer a man unsolicited advice is to presume that he does not know what to do or that he can't do on his own" (p. 17).

"…when a woman offers advice he does not feel she trusts his ability to do it himself" (p. 19).

"Men also become particularly frustrated when a woman talks about problems that he can do nothing about" (p. 38).

"Not to be needed is a slow death for a man" (p. 46).

"A man's deepest fear is that he is not good enough or that he is incompetent" (p. 56).

"It is difficult for a man to listen to a woman when she is unhappy or disappointed because he feels like a failure" (p. 58).

What about women? They are completely different:

"A woman's sense of self is defined through her feelings and the quality of her relations" (p. 18).

To women, "to share their personal feelings is much more important than achieving goals and success" (p. 18).

"To forget her own painful feelings a woman may become emotionally involved in the problems of others" (p. 37).

"The biggest challenge for women is correctly to interpret and support a man when he isn't talking" (p. 67).

In short, men are the *Doers*, the *Achievers*, and the *Problem Solvers*—and, God forbid, don't even question their abilities. Women simply cannot comprehend these simple facts, and want to talk, to discuss, to give advice, and to help men (obviously, because they think that men need help).

Well, of course, the men are also wrong. They do not understand that when women talk, they do not *mean to discuss problems* (therefore do not need men's solutions). They just need loving attention. They want to be needed, to be loved. If both parties understand that they are from completely different planets, the peace is (and relationships are) restored, communication lines are established, and everyone can simply live "happily forever after."

Some of you may remember a remarkable book that was published in the late '60s. It had been a bestseller then. You can still find it in bookstores today, and students still study it in psychology classes. The book's title is *I'm OK, You're OK*, by Dr. Thomas Harris.[3] At that time, back in Moscow, our friends, Zeya and I were fascinated with this book, and spent many hours discussing it.

The book is an attempt to understand one's ways of transaction—the structure of one's communication. The main idea of the book is as follows: Every human being's personality has three distinct components (Dr. Harris calls them *states*). They may be called *Parent, Child and Adult*. The first two are inherited from the early years (0 to 5), when a child is defenseless—depending for most his or her needs on parents. The *Parent* component containing categorical imperatives like "You should long be in bed by now," "Listen to what I am saying," "Be quiet, daddy is watching TV," for example, are inherited. The *Child* component reflects defenselessness, lack of self-esteem, fear of doing something wrong, self-pity. The *Adult* component, on the contrary, is developed during the process of *maturing*. It includes the ability of sober analysis, detailed discussion of problems, objective reflection of one's own and other individual's behavior, and responsibilities.

I remember what struck us most of all in this concept was that communications between people are possible only if the partners are in the same state—*on the same wavelength*—so to speak. Thus *Child-Child, Parent-Parent* and *Adult-Adult* communications are possible and may be successful, while *Child-Adult* or any other *crossover* combinations are simply doomed to failure.

A few funny examples: Man (*Parent*): "Where are my socks? How many times must I tell you that their place is in this drawer?"

Wife (*Adult*): "I just finished my laundry, and your socks are in the dryer."

Or: Wife (*Child*): "You don't love me. I am so tired, and you don't even talk to me."

Husband (*Child*):"You always accuse me (switching to *Parent*). What on earth do you think I am doing now?"

Here is the best example of an *Adult* communication: Husband returns home from a business trip. Wife is not at home, the house is in disarray, and dust is everywhere. He writes with a finger on the dusty polished surface of the dining table (*Adult*) "I love you." It is easy to see the possible reactions of the *Child* ("I work like a dog, and you don't even care…") or the *Parent* ("How many times must I tell you…") level.

---

[3]　Thomas A. Harris, *I'm OK, You're OK: A Practical Guide to Transactional Analysis.* Harper &Row, New York and Evanston, 1969.

When one reads Dr. Gray's book, *Men Are from Mars, Women Are from Venus*, one cannot help but notice in astonishment that almost all the attributes of men's behavior are those of Dr Harris' *Child* mode. Women are closer to *Adult* by their attributes as Venusians. Although being the *Child* in his self-esteem, Dr. Gray's man changes his hat, and in his dialogues with woman typically responds as the *Parent*. The latter just confirms his insecurity and tendency to enhance his macho image. And there is *no Adult-Adult* interaction whatsoever between Dr. Gray's men and women.

Let me give you a few more examples, which I hope will convince you that Gray's man is the *Child*, while, at least in the book's examples, a woman often behaves as the *Adult*. However, in her transactions with men, under the strong man's *Parent* pressure, she often also resorts to the *Child*.

An important place in Dr. Gray's theory belongs to the concept of *Cave*. The *Cave* is where men hide when they need to solve their problems. While in the *Cave*, the man is impossible to reach, and a *dragon* guards the entrance to the cave:

> *"To feel better Martians go to their cave to solve problems alone"* (*p. 31*).

> *"Never go into man's cave, or you will be burned by the dragon"* (*p. 71*). (Lack of self-confidence; fear to endanger his macho image.)

> *"To feel better Venusians get together and openly talk about their problems"(p. 31)*. (Discussion is a typical feature of the *Adult* mode.)

> *"It is difficult for a man to differentiate between empathy and sympathy. He hates to be pitied"* (p. 82). (An obvious emotional underdevelopment of the *Child*.)

> " *"When a man loves a woman, periodically he needs to pull away before he can get closer"* (p. 92), (But that is exactly what little children do when they play with each other.)

> " *"To a certain extent a man loses himself through connecting with his partner"* (p. 97). (For a mature person, connecting with someone dear always enriches life.)

Dr. Gray gives many examples of husband-wife conversations. Here is one of them:

> "When Tom comes home, he wants to relax and unwind by quietly reading the news. He is stressed by the unsolved problems

of his day and finds relief through forgetting them. His wife, Mary, also wants to relax from her stressful day. She, however, wants to find relief by talking about the problems of the day. The tension slowly building between them gradually becomes resentment. Tom secretly thinks Mary talks too much, while Mary feels ignored. Without understanding their differences they will grow further apart" (pp. 29-30).

In this example, Mary demonstrates a typical *Adult* approach. She wants to discuss the problems of the day. With Tom the situation is different. According to what we already know about men, a *stressful day*, or *unsolved problems* mean a wounded ego. He cannot discuss anything with his wife, because any discussion would reveal his *inability*—his frustration as a *man*. He is a typical *Child*. And their crossroads communication is impossible.

What is the solution according to Dr. Gray? First of all, Mary should understand that Tom is in the *Cave*, and leave him alone. What about Tom? When Mary attempts to discuss with him the problems of her day, according to Dr. Gray, she does not, in fact, mean to find any solutions, she just wants his *loving attention* ("she wants empathy, but he thinks she wants solutions," p. 15).

Honestly, if I were a woman, I would get mad at the suggestion that when I am trying to discuss something, I do not really want a discussion. Instead, I just want to attract the precious attention of an SOB watching a football game. The recipes of *successful* interaction that Dr. Gray suggests are insulting to a woman who really wants to discuss something. And the following advice is simply disgusting: "When a man is in a negative state…treat him like a passing tornado and lie low" (p.203).

When your wife begins complaining about the problems at her work, instead of immediate cold advice: "Why don't you quit your job?" (one of the *negative* scenarios to be abandoned, according to Dr. Gray), you should let her talk. Make a sympathizing face and produce—every half a minute or so, while your wife is talking—the syllables like "Yeah?" "Oh." "Really?" "No kidding!" for example (p. 23). In fact, Dr. Gray implies that it is not necessary to actually listen to what your wife is talking about. If you understand the Venusians right, she also does not mean to tell you anything meaningful at all! Talking is just a way the Venusians relax. "…just listening with empathy to Mary express her feelings would bring her tremendous relief and fulfillment" (p. 23). What is important is just to show her that you are listening. Then you will be rewarded. "I love talking with you. You make me really happy. Thanks for listening. I feel much better" (p. 23).

Perform this kind of fraud every day, and your relationship/marriage will be salvaged. Of course, in return, your wife must stop giving you advice on what route to take when you drive to a party, and stop making any remarks regarding your appearance, your shirts or your ties.

What is interesting, in all Dr. Gray's examples—both *negative* and *positive*—when a wife begins her attempts to start *Adult*-type communication, as in discussing her day or her problems, her husband never prompts her for details, never really wants to talk with her, listen to her, to ask questions, to *discuss*. Why? Simply because Dr. Gray's man does not respect the *personality* in his partner, and he is scared to death of unwillingly showing his incompetence, in no matter what aspect of human relations. He is simply *immature*—both emotionally and intellectually.

At this point, I should apologize for the ironic approach I have been taking. But, I am afraid, and perhaps many women will agree with me, that an alternative would be anger.

While reading the book I tried to be as objective as possible. It was difficult, since both Dr. Gray's men and women were so far from people I know, my friends (both American and those back in Russia), as if we, in fact, were from different planets. A reader who accuses me of being *pro-women*, can see that, in most of the examples of Gray's book, the woman is sort of *second class*, not very important to a man as a human being. She is often kind of a *nuisance* (although of course, man, as every child, needs to be needed—to be *loved*). Obviously, she plays no significant role in his emotional life, and in his personality as a whole.

If this *is* true—and the critics in a loud chorus insist that Dr. Gray's book is only a bit short of expressing the century's greatest truth and revelation—then this may well be an explanation of the enormous percentage of divorces in our society today. How can two people live together *as one*, if they mean almost nothing to each other? I must apologize for believing that mostly men initiate divorces. Are men simply *not mature* enough to be husbands and fathers? This is what Dr. Harris, in *I'm OK, You're OK*, says about that: "…the average marriage contract is made by the Child, which understands love as something you feel and not something you do, and which sees happiness as something you pursue rather than a by-product of working toward the happiness of someone other than yourself" (p.155).

In today's America over 60 percent of adult women work. Over 50 percent of university students are young women. It means that the number of women with university diplomas is roughly equal to that of men (actually, by 2008, women with bachelor's and graduate school degrees will significantly outnumber men). Yes, many of women have to sacrifice their career for their families. In addition, if one is to believe Dr. Gray, on top of all their loads of work, family responsibilities, discrimination at the work place, when they return home they must think of how to woo their *Child* husbands. Should they somehow bribe the dragons? Or is it better just to resign themselves and do their best to preserve the family? But is it worth salvaging a marriage that is not based on mutual respect?

Wooing and bribing—that is exactly what Dr. Gray recommends to women as *25 Ways to Superglue Your Marriage* in the June, 1997 issue of *McCALL's* magazine. (I came across that shabby issue while sitting in my dentist's reception room.) I wonder how many women have chosen to follow those recommendations.

Attendees of Dr. Gray's seminars may be quite honest when they write that understanding the man-woman differences has saved their marriages. What is sad is that millions of American couples, even those believing that their marriages are *happy* (i.e., following Dr. Gray's advice, if they believe in the Martian-Venusian theory) are deprived of true happiness, and perhaps have never even known true love.

Here I would like again to mention a book, first published over 50 years ago, but seeming to have been written about our problems of today. This is Erich Fromm's *The Art of Loving*. Our current problems are easily projected on what Erich Fromm was discussing then, and his concepts are fully applicable to our times. The book's prophetic power is so strong that I cannot help thinking that after that book, and those by Viktor Frankl, nothing more should have been written about our decades' long crisis. One should just read them over and over again—these "worn-out theories"—to find answers to the burning questions of our time. But alas, it is human nature—awareness of wisdom is short-lived, and one needs to be reminded again and again about insights that people have always known.

This is what Erich Fromm writes in the forward to his book (p. vii): "…love is not a sentiment which can be easily indulged in by anyone, regardless of the level of maturity reached by him….all his attempts for love are bound to fail, unless he tries most actively to develop his total personality." And further on: "We refer to love as the mature answer to the problem of existence," as opposed to "those immature forms of love which may be called symbiotic union."

Dr. Gray believes that love can be preserved if one follows easy recipes based on the knowledge of inherent man-woman differences. One may be sort of *trained* how to love. This is definitely wrong, for much more is at stake: "*The affirmation of one's life, happiness, growth, freedom is rooted in one's capacity to love*," i.e., in care, respect, responsibility and knowledge" (p. 50; italics are Fromm's).

Thus, once again, the main problem is the lack of maturity—adulthood in man-woman relations. Listen again to Erich Fromm: "Love is possible only if two persons communicate with each other from the center of their existence" (p. 86). "Love…is a constant challenge; it is not a resting place, but a moving, growing, working together; even whether there is harmony or conflict, joy or sadness, is secondary to the fundamental fact that two people experience themselves from the essence of their existence…There is only one proof for the presence of love: the depth of the relationship, and the aliveness and strength in each person concerned" (p.87).

However, is it possible that Fromm's concept of *love* is something absolutely unattainable in our time for ordinary people—for the millions to whom, in reality, Dr. Gray's book is addressed? Has love in our society really disintegrated? (as Erich Fromm claims in the chapter of his book entitled *Love and Its Disintegration in the Contemporary Western Society*). It is true, in a sense, and that is where the most serious problem of our society lies.

And yet, just forget for a moment about Dr. Gray's cosmic theory. Just imagine that Tom and Mary are both *mature* persons. Tom respects Mary as an equal, as a dear and trusted friend. They read books and discuss them. They read a lot to their children. On weekends they (perhaps they have two children) all together go to museums or bicycle or go hiking.

Tom is a computer programmer (but he might well be a university professor, an engineer, a businessman, a carpenter, or a salesman). Mary is a nurse (or she might be a university professor, a department store manager, a medical doctor, a policewoman, a school teacher, or a homemaker working at caring for her children).

If Mary comes home from her work early, she makes dinner, while Tom picks up their children from (perhaps) a kindergarten. Sometimes it is Tom who cooks and serves dinner, while Mary is busy with something else. For Tom, it would be absolutely impossible to grab a newspaper or switch on a TV, while Mary is making dinner or is arguing with the kids.

At dinner, they discuss their day. Children, of course, are first. They tell everything that happened in their kindergarten groups—what books Miss Ann read, and how Betty fell and broke her nose, and what they learned about the dinosaurs.

As parents, Tom and Mary know that in most cases TV is meaningless to their children and even harmful for them. Public television programs are an exception. Although Mary and Tom do not completely agree with the PBS's educational philosophy of learning through entertainment, they actually have no choice.

As for Tom and Mary, while one of them is reading to the children or doing something together with them, the other sometimes watches the *News Hour with Jim Lehrer*—the source of most of the news for them. Unfortunately, they have no time for daily newspapers.

When the children are in bed, Tom and Mary finally have a little time for themselves. They discuss their day. Mary tells in detail what she was doing during the day. Tom knows the names of her colleagues. She tells him of a difficult patient and what she did when her doctor was suddenly called to an emergency room. He tells her about the program he is currently working on. He spent a few hours today trying to fish out a very stubborn bug.

The day is almost over. They may have just 20-30 minutes left for reading in bed. Tonight he reads a recent issue of the *Atlantic Monthly*, while she is absorbed in an article in the *Archeology Review*. Then a hug, a kiss, and the day is over.

Is this a fantasy? In fact, I do know quite a few families like that. My own family is like that. It is normal. It is as it should be.

I would like to refer the reader to the book by Rosalind C. Barnett and Caryl Rivers.[4] As the authors write in the very first chapter, they themselves belong to families very much like that of my Mary and Tom. Their book, based on long and serious sociologic research involving interviewing hundreds of married couples, is a proof of what I am talking about. Mature people—respecting each other, sharing their duties and responsibilities in both the household chores and the upbringing of their children—create a happy, loving family.

True, there may be conflicts and misunderstandings. But what *is* important, my Tom and Mary deeply respect each other. Both are people of high self-esteem and dignity. Both Mary and Tom get angry when she is addressed as Mrs. *Tom* Smith. Tom is proud that Mary is in charge of the family's finances. He will be happy if tomorrow she is promoted and her salary becomes higher that his. (It is already much higher if Mary is a MD, and Tom is a programmer.) In such a situation, Dr. Gray's Tom may develop a heart attack (at least, according to the statistics, the chances of this sad event's happening for him would triple).

What is it that distinguishes Dr. Gray's Tom and Mary from mine? My couple lives a full, although quite difficult life. Each one of their days, each one of their minutes is filled with meaning. They live in a wide world. They belong with it. Reading for them is not just entertainment, but a part, a *mode* of life. It enhances their feeling of reality, their feeling of *belonging*. Their life is full of good music, though they cannot afford to go to concerts of Itzhak Perlman or Evgenii Kissin every time these give concerts in their city.

---

4   Rosalind C. Barnett and Caryl Rivers, *She Works, He Works: How Two-Income Families Are Happier, Healthier and Better-Off,* 1996.

Unfortunately, not many of those who love and need classical music can afford *live* concerts today, especially if a *star* is on stage. For the money, most people (especially college students) are ready to pay for a seat the grand piano is far below and as small as on a TV screen. The quality of sound—and one came to listen to music—is far from what one would like to hear. CDs are more affordable, although the stars' CDs are also too expensive for *ordinary* people to buy without hesitating and procrastinating for a long time. And for those who love classical music, listening to it is not entertainment, but an important and necessary component of their spiritual lives.

The key to a life full of meaning and purpose is in *maturity*. But one does not have to be a PhD or even have a college education in order to live a meaningful life—to feel and appreciate the eternal wisdom of Shakespeare, the beauty of Frederick Chopin, or the quiet elegance of Renoir. Twelve years of public school could offer all this. I hope—I believe—the day when this will come true is near. If not, our civilization is doomed.

Returning to our astronomy lesson: Once again, I did not intend to make this essay a book review. But, in discussing the crisis that our society is facing today, I could not pass up this important issue. Yes, men and women are different. They are different both physiologically and psychologically. Perhaps, to be a policeman or a fighter pilot is easier for a man than for a woman, but a woman would probably be a better gynecologist or a kindergarten teacher than a man.

What is important—and this is the gist of my book—one's life must have *meaning*. Every individual must be able to fully develop his or her personality, to realize one's dreams and aspirations, to achieve goals, to find the *task* of one's life, and even turn it into a *mission*. In this respect the *American Dream*—the dream of affluence and wealth—is not sufficient anymore to bring happiness. Often, having achieved affluence, an individual finds oneself in an existential desert with nothing to do (but, perhaps, make more money), nobody to love, and nothing to hope for.

Another dream that also originates from the very first days of existence of this great country should become an active *American Dream* today. The endless quest for self-development and creativity, the dream of making the world better, of leaving a trace—though modest and humble—that will make the world better than it would have been without one's having lived—is the true way to happiness. This dream and aspiration can have a profound and everlasting meaning in one's life.

With the meaning, comes the whole direction of life. Every day is full. Every day is difficult. You need a friend, a supporter, a spouse. You respect him or her, for you have the same time vector. You develop together, and you are together in happiness and in grief.

Let me repeat: the main problem of Dr. Gray's men is not that they do not understand women as *Venusians*, creatures from a different planet, but that they simply do not respect them as *individuals* and, alas, sometimes even as human beings (hence the cruel abuse, and even murder, of thousands upon thousands of women in America by their "loved ones").

The main problem of Dr. Gray's women is that when they need a man's friendly help, they instead run into a dragon at the cave entrance. Their only chance to attract a man's attention is to play the *Child* with him, only to have the *Parent* in response.

Many more women go to work today not only because families need extra income, but also because they have a profession they love, or they want to develop their personality, widen the horizons of their life, and make it more meaningful. Unfortunately, in our society today, all this for a woman is much more difficult than for a man. Some of the features of our man-dominated society are so ugly, that when you think about them, you simply cannot comprehend how they could have happened.

Only one, but to me, one of the most disgraceful examples: The United States is *the only* democratic country where a woman does not have maternity leave guaranteed by law. In most European countries, a woman has at least a few weeks of paid maternity leave, and she may extend her leave as unpaid for a longer period of time.

Now, when a woman carries her baby there is a man, who will soon call himself this baby's father. He says he loves his wife. But if he does how is it possible that he allows her to drive to her work place and work for eight hours till almost the very moment of birth? And we are the richest nation in the world! Do we know the numbers? Do we know how many miscarriages or birth complications occur because a woman has to work during the last week of her pregnancy? Two weeks? A month? Two months? Has anybody cared to investigate this important issue?

In Denmark, for example, a woman is entitled to take four weeks off prior to giving birth and 24 weeks afterward. The amount of pay received during the leave varies—some places pay full salary during the whole leave; others, a part of it. However a woman is entitled to a minimum of approximately $450 a week from the government if her workplace does not have an "acceptable" plan. However, most workplaces do have reasonably good maternity leave policies. Additionally, a new father is entitled to two weeks off with the baby, which is then deducted from the mother's leave. Quite a few men actually do take the leave. In *less socialistic* Germany, women are entitled to two months of paid maternity leave prior to giving birth and two months after. Then, up to the seventh month they receive from the government approximately $400 a month. The government continues paying up to this amount (depending on the total family income) till the baby is three years old. Of course both the Danes and the Germans pay high taxes. But this is just a case when you get a lot for your money. By the way, they also have free college education.

Why do men not insist, when they elect their congressmen and senators, that a maternity leave law be a condition when voting for the future legislator? Even if they, the men who care for their pregnant working wives, comprise only, say 20 to 30 percent of married men, that would still be millions of them—a strong political force. Yet it is not a political issue. Both those who vote for Republicans as well as Democrats have wives who expect children. Do they not understand that it is simply inhumane and irresponsible in the 21st century to endanger the lives of their as yet unborn children by forcing their wives—their loved ones—to work till the very last day? My brain refuses to comprehend that.

Women are becoming stronger. A social Darwinist could say that women, as a subspecies, have survived in male-dominated societies only because they have developed superior qualities that have enabled them to mature against all odds. The role of women in our society in the 21st century will increase manifold, no matter what the proponents of "the traditional values" would say.

I have a very troubling thought. What if the addiction of our society to guns is, to a significant degree, simply the consequence of the immaturity of good many American men? A child plays with a toy gun—it gives him the illusion of being powerful and strong. I do not want to argue here with the proponents of unrestricted right to own guns, referencing the *Second Amendment* to our Constitution. There are quite a number of authoritative opinions of legal experts that the *Second Amendment* is irrelevant to this problem. Again I challenge the social scientists. Is there any correlation between one's educational level and one's stand on the gun control issue? What percentages of those who do not care to vote are addicted to fire arms? By the way, women mostly support gun control. I wonder why. Is it because they are more mature than men?

Again, what we see as an ugly gender polarization is the result of the same tragic twist of our life. The American educational system does, albeit unwillingly, whatever it can to prevent millions of people from acquiring maturity. As a response to the *popular demand,* the media, and the whole mass culture, like an avalanche, buries the last hope for achieving adulthood. And yet maturity is the necessary condition for a happy, meaningful, and fulfilling life. As in the case of racial discrimination, no training can break the Martian-Venusian relations among men and women. The only remedy is *education.* The *Child* matures and becomes *Adult* only through education. That is why today's America needs a new, thoughtful, and well-developed educational system.

HARLEM HIGH, YEAR 2050: RACISM AND IGNORANCE

> "Sorry, M'am. We respect your voucher, but your kid cannot be transferred to our school. No, it is not discrimination. Your kid's test scores are below the standards of our school, and we do not make exceptions…"
>
> *—Harlem High, year 2050*

What this book is trying to prove is that poor education is the main cause of almost all the problems our society is facing today, in the beginning of 21st century. In this essay I am going to speak about the problems that African-, Hispanic-, and Native Americans are facing in our society every day, and what should, in my view, be done in order to preserve our integrity as a nation. However, I will most be talking about African-Americans.

Polarization, along racial/ethnic lines, is threatening to rip our society apart today. Ninety-two percent of blacks and 84 percent of whites agree that interracial relations today are only fair or poor. A poll also shows that 56 percent of blacks do not think that race discrimination will ever disappear. Only 27 percent of whites agree with this. On the other hand, while 65 percent of whites believe that race relations will eventually improve, only 44 percent of blacks think the same.

Perhaps America is the only nation in the world where the problems of race and ethnicity are so acute. Its uniqueness is, first of all, in its history of a nation created *from scratch*. America's ethnic uniformity was impossible from the very beginning. Waves of immigrants from all over the world brought to this land their ways of life, traditions, and temperament.

But the event of incomparable importance was, of course, *slavery*. First hundreds, and then thousands upon thousands of people were forcefully brought to the New World to support the growing economy of the colonies.

To a student of history, this outburst of barbarity in the 17th and 18th centuries may seem absolutely irrational and ridiculous. It is not that the European nations never knew slavery—it did not disappear from Europe with the disintegration of the

199

Roman Empire or the advent of the Middle Ages. However, in Europe, in the centuries usually referred to as the *Dark Ages*, slavery was not widespread as a socially significant phenomenon. In fact, servitude took the place of the slavery of the previous centuries. The status of slaves, who still could be bought and sold in slave markets, was not significantly different from that of serfs.

Ironically, slavery became more significant on the historic scene with the advent of the Renaissance—the flourishing of arts, the great achievements in science and engineering, intensive trade and travel, and the discoveries of new lands.

It was the intensive travel and the discovery of new lands that opened the new opportunities to acquire a cheap and, in most cases, a reliable, working force. The devastating *Black Death* epidemic in the middle of the 14th century, which took close to one third of Europe's population, was one of the important factors in reviving the slave trade. Laborers were desperately needed even to farm the land. In slave markets of Europe in the 14th and 15th centuries, slaves from all over the known world were traded: Tartars, Slavs, Turks, Circassians, Arabs and Africans.[1]

The European-African slave trade began in the middle of the 15th century when Portuguese ships landed on the Atlantic coast of Africa and raided the nearby areas, or contacted aboriginal slave-traders. Slavery did already exist in Africa. These first African slaves were used by the Portuguese as a work force on their sugar plantations off the coast of Europe and Africa.

Medieval slavery was devoid of racism. "No stigma, racist or other, seems to have been attached to being a slave. It was an accident of fate that could befall any man" (*Slavery*, vol. 1 p.44). It was taken for granted that a slave had been brought from far away. Being a slave meant only some restriction in rights, but did not imply some kind of inferiority. With the growing African slave trade, the attitude toward the slaves as inferiors savages became stronger and stronger.

I did not meet, in literature, a psychological explanation of this phenomenon, which was an unquestionable step backward by the European civilization. It was not just an isolated little step, an error, to be quickly corrected by further development. The reemergence of slavery in the 15th century, and its flourishing in the 17th and 18th centuries have resulted—among other, less significant events—in the creation of a specific social climate in the American colonies, which left its permanent imprint on American society for the centuries to come. Now, at the beginning of the 21st century, the consequences of slavery are, perhaps, the most acute and pressing problems that America is facing.

In the Middle Ages, primitive knowledge of geography, difficulty in communication between nations and very restricted efforts in exploration of land beyond

---

[1]   Milton Meltzer, *Slavery: A World History*, 1993, vol. 1.

the existing borders brought about numerous stories about fantastic lands and their fantastic inhabitants. Detailed descriptions of these creatures—two-headed, four-armed, three-eyed—could be quite often found in medieval books and, presumably, people believed in the existence of such creatures.

The great geographic discoveries of the Renaissance extended both the borders of the existing lands and the minds of people. No monsters were discovered. Rather, those remote and previously unknown lands turned out to be populated by two-legged, two-armed, one-headed creatures and yet different in one respect: their skin was black. These strange creatures led a primitive life—"almost like animals"—worshipped totems, spoke unintelligible languages. In short, in the opinion of the Europeans, they were *savages*.

Of course, the outburst of the new slavery was motivated and prompted by the intensive economic development in Europe and new colonies, and the urgent necessity for cheap labor. But the ease with which the *enlightened* nations succumbed to the moral abyss of mass slavery, albeit against the background of cultural and intellectual growth needs explanation. I think that psychologically the emergence of slavery in the world of quite an advanced humanistic culture was possible only because in the minds of the majority of Europeans the savages were not quite human.

Slavery, however, did not spread throughout the West Indies and the American colonies overnight. European countries—Spain, Holland, France, Denmark and England—began spreading their influence into the Caribbean soon after the West Indies were discovered. The Islands, with their warm climate and rich soil, were excellent for growing many agricultural products, among them, sugar and tobacco. In the 16th century, large plantations were established in the Caribbean Islands. These plantations needed a significant labor force, preferably cheap. The enslaved Africans became that force.

By the beginning of the 18th century, the Caribbean economy had begun to decline, and the Europeans concentrated on the business of exporting slaves to the American mainland. Large European trading companies were established. They flourished due to the enormous demand for slaves in the American colonies.

The very beginning of slavery in America is traced to August 1619, when a Dutch ship sailed into the harbor of Jamestown, Virginia. On board were twenty Africans taken (perhaps bought) from a Spanish ship heading to the West Indies. The twenty people were sold for food, and the ship left Jamestown.

Those people were sold not as slaves but as *indentured servants*. Indenture—a contract that bound a servant to his or her master for a term from two to seven years (typically four years). Quite a few indentured servants were brought to the colonies from England. Being *sold* meant that the terms of contract were considered a payment for a servant's transportation to America. When the contract expired, the servant became free, and, in fact, joined the Colony as a full-fledged colonist. Often the former master gave him a kind of severance pay—some money or clothing or even seeds, to facilitate the beginning of the new life.

Early records[2] show that in 1624-1625 only twenty-three Africans were living in Virginia. The records—until approximately 1661—identified the Africans as "Negro servants," but never as "slaves." Gradually their status turned into that of slaves. This happened between the years 1640 and 1660.

At that time, the African population was split into three categories: freemen, indentured servants, and slaves. The latter category continued to grow until, by the beginning of the 18th century, the first category had completely disappeared. The golden age for slave traders had begun.

Of course, the process of enslavement in the colonies was prompted by the needs of flourishing tobacco economy. However this process was significantly facilitated, if not motivated, by the psychological twist I mentioned above, which resulted in discriminatory and cruel treatment of black African servants, in contrast to that of their white counterparts. One of the first mechanisms to turn servants into slaves was punishment of runaway servants. The white runaways were typically punished by whipping. The Africans were punished both by whipping and extending their contract to life. From the legal point of view, the white servants were the subjects of either the English Crown or another European nation, and therefore were protected from arbitrary punishment. However, nobody defended the Africans. Eventually, appropriate laws were enacted that made slavery a legitimate form of life in the American colonies.

The evolution of the laws can be seen from the following examples (*The Black Man in America*, p. 18):

> "Children got by an Englishman upon a Negro woman shall be slaves or free according to condition of the mother" (Virginia, 1662).

> "All servants, not being Christian, imported into this country by shipping, shall be slaves for their lifetime, but such as come by land shall serve, if boys and girls till 30 years of age, if men and women, 12 years and no longer" (Virginia, 1670).

> "…all servants imported and brought into this country by sea or land, who are not Christian in their native country shall be accounted and be slaves, and as such be here bought and sold

---

[2] See, e.g., F. Jackson and J. B. Jackson, *The Black Man in America: 1619-1790*.

notwithstanding a conversion to Christianity afterwards"
(Maryland, 1705).

Eventually the anti-slave laws crystallized into what was known as the *Black Codes*. The function and objective of the codes were to protect the right of slave holders to their property. The slaves were not considered to be human beings. "Every aspect of the slave's life was controlled by the Black Codes. They varied in particulars, but at the heart of the codes was the belief that the slave was not a person but a piece of property. The way to safeguard property was to ensure the domination of the slave by his master and to protect the master from any insubordination of the slave" (*Slavery*, vol. 2. p. 201).

All the Northern colonies had also legitimized slavery. The only difference from the South being that they did not need that large a labor force, since their economy was not of a purely agricultural character.

In a sense, America had been *infected* by slavery. It could have rejected this form of labor from the beginning, but was unable to do this. Apart from the obvious economic reason, there was also a deep psychological one—the one that I have already mentioned: the failure to recognize the African-Americans as *humans*.

Hunting down the savages—or buying from local slave-traders, loading the ships with them, and then selling them in numerous slave markets in America— perhaps did not seem either immoral or unlawful in those times. So strong was the conviction that the blacks were inferior, that neither the above-average educated people nor even the church, more enlightened than the general populace, seem to be willing or able to raise any moral barriers to slavery in the minds of Europeans and American colonists.

Long after the European slave trade had been abolished, slavery in America continued to flourish. In spite of the fundamental contradiction between the principles of *natural* rights and slavery, the Founding Fathers were unable to include the abolition of slavery in the Constitution of the young United States of America. Even intellectuals found very sophisticated justifications for slavery, such as "bringing the savage within the pale of civilization and Christianity." [3]

Again, I see only one explanation for this ridiculous twist of history. These people—these colored slaves—were so very different, so much unlike the whites. True, they were no monsters, but were they really *human beings*? Or were they just kind of *subhuman animals*? The minds of people in the 16th century were

---

3   *Charleston Mercury*, Nov. 1854, as quoted in Ronald. T. Takaki's, *A Pro-Slavery Crusade: The Agitation to Reopen the African Slave Trade*, 1971.

well prepared to reach such a conclusion. Unfortunately, the *enlightened* 17th and 18th centuries did not significantly change that ideology.

I am afraid that was the only moral reason that had prevented civilized Europe and America from abolishing the newborn slavery immediately. The irrational conviction that the colored people were *subhuman*, in at least some respects, was not shaken even by the development of science and culture in the 19th and 20th centuries.

In fact, this kind of reasoning is, and has always been, the foundation supporting all the white supremacy movements (the Nazis being the most bestial of all time), as well as everyday racism, anti-Semitism and xenophobia throughout the world.

In my view, the feeling of mistrust or fear or even hatred toward someone who is not *like you and me*, is a fundamentally biological feeling. In the animal world, this sense helps a species to survive the ruthless process of natural selection. Some animals even kill their own handicapped or other mutants, whose appearance does not fit the genetically imprinted image of a *friend*—for all the others are *foes*. Perhaps, this purely animal feeling in men helped at least the Stone Age society to survive. Social Darwinists of today would probably shun this explanation of racism as politically incorrect, although the evolutionary quality of the mistrust of the different can hardly be argued against.

It is interesting that this rudimentary behavior can be readily observed among children. They use to stigmatize, call names, reject from their activities and even exert physical violence on those who look *different*: the redheads, the lame, the infirm (in Russia, also the lefties), and even the nerds.

The history of human civilization is the history of how people have fought the animal instincts within themselves. Sometimes we win, sometimes we lose. The 20th century is filled with devastating victories of the animal in men. And now, on the beginning of the high-tech 21st century we are facing the same old enemies: xenophobia, ethnic strife, and the king of *ultimate hatred*—racism.

The history of America teaches us an important lesson. In the unending quest for human rights against all kinds of discrimination and, above all racial discrimination, who were and still are in the forefront?—The educated. And it is easy to understand why.

As I have discussed elsewhere, education, not training, is the opening of a window on the world. It allows us to see who we are, where we have come from, where we are heading. It gives us a gulp of fresh air, even if one feels there is nothing left to breathe. It tells us something about ourselves that we did not know before. It strengthens our soul. It makes us feel responsible not only for ourselves and our loved ones, but for the whole world.

Typically, historians explain social cataclysms as wars between the rich and the poor. In my view, however, at the heart of too much social strife is the war between the educated and the ignorant. The event on the global scale, the wave of Communist revolutions throughout the world, does confirm my point.

What were the revolting Russian peasants doing back in 1917-1918? They were burning books in the landlords' houses. Vladimir Lenin was an ardent anti-intellectual. In 1921 he wrote to the famous writer, Maxim Gorkii: "You are saying that the intelligencia is the pearl of the nation, but they are shit." The Chinese's infamous *cultural revolution* was aimed at only one enemy: the educated. The Red Khmers in Cambodia were infamous for having literally exterminated the educated—doctors, engineers, and even university students. And, of course, the Nazis burned books…

These are the extreme examples of what an organized and armed ignorance can do to human civilization. In everyday life ignorance is not that dangerous, of course. But racial hatred among uneducated masses is, and since the beginning of time, was the immediate consequence of ignorance. And there is only one way to fight it—*education*.

If I am right, and I hope I am, then we have not just one problem at hand, but two. I do not know which one is the more difficult nut to crack. Besides they are tightly interwoven.

We do already have a vicious cycle. African-Americans are not motivated to become educated, because of the racism of American society. No matter how good you are, *the white man's society* will reject you. However, the African-American (as well as other minorities, who feel underprivileged) simply have no other option but to wage a massive *educational revolution*.

The second problem is of course the whites. The poor state of education in America is on everybody's lips. But nobody even mentions that the *inherent* racism in America is the direct consequence of the extremely low general educational level of our society. Stereotyping and stigmatizing are the two arms of racial mistrust.

Racism, in all its manifestations—including mistrust, mutual suspicions and accusations—will disappear as a dangerous social phenomenon only with a good education, perhaps *excellent* education. No *education about racism* can do this. An *anti-racism* (or even *human rights* or the so-called *diversity*) training does not make more sense than the *prevention of sexual harassment* training does. In two hours you would not convince a white supremacist (who, by the way, also hates the government and the whole social structure of law and responsibility), or just someone who accepts cheap racist stereotypes—that a black man, although different, is not in any way *worse* or *inferior*. In the same way, you would not convince a male chauvinist, who simply does not respect personality in a woman, that women, although different, have the same rights that he has.

One of the evils usually blamed for the distress and nihilism of black youths is the lack of self-esteem. The revival of some traditions from ancient African culture is, probably, a necessary step toward raising self-confidence and cultural identity of the young African-Americans. However, the recent Africanization of the pop culture has very little to do with the ancient African culture. The latter was based on deep religious believes, rituals, and oral tradition. While the present pop culture stresses only the antagonism with the contemporary white-dominated society, and the resistance to true cultural advancement. The proliferation of rap, with its violent anti-societal lyrics, is a pronounced example of this trend. As for the epidemic of tattooing and body piercing, it reflects only the existential vacuum and nihilism of people, and has nothing to do, even remotely, with the ancient African culture.

Unfortunately, such a "return to African traditions" will undoubtedly lead to a dead-end, and will result in exacerbating the inter-racial polarization in American society, unless it is accompanied and supported by a strong educational drive.

In my view, the attempts of liberally minded people in America to get rid of racism in education by forcefully eliminating the disparity in the education of whites and blacks, were counterproductive and actually failed. *Desegregation* of schools—bussing inner-city children to suburban schools—has not raised the children's level of education but, rather, has lowered the educational standards and capacity of suburban schools. Moreover, it has resulted in the increase of racial strife between both the children and adults of inner-cities and suburbs.

The response of many of those most concerned has been to abandon the public school system for a better education of their children wherever possible. As a result, in many school districts, the school system has become as segregated as the most segregated schools prior to the beginning of this fiasco.

In my view, instead of reinventing quasi-desegregation, the main emphasis should have been first placed on improving the predominantly black schools and raising their standards to a high enough level. As in any revolution, the educational revolution needs thousands of people willing to devote their lives to *the common cause*. This revolution will need thousands upon thousands of devoted black teachers.

If you tell me that it is naïve to expect and therefore impossible to achieve, I will again refer you to history. The educational revolution did occur in the Soviet Union within two or three decades after the Communists took over in 1917. It was accomplished by the many thousands of idealistic men and women who went to remotest villages of the enormously vast Soviet Union to teach both children and adults. In today's former Soviet Union, illiteracy is unheard of. As for education in general, in many respects today it is much superior to what it is in America.

The educational revolution in the Soviet Union was necessary for the Communists, not because they praised the culture or wanted to promote education. It was simply because the scale of ignorance and, as a result, the semi-animal existence of tens of millions of peasants (I address the reader to Anton Chechov's short novel *The Peasants*) were monstrously inadequate, even for the social purposes of the totalitarian regime the Communists wanted to create.

What I want to say is that hungry, barefooted Russia, destroyed by the devastating civil war, found resources, both material and human, to wage the educational revolution. Why cannot today's America, the richest and the most powerful nation in the world, do the same? In spite of today's tendency to decentralize education, I believe that undertaking this revolution in education on a national scale is impossible without a center, a heart and a brain.

Should it be the government? Probably not. Not only because the bureaucratic behemoth of today's government has compromised itself by its inability to do a good job. The whites—and no matter how many cabinet secretaries in the government are from minorities, the government remains *white*—cannot do it. No matter how much the white enthusiasts would like to destroy the black ghettoes, they will not be able to do that. Simply because they are *strangers;* they are not trusted, and they do not know what direction to take. The blacks *must do it themselves.* If not they, then nobody can.

No matter how enormous that task seems to be, when people are full of determination to change the situation and put their energy and passion into that cause, they win. Here is one of the success stories, as told by the former Secretary of Education William Bennett[4] in his book (p. 67): "One of the best is the public system in local District 4 in New York's East Harlem. In the early 1970s, District 4 was an educational basket case. It ranked last in reading scores among the city's thirty-two school districts. Then, under the leadership of superintendent Anthony Alvarado, the district allowed parents to choose for their children among a wide variety of newly restructured schools, each offering a particular instructional focus. In some instances, several mini schools were created within the same building. Before the choice program began, only 15 percent of the students in the district could read at grade level. Recent test scores show 64 percent at or above grade level in reading and 53 percent at or above grade level in math. According to William C. Myers of the *Free Congress Foundation*, the number of

---

4   William Bennett, *The Devaluation of America: The Fight for Our Culture and Our Children*, 1992.

students from the district who qualified for admission to one of New York's prestigious specialized high schools increased from ten to three hundred, and today 96 percent of East Harlem graduates are admitted to college."

A few more examples are given in W. Bennett's book. Among them, the story of Joe Clark, "America's most famous principal" that was the basis for the script of the movie *Lean on Me*. By the willpower and determination of one person, supported by the efforts of a few enthusiastic teachers, the destiny of hundreds of teenagers had been changed for good.

I am not in a position to say, "Hey, guys, why don't you get together and decide how you are going to do it?" Should it be the NAACP or some other organization? Or, perhaps, a Council of African-American Athletic Stars (yet nonexistent) who will lead? But it must be a body the people will agree to listen to, will want to believe in, will entrust their lives and careers to.

It is true that the revolution will require enormous material resources—funds not only to pay thousands of new teachers, building and equipping new schools, but also to create a network of summer camps and boarding schools. The latter may be necessary to break the vicious cycle of inner-city ghettoes' social reality.

Of course, a necessary condition for the minority schools to be able to dramatically raise their quality of education is good financing. Success will probably be impossible unless the federal government takes over the financing of schools—all schools. What I mean is financing the construction of new school buildings and their maintenance, providing the necessary funds to pay teachers and to pay for the necessary teaching equipment (computers, for example), paying for other expenses necessary for the teaching process be a success—such as field trips, excursions, for example.

The schools will not lose their *independence* within their school districts, but all the schools will have equal opportunities to deliver the highest possible education to all children, irrespective of the wealth of the neighborhood. This idea may seem too revolutionary for today's America. But, in fact, there is nothing revolutionary about it. To realize it, is just a matter of common sense. Nobody questions why Medicare—the program that provides the means for sustaining physical health to all retired Americans—is directed by the federal government. Why should not federal government provide the necessary means for sustaining conditions for intellectual, emotional and spiritual health—through good education—for *all* American children?

I do not know what part of the enormous funds needed for the educational revolution can be raised by the African-American superstar athletes, movie and TV stars and businesses. The contribution of the government will probably have to be enormous. A special *educational tax* may be necessary. I am afraid it will be necessary, in any case, in order to significantly improve the whole

American educational system. But, first of all, the African-American community, at some high enough level, has to make the decision.

Just imagine that on our 1040 tax forms the box "do you want to donate $3 to the Presidential election Fund" has been abolished, and instead, a new box appears: "Do you want to donate to the Educational Fund: $1, $3, $10, (other)?" This Fund could raise hundreds of millions of dollars, and would cost most Americans less than a six-pack of beer. Possibly millions of Americans would choose to fill in the *othe*r box with two or three digit donations.

I am afraid, and I think that many will agree with me, that so far the leaders of the African-American community have not given it the *right* direction. Heavy rhetoric is aimed against white racism and discrimination, against attempts to reduce the entitlements and the affirmative action. The radicals even insist on establishing some kind of *reparations* that the whites must pay to compensate for slavery. Against this background, sober voices really concerned with the future of the African-Americans are not heard at all.

At the same time, since the racial climate in today's America has drastically worsened in recent years, responsible people in both camps insistently call for *dialogues*—for intensive and constructive discussions of the racial problems in America. Dialogues and discussions are always helpful. But this call seems to be as naïve as the *Just Say No* call to stop the drug epidemic.

When people talk about dialogues they mean some kind of meeting, or exchange of opinions in the press or on TV. No doubt, honest and competent people will organize and participate in such discussions. However, what about the millions of blacks who are bitter and disgruntled, and the millions of whites who not only do not trust the blacks but even hate them? How about the stereotypes—on both sides—that are being constantly reinforced by the ugly reality? Can discussions break this vicious cycle?

Very unlikely they can, although again, it is important to be involved in a dialogue. What I do think will be really helpful are discussions on how to bring about the cultural and educational revolution. Unlike the *abstract* discussions on how to "improve the racial climate," "enhance mutual trust," for example, these discussions should be like meetings of a military general staff: constructive discussions and analysis of options, strategies and distribution of roles among various units before the general assault.

In October 1995, something that could have become very important for the future of our society as a whole, and especially for the future of the

African-American community, took place. I mean the *Million-Man March* in Washington DC, organized by the head of the Nation of Islam, Louis Farrakhan.

Farrakhan, infamous for his bigotry and heavy anti-Semitic rhetoric, might have had as his main objective just to prove that he was the man who could make that unprecedented event happen. But both for the majority of blacks (72 percent) and whites (53 percent), this rally—the call for black self-help—looked as an important step toward the integration of our society. At that time, although the media was debating whether *the wrong* (Farrakhan's reputation as a bigot) could be made *right*, everybody agreed unanimously that the ball was then in the court of the black communities. It was hoped that the local leaders, under the pressure of those hundreds of thousands of people having personally experienced the enthusiasm of that rally, would take the initiative in this process of self-healing. Together with millions of Americans I did believe then, and continued to hope that this would happen. It seemed then that the powerful *Million-Man March* might be the beginning of the revolution I have been discussing.

Unfortunately, nothing significant has happened since. The African-American establishment have not been doing anything in the right direction at all. The ideas of the *Million-Man March* are dead. Instead of a call for self-reliance and a breakthrough in education, the intellectual Left—by supporting extreme forms of Affirmative Action and other forms of Afro-centrism on American campuses—enhanced by anti-democratic (and, in my view, anti-constitutional) *political correctness* campaigns, has antagonized a significant segment of Americans. And the reality today is even uglyer that it was before. School drop-outs among African-American youth is higher than before, and 25 percent of African-American males are either behind bars or being in conflict with criminal law.

In concluding this essay, let me explain something important. Every year, at Passover, all over the world and, of course throughout America, Jews gather at a *Seder*, the solemn Passover meal. Passover commemorates the event in Jewish history that not only cemented the Jews into an unbreakable entity, but also shaped the whole future of the Jewish people. This event was the exodus of the Jews from Egypt in the 13th century BCE. Many times, during this Passover night, millions of voices throughout the world repeat the same words: "…because we were slaves of Pharaoh in Egypt…" We the Jews once were slaves, and we remember that. That is why the Jews have always been in the forefront of struggle for human rights. The African-Americans in this country do not have an ally more reliable and more devoted to their cause than the Jews. It is very regrettable that today anti-Semitic sentiments are spreading among the African-American community. What is most regretful in this trend, however, is that African-American intellectuals (both university professors and students) are in the forefront of disseminating all kind of anti-Semitic accusations against Jews (like the accusation of Jews having been active slave traders).

In any war, it is unwise to reject the support of an ally. In the war to come—the revolutionary war against ignorance—the blacks will need not only all their spiritual energy, determination and integrity, but also all the possible help they can solicit. And, they do not have to solicit help from Jews. When the educational revolution I am talking about begins, the Jews will be there, giving all their knowledge, passion, and even lives.

Nobody can predict what the future has in store. But, if what I have been talking about is true, then the educational revolution in America is not just *desirable*, it is *a must*. If it happens, within a generation or two, the educational level of both the whites and the African-Americans will dramatically rise. Then the imaginary conversation of the epigraph to this essay will be an everyday reality. But in order for this to happen, a lot must change in our society. And, first of all, that change must happen in our heads

ALIENS ARE COMING:
AMERICA'S MORAL DILEMMA

"End never justifies the means, but it's the means which determine the end".

—*Mahatma Gandhi*

Not long before the KGB searched our apartment in May 1977, I wrote an essay, actually a letter, to President Jimmy Carter—a letter I have never mailed. There, I discussed the fundamental difference between the Soviet (totalitarian) ethical system and that of a Judeo-Christian civilization.

Judeo-Christian ethics are based on the Bible's Ten Commandments, and are fundamentally an *absolute* morality. The Commandment's prohibiting clauses are but the definitions of *absolute Evil*. It is *never* good to commit murder, it is *never* good to steal (no matter from whom), it is *never* good to bear false witness, and it is *never* good to commit adultery.

The popular translation of the Sixth Commandment: *Thou shalt not kill* is wrong: In Hebrew, as in English, there are two different words for *to kill* (*laharog*) and to *murder* (*lirtsoakh*). The original Commandment is *Thou shalt not commit murder*. Obviously, the wrong translation invites abuse and misinterpretation of the Commandment.

The Communist moral code rejected absolute morality as *bourgeois*. *Good* and *Evil* might change places, depending on what was good or bad from the *class point of view*. To murder, to steal, to bear false witness, to betray were good, and even a matter of highest virtue, if they served the totalitarian regime's purposes.

212

In that letter, I wrote that sooner or later we would encounter an alien civilization in space. For us to make successful and constructive contact with it, it would be unimportant if those creatures were *humanoids*—like you and me (perhaps, with some variations—see *Star Trek*), or if they were spiders with six eyes and twelve tentacles. The only matter of real importance would be their perception of *Good* and *Evil*. If their concepts of *Good* and *Evil* were like ours, we would be friends. If they were different, we would be adversaries.

I further wrote that scientists were holding conferences and symposia, discussing the possible outcomes of that encounter. However, we do have such an encounter right here, on our Earth. The aliens are here. They are the creatures of the Communist civilization. We just refuse to recognize them as *alien*, evil and dangerous.

I called on President Carter to keep in mind the fundamental difference in moral approaches to the problems between the West and the Communists. In order to survive, the Free World would have to call on all its intellectual resources, mobilize its best think tanks in order to *overplay* the adversary. Obviously, what I meant was to be sterner regarding the terms of détente, more insistent on fulfillment of the treaties on the Free World's terms.

> I had given that letter to a friend to read just a few days before the KGB's search of our apartment. If it had been found (with "Dear Mr. President…" and that *aliens* stuff), I would definitely have gotten a severe prison term…

Now that I understand better the political climate of the détente, my attempt to share with President Carter the important thoughts about the Soviet regime seems to be childishly naïve. President Ronald Reagan later understood all these, almost obvious, ideas. There is no doubt in my mind that the Communist Empire collapsed only because Reagan made America strong again, scaring the *aliens* to death with the possibility of developing an absolute defense weapon. For not only would the development of the *Strategic Defense Initiative* (SDI)—*Star Wars*—weapon make the nuclear weapons obsolete, it would make the Communist regime obsolete, simply because the regime would not be able to expand anymore. Gorbachev and his buddies grasped that danger very quickly.

The rest is now history. Gorbachev has been awarded a Nobel Prize for letting his system collapse. However, this happened not because he wanted it to collapse, but because, in a panic—facing the imminent end of his empire if the

Star Wars program were a success—he and his buddies mismanaged and screwed everything up.[1]

I remember, in August 1968, the Soviet tanks invading Prague, bringing to an end the *Prague Spring*—a symbol of our hope for the future. I was sitting in the tiny kitchen of our Moscow apartment with my two good college friends (one of them died of a heart attack a few years later, the other is now a professor at one of the leading American universities). The invasion of Czechoslovakia was like a personal tragedy to us. (We would have the same feelings, almost seven years later, when Saigon fell.) We were desperate. We were trying to develop a scenario of how Communism could have been stopped, for we saw that the West was not willing to interfere with the expansionist policy of the Communists. It was like a brain storming: "*Any* idea, please, *anything...*" And the only *anything* we could have come up with was a fantastic scenario. There were rumors that the Americans had managed to develop a new laser, much more powerful than the existing ones. If the Americans could make an anti-missile laser weapon, that would be the end of the Soviet Empire. I remember our reasoning as if it were just yesterday. The Soviets have always suffered a severe inferiority complex toward America. Even if the efficiency of the new weapon were only 10 percent, they would know that it would just be a matter of time before it would be 60, 90, and then 100 percent. And that would be the end of their system. A mugger is brave and daring only so far, as he knows that his victim is unarmed. If there were even an unknown chance of retaliation, he would think twice before attacking. That was our pipe dream scenario of 1968—for those rumors about lasers most likely had been spreading by desperate people like us. Fifteen years later, Ronald Reagan made it a reality. My family was already in America, but we knew that the end of the *Evil Empire* was close. I also remember a clash with an MIT physics professor at a lecture on SDI, who called Ronald Reagan a criminal who must be stopped.

---

[1] Of course, there were some other factors, apart from SDI, but the latter had doubtlessly played a crucial role. For those interested in an objective analysis of the last decade of communism and the role of the Reagan Administration in accelerating the end, I would recommend the book by Peter Schweizer, *Victory: The Reagan Administration's Secret Strategy That Hastened the Collapse of the Soviet Union,* 1994.

Ultimately, historians will dig out the truth. At the present time, however, we live with the theory that President Reagan could have brought the world to catastrophe with his SDI, had it not been for Gorbachev's *wisdom*. As for the CIA, it had been deliberately lying to the American people for decades that Communism was strong. Whereas, in fact it was about to collapse, which it did the moment Gorbachev made that crucial decision that Communism must go.

> The day Gorbachev resigned as the President of Russia, the *Boston Globe* carried across the first page in huge letters the heading: "The End of Dreamer." But the legend is growing. In April 1996, Gorbachev was awarded the *King David Prize* by the New York Jerusalem Foundation for his liberating Soviet Jews. Why not posthumously award the pharaoh of 13th century BCE for *liberating* Jews from Egyptian slavery?

Returning to the aliens: At that time, in 1977, that theory of mine had not won unanimous approval among my close friends. Had I meant that we and all those people, with whom we worked—into whom we ran on streets or in stores—were a kind of *Martians*? What about Americans or Germans? Did they also not attempt to maximize their advantages in every situation? Did they not exercise different moral judgments when encountering different dilemmas, depending on what was more profitable in no matter what sense? Don't they cheat, steal, and bear false witness? Don't they ever *fiddle around*? People are people, and they are alike everywhere. I did not know America or Germany therefore I had chosen not to argue.

I did not know then that, at that very time, a book was published in the United States, written by a University of California, Irvine, psychologist. His name was Vladimir Lefebvre. He had left Russia just a couple of years before, but I had known him for years, and for a short time before his emigration we used to meet rather often. The book[2] was an attempt to use mathematical methods for analysis of human moral cognition. This attempt was quite successful, and in 1982 (when my family was already in America), a second book, *The Algebra of Conscience*, was published[3] comprising the results of the already matured and developed theory.

[2] V.A.Lefebvre, *The Structure of Awareness: Towards a Symbolic Language of Human Reflection.* Sage Publications, Beverly Hills, 1977.

[3] V.A.Lefebvre *Algebra of Conscience.* D.Riedel Publishing Company, Dodrecht-Boston-London, 1982. For references to other Dr. Lefebvre's works and numerous papers originated from his ideas, see the book: *The Structure of Human Reflection: The Reflectional Psychology of Vladimir Lefebvre.* Ed. by Harvey Wheeler, American University Studies, Series VIII, Psychology, Vol. 17. Peter Lang, New York, 1989.

In his books, and in numerous papers in professional journals, Dr. Lefebvre claims that an ethical system can be described in the language of mathematics. The language he uses, the so-called *Boolean algebra*, operates with quantities that can take only two values: 1 and 0—the same *binary logic* that is the basis of computer science. In fact, it is the *logic* of all our PCs, and is also believed to be the logic behind the functioning of many biological systems, including our brain.

At first sight this idea, to even attempt to explain human behavior by mathematical equations, seems absolutely ridiculous and crazy. Ethical values change from civilization to civilization, from culture to culture. People live in different conditions, their motivations for making decisions are also different. Besides, they have free will. How can one describe all this universe of motivations and goals by a mathematical equation?

Here is what Dr. Lefebvre's reasoning is. No matter what culture, it does have clear-cut concepts of *Good* and *Evil*. No matter what the physiological mechanisms of brain functioning, an individual, inside his or her personality, has a prescription, *an algorithm* of how to choose between *Good* and *Evil*, and to judge both his or her reaction and that of another individual *vis-à-vis Good* and *Evil*. Is it possible to somehow formalize this algorithm, to see if it can be universal?

In the Introduction to his first book, Dr. Lefebvre writes: "In this book I try to demonstrate that the evaluation between good and evil which is a norm for any given culture, predetermines the typology of individual belonging to that culture. There is a certain connection between the ethical philosophy of an individual and his psychological type. This connection can be expressed formally in strict mathematical language" (p. xiii).

The main idea of Dr. Lefebvre's theory is to represent an individual as an abstract *automaton*. The automaton's inner structure can then be represented by mathematical formulae, connecting the inputs and outputs. The fundamental elementary concepts of the structure are *Good*, which is assigned the value 1, and *Evil*, which is assigned the value 0 (it could be the other way around, but then the equations would be different). Like computer automatons, Dr. Lefebvre's automatons are also governed by binary logic. Having made this assumption, the first, and, in fact, revolutionary result immediately follows: *there exist only two distinct "ethical systems"*: the algorithms of connecting inputs and outputs, and relating *Good* and *Evil* in the automaton's behavior. If this theory is applicable to all *thinking* systems, which are binary—and it looks as though it is—then, the existence of only two distinct ethical systems is also a universal feature of, perhaps, the whole universe.

Dr. Lefebvre's automaton ("an individual") is represented by the formula of a specific hierarchical structure, the "inner world." The individual's inner world may consist of images of this individual, of his or her partner in interaction, and of relationships between them (confrontation or compromise). These images, in turn, may have their inner words—an image of one's partner's image of oneself, for example. These images may be either correct or incorrect. A "situation" is represented by a formula expressing two individuals and the relationships between them. Such concepts as image of oneself, image of one's enemy, feeling guilty, feeling satisfied, suffering, sacrifice—as examples—are strictly mathematically defined. A concept of ethical status is also introduced—a perception of one's stance, confronting ethical choices. Ethical types named "hero," "saint," "Philistine," "dissembler" are also mathematically defined, depending on one's evaluation of one's ethical status.

The two distinct ethical systems mentioned above are based on two pairs of fundamentally different principles (they are expressed as Boolean algebra axioms in Dr. Lefebvre's theory):

1a. Compromise between *Good* and *Evil* is evil
2a. Compromise between *Good* and *Evil* is good

These two diametrically opposed statements describe the possibility of using a bad means to attain good ends (the compromise of good and evil). Complimentary to them are statements describing the attitude toward the prohibition against the use of a bad means to attain good ends (the confrontation of good and evil):

1b. Confrontation between *Good* and *Evil* is good
2b. Confrontation between *Good* and *Evil* is evil

Here *confrontation* and *compromise* are within the same person, rather than between persons. And one can, in fact, see that there are no other *non-contradictory* ways of connecting *Good* and *Evil* but the above two logical propositions.

Dr. Lefebvre refers to the ethical systems corresponding to these principles as the "first" (principles 1a + 1b) and "second" (principles 2a + 2b) ethical systems. He then offers experimental and empirical arguments showing that the first ethical system is realized in Western culture whereas the second ethical system is realized in the culture of the Soviet Union. Actually, what Dr. Lefebvre demonstrates is that the difference between Western society and a Soviet-type society is much deeper than is actually assumed. This difference touches upon the fundamental structures connecting the categories of *Good* and *Evil*.

The latter conclusion is extremely important. Although the Soviet Union does not exist any more, and the threat to the Free World from the Evil Empire has disappeared, the conclusions Dr. Lefebvre has arrived at are of enormous value today to both psychology as a science, and to our understanding of ourselves and the society around us.

In slightly different terms, the *first* ethical system is one in which the principle, *The Ends Justify the Means* is rejected, while in the *second* system, this principle is accepted and followed. In fact, the ethical foundations of the *first* ethical system are not just those of "Western" society, but also those of the whole Judeo-Christian civilization. The *Great Commandments* are but the direct consequences of the fundamental principles of the first ethical system.

On the other hand, Dr. Lefebvre claims that the "Soviet" ethical system is not historically unique. His analysis of Icelandic sagas suggests that pre-Christian Europe might have belonged to the *second* ethical system. In the 20th century, the *second* ethical system has been espoused by all the totalitarian regimes, both secular and religious, and by not a single democratic society. Dr. Lfebvre supplements mathematical definitions, formulas, and their interpretations with the analysis of literary characters of Shakespeare, Dostoevsky, and some authors of Communist literature.

Dr. Lefebvre's theory predicts some interesting features that are observed in real societies. It analyzes such categories as the connections between "being in doubt" and "being guilty," and finds that feelings of guilt appear more often in the *first* ethical system than in the *second*. The absence of doubts, as to correctness of one's image of oneself, results in the loss of feeling guilty in the "Soviet" system but not in the "Western" system.

As one of the main results of the work, the theory predicts a kind of ethical paradox. An ideal individual, of the *first* ethical system, rejecting the compromise between *Good* and *Evil*, nevertheless has a tendency to compromise with another individual, even in a situation of conflict. Whereas an ideal individual of the *second* ethical system, who accepts a compromise between *Good* and *Evil*, has a tendency toward confrontation with a partner.

Dr. Lefebvre and his collaborators also performed an interesting experiment. Two groups of volunteers—one group of recent émigrés from the (then) Soviet Union (ages 19-66; 42 males and 42 females), and the other group of people born in America (ages 17-67; 27 males, 35 females)—were asked to fill out a special questionnaire. The questionnaire consisted of four groups of two statements about situations requiring to correlate the ends and the means. The first statement in each group reflected compromise, while the second reflected confrontation between *Good* and *Evil*. Results are shown in the table below (*Algebra of Conscience*, p. 7):

Comparison of "Soviet" and "American" Preferences in Separation of *Good* and *Evil*

Group Number	Statement	Percentile of Agreement: "Americans"	"Soviets"
1	A doctor should conceal from a patient that he has cancer, in order to diminish his suffering.	8.0	89.0
	A doctor should not conceal from a patient that he has cancer, in order to diminish his suffering.	80.5	15.8
2	A malefactor can be punished more severely than the law requires, if this may serve as a deterrent for others.	11.5	84.5
	A malefactor cannot be punished more severely than the law requires, even if this might serve as a deterrent for others.	83.6	28.0
3	One may give false evidence in order to help an innocent person to avoid jail.	19.9	65.0
	One must not give false evidence in order to help an innocent person to avoid jail.	82.3	42.5
4	One may send a cheat sheet during a competitive exam to a close friend.	8.0	62.0
	One must not send a cheat sheet during a competitive exam to a close friend.	90.3	37.5

From this table, one can see the dramatic (and statistically reliable) difference in the responses of Americans and Soviets. Americans evaluated statements reflecting moral compromise negatively while Soviets evaluated them positively. At the same time, confrontation between *Good* and *Evil* was evaluated negatively by Soviets, and positively by Americans.

This experiment confirms the validity of the fundamental ethical principles formulated in Dr. Lefebvre's theory. Other experiments also agree with some subtle differences with "normative" behavior of personalities of the *first* and *second* systems, predicted by the theory.

Dr. Lefebvre, however, writes: "The author is far from the thought that everyone living in the United States and everyone living in the Soviet Union has the peculiarities described above. Neither the American nor the Soviet culture is a homogeneous unit generating individuals of strictly one type. Moreover, each of these societies today is a battle arena between the two ethical systems. But we can establish the predominant ethical philosophy and the predominant normative character of an individual, which is predetermined by a specific style of upbringing and education. Thus, when we say that in American society the *first* ethical system is realized and in Soviet society the *second* ethical system, we emphasize the fact of the predominance of the ethical system in a given society. In addition, in each culture there may exist subcultures belonging to another ethical system."

Examples of such subcultures are many. Below I'll address some patterns of the *alien* subculture in our life today. But such hostile ethical islands always existed even within official Christianity that might be expected to reject the *second* ethical system outright. For centuries, it had been believed that all means are allowed in the struggle for the *purity of faith*, against heresies, against the unbelievers. Forceful conversions and persecution of heretics by the Holy Inquisition (with the Jesuit Order as its powerful arm) are just two examples.

Acknowledgment of existence of different subcultures is very important, for it rejects the dogmatic approach to a society's ethics. Both the American and the former Soviet societies today are, in fact, battlefields between the two ethical systems. In the former Soviet Union the fundamental reevaluation of all the moral concepts is in progress. But this does not concern me in this essay, although the outcome of that battle may play a crucial role in the future of not only America, but also of the whole world.

What interests me now is the situation in America. This aspect of our culture—the confrontation between the *first* and *second* ethical systems is quite new and unknown even to experts, but it may reveal and explain many phenomena of our life. Dr. Lefebvre's work, in my view, a piece of genius, will undoubtedly make a significant impact on contemporary cognitive science, and possibly even on the new branch of computer science called *robotics*.

It also follows from Dr. Lefebvre's work that robots of the future, apart from obeying the fundamental principles formulated by Isaac Azimov in his series of brilliant science-fiction novels and short stories, may be also programmed to belong to two different (and adverse) ethical systems. A well of ideas for one who is going to write about robots!

I am not in a position to perform a detailed and comprehensive analysis of this ethical struggle in America. But some of its features are so obvious that one does not need to be an expert in order to notice them.

As a kind of *quiz*, let me give a few examples of everyday situations (and you, my reader may add perhaps a hundred more to my list), and ask you to evaluate them and decide, if their ethical attitude belongs to the *first* or to the *second* system. A hint: in all the examples: the end is *good*—no question about it—for the people exercising these judgments, while the means are definitely *evil*—and those who use them, are aware of that. However, the people in question do not regret being involved in an obvious moral compromise typical of totalitarian ethics.

- You receive in your mail an offer to open a credit card account. Some of the terms (sometimes very important) are in fine print. It is obviously meant by the authors of the document that you enter the contract without understanding some of its important provisions. The credit card business is profitable. But do you think the ends justify the means?

But what shall they do if the offer or the advertisement is oral rather than written? There is no *fine print*, is there? Oh, but there is. The announcer begins to speak so fast that one cannot comprehend what it is about. The *fine print* objective has been achieved!

- A company reports losses, and fires some workers. At the same time, the executives continue to receive fat bonuses (of course this is not widely advertised). As a CEO of such a company said in a TV interview, his main responsibility was the interests of the stockholders, and the *bonuses* were simply the consequences of the increased values of the stock. The ends are good: make the stockholders rich. But do the ends justify the means?

- As a part of a downsizing process, a company lays off a hundred of its workers and then hires a hundred new ones, but this time at lower salaries and without benefits. Of course the company somewhat recovers economically. But do the ends justify the means?

- The owner of a factory that employs virtually all the small town's adult population decides to transfer the factory to Mexico (an international agreement inspires and facilitates this transfer). Because of the cheaper labor and favorable tariffs, this would somewhat increase the company's competitiveness and its profit. But do the ends justify the means?

- "Abortion is murder. Over a million unborn children are killed every year." In order to stop this "mass murder" all means are good—from insults and intimidation of patients and doctors even to murder. Do the ends justify the means?

- "A woman has a 'right to choose.'" In order to preserve their lifestyle and sex habits, some women choose to undergo as many abortions as they can. Regardless of whether a fetus is already a *human being* or not—and thus the abortion may or may not be a murder—in a few months that bundle of multiplying cells would have been a beautiful baby; in fifteen years, a teenager looking for meaning; in twenty five years, a happy parent; and in sixty years, the head of a huge family. Do you think that in this case the ends justify the means?

If the protesters at abortion clinics, instead of shouting insults, just silently exposed placards with exactly the same words: "In a few months this bundle of multiplying cells that you are going to get rid of would have been a beautiful baby; in fifteen years, a teenager looking for meaning; in twenty five years, a happy parent; and in sixty years, the head of a huge family," this could have a much stronger effect on women-patients, for conscience is never awakened by threats and violence.

In the examples above, it was important that the people involved believe that the ends were good (although others might naturally question those judgments). While they also knew (and there was no doubt about this), that the means were bad—in some cases the means were even concealed (all the liars know they lie, the crooks know they cheat, the murderers know they murder). And yet people agree to the moral compromise, and that is exactly what distinguishes the *second* system from the *first*.

I have deliberately chosen examples from diverse fields and of different societal significance. However, from the ethical point of view, any violence—a worker's lay-off or primitive cheating—are indistinguishable, for what is important is not the concrete action but the (sometimes subconscious) *reasoning* behind it. I do not want to say that the president of a company who pitilessly fires a dozen workers in order to pay himself a bonus will shoot a doctor at an abortion clinic. But he, and that murderer, are *brothers*, for they believe in the same *eternal truth*: if their ends are good (for them!), then a wide variety of means are allowed although some of them are obviously evil.

In all my examples, except those that deal with violence, there is no law that would prohibit the obviously *amoral* behavior of the people. You cannot appeal to a court or submit a complaint to an attorney general. Conscience is the only judge. If fewer and fewer people have that internal judge inside, we are in trouble. You know how it is. First the glass is full, then gradually it is only half-full, then it is half-empty, and then there is nothing left.

I would like to give two more examples. They relate to important social phenomena of our time and, as such, are to be evaluated.

There is an industry in our society that has been completely taken over by the "aliens"—actually, it had been created by "aliens." This is the *Litigation Industry* (see essay *Beware of the Indifferent*). Even the more innocent component of our jurisprudence, defense, is also being gradually taken over by the aliens. More and more often a defense lawyer sees, as his or her main objective, letting the client get away, rather than serving justice. In fact, the lawyer becomes a *coconspirator*, doing his or her utmost to conceal the truth from the jury. As a witness, this would be a punishable offense. If the criminal is freed (or gets away with a lighter sentence), no matter whether the lawyer receives a fat honorarium right away or not, his or her reputation on the litigation or defense market will significantly rise (together with its future monetary compensations)—the main objective and motivation behind the lawyer's efforts. The accused has the right to a fair trial. But this end does not justify the means used.

Politics has always been believed to be a "dirty" business—"unprincipled" and "amoral." Nicolo Machiavelli, a famed Renaissance statesman, military leader and philosopher, and one of the most powerful proponents of amorality and cynicism in politics, diplomacy and international affairs, actually elevated the ends-justify-the-means-motto to the status of a principle. No matter how strongly society may oppose other forms of *amorality*, politicians always acquire a kind of immunity. When an American Secretary of State declares:[4] "…we have consistent principles and flexible tactics. We consistently speak against human rights violations whether they are in China, Burma, or Cuba. We, however, have to have a flexible approach to how we deal with it depending upon what our national interests are," is not that an uncamouflaged expression of the aliens' relative morality? One may argue, "Well, in case of our national interests, perhaps the ends may justify the means." The thing is, however, that "national interests" may be and, in fact, are formulated according to our politicians' moral standing. The quoted statement was issued in the midst of a controversy having to do with Chinese and Burmese human rights violations, but fundamentally different US responses. This debate, however, has shown that such a thing as *moral integrity* among politicians does exist.

A much more serious moral controversy arose after the 9/11 terrorist attack. The response of the US government to the terrorism was immediate, pitiless, and efficient: Al-Quyda network in Afghanistan was destroyed, and the whole world terrorist infrastructure severely damaged. One "brand" of terrorism was, however, left with almost legitimate tolerance (if not even approval in the UN): the terrorism against Israel.

Not only is the terrorism against Israel tolerated—even the attempts by Arab nations in the UN have been undertaken to exclude anti-Israeli attacks from the definition of terrorism—the point of view in the Left is circulating that the 9/11 attack can be understood, and could have been avoided were not the United States' policy of supporting Israel in its "genocidal" occupation of "Palestine."

But the most incredible, if not shameful, fact is that the American administration has also accepted the "two terrorisms" theory. We do not have "guts" to say directly and unequivocally to the Arabs—including our "allies" like Egypt, Jordan, and Saudi Arabia—"No! Palestinian's attacks, including the suicide attacks highly valued in the Arab world, are not excluded from what terrorism is

---

[4] Madeleine Albright, quoted in NPR's *All Things Considered*, 22 May 1997; downloaded from the Internet.

in our understanding. They are the worst kinds of terrorism, for they are based on compromising the fundamental principles of human life."

The origin of this compromise between good and evil is obvious. We depend on Arab oil. Period. Unfortunately, as I mentioned elsewhere, our response to that oil dependency is the proliferation of SUVs with incredibly low gas mileage, as if we were bathing in oil and simply did not know what to do with it.

In spite of this shameful twist of the American policy toward world terrorism, to the honor of America, there are congressmen and senators (and not only among Republicans) who passionately opposed this *national interest* approach. As for the reaction of *us, the people,* it is muted. Without doubt, the *amorality* of politicians corrupts their constituency. On the other hand, politicians are morally corrupt only to the extent that their constituency is ready and agrees to tolerate. But for how long will it be tolerant?

Everybody knows what I am talking about. Consumer protection organizations warn us again and again about car salesmen who cheat, about the necessity of reading the fine print, about the necessity of carefully reading advertisements and product labels. For, in many such cases, there is an element of fraud—the moral compromise between good ends (for the manufacturers or sellers) and evil means (for the consumers).

Does that mean that our society tolerates the situation when a minority of "aliens" takes advantage of the majority of people who, although aware that they are being cheated, do not understand the seriousness of the situation and thus indirectly support it? Or do we, the majority, believe that moral compromise between *Good* and *Evil* is all right? You may say, "Well, it was always that way. Society is not ideal. Besides, in Dr. Lefebvre's tests, the majority of Americans do give *correct* answers, identifying themselves with the *right* morality. Can't they just *sin* from time to time?"

That is true. And yet, there is a permanent struggle between these two systems inside every person. The question is, who wins? My concern is—and that is why I decided to write this essay—that more and more often the "aliens" win.

But what has this "aliens" morality to do with our current crisis? Most of the examples I gave above would have been unheard of, say 30 to 40 years ago. American capitalism has not always been as greedy as it is today. America is the cradle of contemporary capitalism. Other countries have studied and realized capitalism based on our example. But if you now compare the gaps between the salaries of top executives and ordinary workers in this country and in the countries of Europe or Japan, the picture is ashamedly striking. Ratios of large corporation CEOs' salaries to average salaries within corporations are: in USA—119:1; in Europe—25:1; in Japan—18:1. And mind you, we are not ahead of other industrial countries in production and quality of many goods.

Is it possible that money today is a way of filling the existential voids in our lives? Unfortunately, the answer is *yes*. Viktor Frankl writes:[5] "Sometimes the frustrated will for meaning is vicariously compensated for by a will to power, including the most primitive form of the will to power, the will to money." We believe that money can be both the ends and the means. We believe that money can make us happy. We believe that *making money* may be a reliable way of filling our lives.

I am unable to discuss the psychology of greed. It seems, however, quite plausible that a person with no direction, no meaning, lost and lonely, may turn to making money, or gambling, or just spending money—for the sake of spending—as the only way to bring *meaning* into his or her life.

In response to this powerful demand, the free society supplies us with the means to fulfill our passion for money. A gambling craze, from a growing chain of casinos to numerous state-sponsored lotteries, and an epidemic of sweepstakes promising quick enrichment—no doubt operated by the "aliens"—is something quite normal today. The flood of greed, unheard of before, coincides in time with the decline in our education, growth of crime and proliferation of drugs—the sure symptoms of a serious crisis.

> In numerous discussions on whether or not gambling should be legalized, people usually argue about the economics, the proliferation of crime, the addiction to gambling—and not a single word, or any attempt to pose the question *why*. The easiest way to deal with the problem, the opponents suggest, is to either regulate or prohibit gambling altogether. It is the same easy and meaningless solution that is suggested when the drug problem is in question. By the way, the majority of people who sustain the multibillion gambling market belong to the less affluent. When the supporters of gambling argue that the states have significant revenue through taxes that just means that the poor pay additional indirect taxes on their income, already quite low. As for the main chunk of the revenue, it goes to the "aliens". Meanwhile, in 2003, Americans lost $3 billion by gambling on Internet sites (and by 2006 this figure will double). One does not need to drive to an Indian reservation any more—the means to gamble is here, 24 hours a day, at one's bedside. An expert's view: "Internet gambling is probably the most dangerous thing we've got going.[6]"

[5] Viktor Frankl. *Man's Search for Meaning*, p. 129.
[6] Amie Wexter, an expert on psychological problems of gambling. Quoted in *The Week*, September 5, 2003, p. 18.

When an individual loses direction, the only roads left are the easiest ones, the ones that do not require *purpose*. Money is just such a road. Another road is sex. The advent of the *sexual revolution* also coincides with the beginning of our cultural crisis. Sex is even easier to handle than money—everybody has all that is necessary. The so-called *experimenting with one's body* has nothing to do with the proud meaning of *experiment* as an integral part of science. It is simply another manifestation of the *sexual inflation* that has struck our society. It is but a wandering in the darkness of meaninglessness. Neither money nor sex is the substitute for happiness.

As for the now "infamous" Commandment, *Thou shalt not commit adultery*, it now seems totally absurd. What used to be one of the highest manifestations of human responsibility, honesty, and dignity is now a mockery of common sense. For the ends justify the means.

Returning to Dr. Lefebvre's theory: No matter how idealistic or even naïve the quest for morality may seem to some people, there is yet something to think about. The moral principles of the Judeo-Christian civilization—actually originating from the refusal to compromise *Good* and *Evil*—are unreachable for many individuals. Often, it is more profitable to compromise this moral integrity. Perhaps, in the past, it was mostly the fear of God that had made people behave according to the requirements of the first ethical system. But who fears God today?

The problem of moral values is extremely controversial today. As I claimed elsewhere (see essay *Training or Education?*), explicitly teaching moral values at school is very unlikely to result in acquiring these values. However, the educational system based on the *Progressives'* ideas going back over a century—the prevailing educational system in America today—is implicitly directed at teaching and enforcing the relativism of moral values. As I already discussed, our educational system rejects imposing on children any absolute goal or knowledge, "unless it is social progress attained through individual freedom." Thus children are free to develop their own attitude toward (or against) moral problems. The values emerge as personal preferences, and thus no one set of values is better than any other.

The effect of implementing these ideas on both our high school, and college students is quite devastating. For example, students do acknowledge the fact of the Holocaust, but they refuse to unequivocally agree that the killing of millions of people is wrong. Typically, they deplore what the Nazis did, but they express their disapproval not as a matter of moral judgment, but as a matter of personal preference or taste. It is possible that 10 to 20 percent of students think this way.[7]

---

[7] John Leo. "A No-Fault Holocaust." *US News & World Report,* July 21, 1977.

Moreover, sometimes students are unwilling to reject as absolutely inadmissible even such moral horrors as human sacrifice, ethnic cleansing, or slavery. They claim that the moral views of another group or culture should not, in fact, *must not* be criticized. Today to condemn human sacrifice is politically incorrect because the Aztecs practiced it. As a cornerstone of the prevailing postmodern ideology on our university campuses the existence of any absolute truth is denied. No moral knowledge exists. Opinions are only clashing perspectives.

Since religion, for millennia, used to be the foundation of morality, perhaps a few words are due on where we stand today with respect to faith.

From what I have said above, it is clear that a secular ideology based on relativity of knowledge cannot support absolute moral values. Therefore, to insist that morality is impossible without religion is quite controversial these days. But it was not so to George Washington, who, in his Farewell Address in 1796 said, "And let us with caution indulge the supposition that morality can be maintained without religion. Whatever may be conceded to the influence of refined education on minds of peculiar structure, reason and experience both forbid us to expect that national morality can prevail in exclusion of religious principle."

Although, any president, any senator or congressman, either from the Left or the Right, cannot avoid ending virtually any speech or address with the magic words, "God bless America," in 99 percent of the cases it is just lip service, if not hypocrisy.

If they did care for God's blessings, then the *separation of church and state*, undoubtedly necessary in order to prevent any interference of the state into citizens' spiritual lives, would be of a completely different character. In spite of the fact that over 90 percent of Americans acknowledge, at least in some degree, the existence of a Higher Being, no public school curriculum provides any course in religion, or even in the history of religion, either the Christian religion, or any of the contemporary religions in the world.

In fact, in our public schools it is simply prohibited. But it was not always like this. In 1913, the *Released-Time Religious Education Program* was initiated in the United States (first, mostly by Protestants, but later supported by Catholics as well). It took various forms, but typically, public school students were released for one class period during the week for instruction in the faith of their choice.[8] In 1948 the Supreme Court, in its decision in the case of *McCollum vs. Board of Education* declared unconstitutional the *Release Time Programs* in American public schools.

At the same time, other democracies—England, Scotland, Canada, Germany, and the Netherlands—do have quality religious education in their schools. Such

---

[8] See, for example, Everett J.Kirchner, *Religion in Public Education*, in *Foundations of Education*, ed. by George K.Kneller, John Wiley & Sons, New York, 1968, p. 225.

courses do not teach moral values, but give children the basic understanding of the role of religion in various spheres of human life, and the evolution of this role throughout the history of mankind.

If a kind of general religious education—in the form of the history of world religions and their main ideas and teachings—were reestablished in American schools, it would serve another goal, apart from the educational and developmental. It might teach tolerance and understanding of the religious beliefs of others.

> In Germany, religious studies as a mandatory subject, is taught in public schools in all grades. In Bavaria, one of Germany's lands, religion is taught two hours a week in first grade, three hours in grades two through four, and two hours in higher grades. In Baden-Wurtenberg, a different land with its own laws, religion/ethics is taught two hours a week in grades five through eleven.

Weakening of the faith in God, in our time, cannot be explained as resulting from the tremendous success of science. Paul Davies, in his book *God & the New Physic* (1983), wrote: "…if religion has been displaced from people's consciousness, it has certainly not been replaced by rational scientific thought. For science, despite its great impact on all our lives at the practical level, is as illusive and inaccessible to the general public as any exclusive religion."

In spite of this weakening of faith, as I mentioned above, over 90 percent of people in this country claim that they believe either in God or a Universal Spirit, even if they do not belong to an organized religion.

At the same time, the amount of crime and violence that is flooding our society today is not committed by only that remaining 10 percent (among them a good majority are probably uncompromising atheistic intellectuals, who would never commit any crime). Just one example of the thousands of examples that our media supply every day: half of all women in the US will be battered by their intimate partner at some time in their lives. Battering an *intimate partner* is one of the worst cases of moral compromise, second, possibly, only to child abuse. And who knows how many children are being abused every day?

One explanation for this obvious moral contradiction is that for most of those people who claim to be believers, the religious belief is too shallow. Discussing the problem of religion in this country, Jeffrey L. Sheler wrote:[9] "…if Americans would only replace their 'surface religion' with a deeper, more committed faith,

9 "Spiritual America." *US News & World Report*, April 4, 1994.

the morality of the nation overall would be heightened and many of its most pervasive social problems presumably would subside." This *shallowness* of faith is, without saying, a direct consequence of the lack of general education, on the one hand, and the virtually total absence of religious education in this country, on the other. Both are the results of the degradation of our educational system.

Unfortunately, I do not see how a *religious revolution* can take place without sweeping improvement in our education. High educational level of an individual (including that in science) cannot be an obstacle in developing new attitude toward religion (see essay *Science and Society*). Perhaps, from the point of view of both the society and the individual, the return of profound faith would mean not only the strengthening of moral values, but also a reliable way toward restoring meaning in one's life.

Erich Fromm wrote:[10] "...in religious cultures, like those of the Middle Ages, the average man...looked at God as to a helping father and mother. But at the same time he took God seriously also, in the sense that the paramount goal of his life was to live according to God's principles, to make 'salvation' the supreme concept to which all other activities were subordinated. Today nothing of this effort is present. Daily life is strictly separated from any religious values. It is devoted to the striving for material comforts, and for success on the personality market. The principles on which our secular efforts are built are those of indifference and egotism...Men of truly religious cultures may be compared with children at the age of eight, who need father as a helper, but who begin to adopt his teachings and principles in their lives. Contemporary man is rather like a child of three, who cries for father when he needs him, and otherwise is quite self-sufficient when he can play."

If Dr. Lefebvre is right—and I believe he is, for his proofs as a scientist seem flawless—then the problem that we have now—a gradual proliferation of relative, alien, morality—may become a serious obstacle to our future development as a humane democracy. That is something to think about. However, I also believe that one day we will be healthy again, but this will not happen without a radical revolution in our educational system.

---

[10] Erich Fromm. *The Art of Loving*. Bantam, 1963, pp. 87-88.

BEWARE OF THE INDIFFERENT

"Don't be afraid of your enemies: the worst thing they can do is
to murder you. Don't be afraid of your friends: the worst thing
they can do is to betray you. But be afraid of the indifferent, for
it is by their silent consent that all the murders and betrayals in
the world happen."

—*Bruno Yassensky "King Pithecanthropus the Last"*

There is an old joke that you have probably heard: "What is worse, ignorance or
indifference?" "I don't know, and I don't care."

This question—what is worse?—does make sense. And the most proper
answer to it is the same as the Communist dictator Joseph Stalin gave in the '30s
when he was ruthlessly crushing all political dissent. A journalist asked him:
"Which opposition is worse: from the Left or from the Right?"

"Both are worse," was the answer.

Both the ignorance and the indifference are worse. They are like siblings. But,
although indifference is almost inevitably a quality of the ignorant, the educated
can also be indifferent. And again, both varieties of indifference are *worse*,
although, perhaps, the indifference of the educated may be much more harmful
to society, for the ugliest side of that indifference is *irresponsibility*.

In this essay I will touch on just two aspects of the indifference in our society:
civic indifference—a direct consequence of our population's low educational
level—and the indifference of the "educated." As I have mentioned in the *Preface*,
the indifference of that kind transforms into an irresponsibility on a scale
unheard of before in America. *We, the people* are victims.

A Civic Void

"The people who vote least and who care the least about political issues are not so much the poor as the uneducated, whatever
their income or occupation."

—*Richard J. Herrnstein, and Charles Murray, The Bell Curve:*
Intelligence and Class Structure in American Life

Unlike some other societal categories that are difficult to ascertain, the indifference as a *citizen* is easily detected. Just look at the percentage of eligible voters
who cared to vote in the recent elections. In 1998, 186 million Americans were
eligible to vote (citizens older than eighteen). Of them, about 123 million were
registered as voters, but only 67.5 percent of these turned out. The latter amounts
to close to 83 million, or a little over 40 percent of all eligible voters. In the 1994
elections the turnout was 45 percent. Fifty-four percent of the eligible voted in
1996. A dramatic drop in turnout—close to ten points—occurred in the '60s,
from 63 percent in 1960 to 55 percent in 1972. Since then, the turnout figure
has been oscillating around the 50 percent level. Only the most recent, 2000
presidential election showed "unprecedented" voter turn out: 59.5 percent.[1]

In 1992 Bill Clinton got 43 percent of the vote, which means that he had a
"mandate" from only 24 percent of *us, the people*. Does that, in any sense, have
anything to do with Clinton or the Democrats? Not at all. In 1994 the
Republicans got 53.5 percent of the vote, and thus, with the majority in both in
Senate and the House they got a mandate from…just 21 percent of Americans.
The 2000 presidential elections beat all records. After the Florida scandal and
interference of the Supreme court, the victory was awarded to George Bush, in
spite of the fact that he got only 47.9 percent of the popular vote, while Al Gore
was 0.5 percent ahead with 48.4 percent of voter support. Does George Bush
have a "mandate" from *us, the people?* Obviously, we are not a "representative
democracy" anymore.

These figures are threateningly depressing. Whatever is going on in this country on the legislative or governmental level has been reflecting *the will* of a stunning minority of Americans. If one also takes into account that the voter turnout
is crucially dependent on the voter education level—the higher the education, the
higher the turnout—it follows that the mandate shifts almost completely to the
upper and upper-middle classes. In 1994, 80 percent of Americans had nothing

---

[1]   *US Census Bureau. www.census.gov/population/socdemo/voting/*

to do with the alleged Republican "contract" with them, and 83 percent of Americans did not care what the Democrats' alternative would have been. And close to 62 percent did not give a damn about either program, for they did not care to vote at all. After the 2000 election, President George W. Bush did get a mandate from over 60 percent of Americans, who showed that out nation can unite and support its president in times of crisis—the 9/11 terrorist attack, and the subsequent Afghanistan and Iraqi wars.

When a president wants to address the nation, he should be very careful in scheduling the *right* time for his address. There must be no football game at the same time, otherwise he may lose a possibly significant part of his audience. Ninety million Americans regularly watch a Superbowl game, while in 2000 only 110 million chose to vote, but 75 million refused. I do not know what to make of these figures. It is just very distressing.

Politicians understand that the number of voters has to be increased, some-how, by a proper election campaign that would boost their chances of being elected. For them, the level of *citizenship* of the electorate does not matter. A potential voter may know nothing about our Constitution, for example. All that is unimportant if the political campaign is *populist* enough, if it touches on sensitive nerves and is as blunt, aggressive and even negative toward the opponent as possible. The *Motor-Voter Registration Act* enables one to be automatically registered when a driver's license is issued or renewed. Thus, the number of registered voters grows. People register, but nevertheless, they do not care to vote.

Why? Is it because people cynically believe that their vote would not change anything? A definite level of responsibility is necessary—and is lacking—for a person to be willing to care for something that is not just the self and the immediate family? The statistics insist that under-education is the decisive factor in voters' indifference. Herrnstein and Murray, in their book, *The Bell Curve: Intelligence and Class Structure in American Life*, write: "Poor and humble workers, it is sometimes argued, are disenfranchised whether they vote or not, because the government does the bidding of the rich and well-placed. It is small wonder, then, that they do not vote, the argument continues. But the evidence shows that it is not so much the poor and humble who fail to vote; it is the undereducated" (p.261).

There is, however, a group of people (and, in 2000, they comprised 20 percent of those refusing to vote), mostly moderately or even highly educated, who refuse to vote because of their disappointment in our political system as a whole. Among my friends and colleagues who I dared ask the rather personal question: "Who are you going to vote for?" those who said they would not vote at all, explained why. They said that both on the Right and the Left, the politicians were dishonest and mostly pursued the interests of some interest groups. Both presidential candidates, in their election platforms, promised something they could not deliver, and did not focus on what was really important and pressing, for example.

The motives of those disappointed and distressed people seem to be far from being a kind of indifference. At least it is not the indifference of somebody who "does not know and does not care," and yet, it is *indifference* all right, but of a different kind. It is called *irresponsibility*, and I will be addressing this vice below at some length.

I do not disagree with the motives of those who refuse to vote. The problems they mention are the result of the serious crisis in our society. However, refusing to vote for a candidate, who one does not believe in, is not a solution to the problem of who will be directing the country for the years to come. In such a situation, more then ever, a scrupulous analysis is needed of who will indirectly benefit as a result of one's refusal to vote. Which evil is worse? There is also a moral aspect. By refusing to vote, one also loses the right to criticize the policy of the representatives who have been elected by somebody else.

> Oriana Fallaci, a distinguished Italian journalist writes[2]: "...the non vote is a vote. A legal vote, a legitimate vote. A vote to say to-hell-with-you-all. But at the same time it is the most tragic vote that exists. The gloomy vote of a citizen who does not trust anybody, does not identify himself with anybody, does not know how to be represented by somebody, and consequently feels abandoned defrauded alone."

Therefore, a piece of advice (unsolicited) I usually give to those who are contemplating not voting: just decide whose election platform is more adventurous and less responsible, and vote for the opposing candidate—even if what that candidate promises or is really going to deliver is far from what you think is necessary or would be good for both this country and yourself. A much greater evil can then be prevented.

But let us return to those millions of indifferent, and possibly poorly educated people who do not care to vote. We do not understand why they do not care to vote—why a low educational level transforms into indifference. But we also do not understand—in fact, do not know—*who* they are, what their *political views* are, what their aspirations are, or *what* they are.

The *US News & World Report* issue of 19 July 1995 carried an article under the sensational title, *The New America*. The article was based on the new poll which,

---

2   Oriana Fallaci, *The Rage and the Pride*. Rizzoli, 2002 (p.162).

as the author claimed, "shatters old assumptions about American politics." The article was interesting, and it did reveal many aspects of Americans' political affiliations. The analysis was based on the bipartisan nationwide poll that involved 1,045 *registered voters*. There was no information on the political views of those who did not care to register (I wonder, what the pollsters used to say if they came across someone who was not a registered voter—"Sorry, Ma'am (or Sir), we are not interested in your views" or what?). Only half of the registered voters actually cared to vote, but there was no mention of that in the article, and one could only guess which of the seven *political tribes* America consists of, according to the article, contributed most to that group of the indifferent.

As I mentioned before, the political scientists know that the less educated will probably less frequently get registered and go to a voting booth. But that is all we know—at least we, the people in the street, like me. Do those indifferent oppose gun control and support the *National Rifle Association* (NRA)? Adding up the numbers in the above-mentioned article, one easily finds that 70 percent of the registered voters are against owning guns and do not support the NRA. Does that mean that the power and the influence of the NRA comes mostly from those whose citizenship is at the lowest, for they do not care even to register to vote? What do those indifferent think about our government and our political system as a whole? Hundreds of questions, and no answers.

The politicians do not care, for what they care for are the *real* votes they can rely on, even if these comprise a stunning minority of eligible voters and constitute virtually no mandate.

We already know that the situation is dangerous. American terrorism has emerged, disguised as patriotism, quite unexpectedly for everybody. Neo-Nazi cells are penetrating our armed forces. But it should not have been unexpected, for there are millions of people whose attitude toward American democracy, our social institutions, and law and order in general, is at least unknown, with a high probability of being hostile. If one day they decide to vote, who will they vote into power?

According to figures released by *Klan Watch*, the anti-government Patriot Movement has grown to 858 groups across the country. Of that, 380 are considered armed militias. The number of bombing incidents in the United States increased from 847 in 1985 to 2577 10 years later—the same year as the Oklahoma City bombing[3].

---

3 PBS' *News Hour with Jim Lehrer*, Internet On-line Focus, April 1 and 3, 1997.

One of the consequences of our existential crisis is the decline in active citizenship, almost unheard of in the civilized world. A recent survey of voter turnout shows that the US is almost at the very bottom of the list of 163 nations. Only 25 countries, most of them poor African and Central American nations, are behind us. Our closest allies and friends, the European democracies, are well ahead of us. In Italy 90.2 percent of registered voters vote. In Belgium, Israel, Sweden, and Denmark, between 80 percent and 85 percent; in England and Germany, around 72 percent. Our media are alarmed. What can be done?

Two possible remedies are suggested: to make voting mandatory (some democratic countries *force* their citizens to vote), and/or to make the Election Day a holiday. The first remedy has absolutely no chance of being administered. Americans do not like to be forced, besides, we cannot make even geography in our high schools a mandatory subject!. The second remedy may be easily administered (everybody would like to have an extra holiday), but it is very unlikely to bring the desired result. People fail to vote, not because they are too busy, but because they simply do not care. This is something to think about.

Responsibility

"Freedom is only half of the story, half a truth. On its own, freedom is a negative concept that has to be complemented by its positive counterpart, responsibility, an awareness of being responsible. Freedom threatens to degenerate into arbitrariness or license if it is not lived in terms of responsibility. This is why I have been suggesting to my American friends that the Statue of Liberty on the East Coast be complemented by a Statue of Responsibility on the West Coast"

—*Viktor Frankl, an interview*

Responsibility is a fundamentally human quality. It is usually interpreted as a kind of *duty*—something that has been imposed from the outside. But actually, as Erich Fromm puts it, "responsibility, in its true sense, is an entirely voluntary act; it is my response to the needs, expressed or unexpressed, of another human being."

One has that quality only if one is able to *respond*, if one *cares*. Responsibility, as one of the most important qualities of humankind, has been discussed by philosophers and scholars from time immemorial. Cain's question to God: "Am I my brother's keeper?" and the implied but unspoken answer, "Yes, you are. *We all are our brothers' keepers.*" is, in fact, an important component of the foundation of Judeo-Christian civilization.

In a cynical society, the latter maxim is inevitably an object of mockery and disrespect. However, having rejected that maxim, one immediately brings oneself into the state of *existential vacuum.*

A full and fulfilling life ultimately means taking responsibility—every day, every minute—to find answers to the questions that life poses to everyone. Finding *meaning* in one's life—*the* meaning—is impossible if one is unable to rise above oneself, is unable to give oneself to "a cause to serve or another person to love"[4] . The person lacking meaning then has two surrogates for meaning: the will to pleasure and the will to power, and "the most primitive form of the will to power, the will to money" (p.129). These two wills are always the motivation of the irresponsible.

Responsibility is incompatible with indifference. Moreover, perhaps the most dangerous form of indifference *is* irresponsibility. Here I am not going to discuss the problem of irresponsibility in American life in all its scope and complexity. I will touch on some of its aspects in other essays in this book. Irresponsibility has infected all spheres of American life and virtually all its institutions—the government, the legislature, the judiciary, the media, to say nothing of politicians at all levels, interest groups and businessmen. Here, as examples, I would like to discuss only the most blatant manifestations of irresponsibility, mainly by those who have political influence and power.

Battered the First Amendment, Forgotten the Ninth

In 2001, Rock Star Game released a new sequel to its *Grand Theft Auto* video game: GTA3. Now the game is available for PC. According to news agencies, thus far the game brought to their makers and distributors well over $200 million.

Like in all the industry supplying violent entertainment, in order to survive the fierce competition, each new product must be more thrilling, more violent. In its ruthless violence, GTA3 well surpasses its predecessors. Killing is indiscriminate, including killing both and innocent by-standers and cops (and this is, by the way, a federal crime leading to the death penalty). One of the episodes invites player to kill a prostitute after having sex with her. The latter prompted the Australian government to ban GTA3 from distribution in Australia. In December

---

4   Viktor Frankl, *Man's Search for Meaning*, p. 133.

2002, Honduras banned violent video games. Germany is also moving in that direction, and there is even a movement for the international legislation to ban sex and violence video games.

The level of violence the game's players face is so high that our legislature was also to interfere. The *Protect Children from Video Game Sex and Violence Act of 2002*, introduced to Congress in May 2002, would make it a federal crime to sell or rent the violent video games to minors. However, the language of the bill is vague: to begin with, the concept of being *a minor* is not properly defined. It is also unclear how the law, if passed, could be enforced. (How can the Internet sale of the game be controlled?)

If one looks into bulletin boards, where the game and the proposed legislation are being discussed, one can see the general hostility of people toward "government's" interference. The main motif is: "It is not the government's business to control what games children play, it is the parents' business." With only a few objections like: "But should not the government interfere if parents do not care? Should not the government be the second line of defense when the first—namely family—has been overtaken?"

Unfortunately, people forget that it is not the *government*, but rather their own elected representatives who are attempting to stop the proliferation of violence among children!

We are so used to the presence of violence in our entertainment industry and our media that nobody of those who care and want their voices to be heard even mention the impact of the new game on *non-minors (*the age of 18 is often mentioned as the border of being a "minor"). It is taken for granted that the right of adults to be immersed into the atmosphere of violence, as a manifestation of our *freedom of speech*, is guaranteed by our Constitution.

Even leaving alone the emotional hostility of people toward *any* restrictions of their freedoms, the restriction of the most fundamental freedom—the freedom of speech—guaranteed by our Constitution's *First Amendment*, seems to be absolutely intolerable.

Following Australia's footsteps—banning the GTA3 and similar violent video games from being distributed in the US—would strip America's violent entertainment industry of hundreds of millions, if not billions of dollars. Even if the American public would understand the necessity of that act (which is impossible today), our powerful ideological and political interest groups would not tolerate it. As they would not tolerate ratification of any anti-violence international agreements.

Very rarely, however, do the objectives of these groups have anything to do with the interests of *us, the people*. They have their own agenda, and the politicians who succumb to their pressure, willingly or unwittingly fully exercise their right to be irresponsible to the true needs of our society.

Almost none of these acts of irresponsibility—disguised as virtues of high morality—are *anti-Constitutional*, and therefore cannot be stopped. And most of these irresponsible people—at least a good majority of them—claim the *First Amendment* to our Constitution as the basis and justification for their actions.

The proliferation of violent video games, under the protection of the *First Amendment* armor, is just one, albeit a very important, example of the abuse of the greatest article of our Constitution.

Abused and Exploited. This article of the American Constitution is perhaps the most abused in our political and judicial life today. In fact, its abuse knows virtually no limits, verging sometimes on the farcical.

This is how the *First Amendment* (without additional interpretations) reads:

> *Congress shall make no law respecting an establishment of religion, or prohibiting the free exercise thereof; or abridging the freedom of speech, or the press; or the right of the people peacefully to assemble, and to petition the Government for a redress of grievances.*

The freedom of speech part—the one usually meant when claiming *First Amendment* rights—is interpreted as unrestricted freedom of speech in all its forms: oral, handwritten, printed, sung, transmitted by electronic media, and even just contemplated, although not yet realized. If interpreted that broadly, the *Amendment* simply invites abuse. *We, the people,* are so used to it that we never ask any questions and do not even recognize the abuse of it as such. Here are a few examples:

- Racial, religious, or ethnic slurs, so-called "hate speech," is OK, in spite of the controversy over it that has persisted for decades. Samuel Walker, in his book, *Hate Speech: The History of an American Controversy* (1994) writes: "Most countries prohibit the expression of offensive racial, religious, or ethnic propaganda. According to Human Rights Watch, 'The United States stands virtually alone in having no valid statutes penalizing expression that is offensive or insulting on such grounds as race, religion or ethnicity'" (p. 4). In the paragraphs that follow, the author quotes from the corresponding laws of Britain, Brazil, Turkey, Germany, and Canada, as well as from several international human rights declarations.

- Burning American flag is OK. In spite of numerous attempts by the Congress to enact a law prohibiting desecration of the national flag, the Supreme Court insists that flag-burning is a kind of *speech* and therefore protected by the *First Amendment.* If it is a "speech," it is a variety of a hate speech expressing hatred of our political system, our symbols, and our traditions. As speech, it does not contain any positive meaning. Its sole intended objective is to insult both millions of people to whom our traditions and values are dear and, what is worse, to insult the memory of all who have given their lives defending those values. The flag haters, at least, had decency not to have attempted to burn the flag salvaged from the ruins of the World Trade Center.

What about cross-burning—the infamous KKK ritual? It is no good. After decades upon decades of that disgusting practice, in April 2003, the Supreme Court ruled that burning crosses is not supported by the *First Amendment* as a free speech right, because it is "an instrument of racial terror." But racial slur and insults are still OK.

- Violence in the media and entertainment industry. Violence never occurs without hate—in fact, it is initiated by hate. But since the propaganda of hate, any hate—as a form of "speech"— is OK, why should violence not be OK? It is the true expression of hate. It is the *propaganda of hate* by direct action. So it is a kind of *speech,* all right, and therefore it is OK without saying.

The violent video games I have already mentioned are just tiny drops in the ocean of violence our society is exposed to. From the Internet page, *Rising Subculture Iceberg* (http://logosresourcepages.org/subcultr.html), I have learned that "a six-volume set of books on killing techniques is available in America but banned in Canada. This set is found in the hands of young skinheads, gang members, serial killers, psychotics, for example. Many lesson plans come with each volume. This set of books is protected under freedom of speech in America." For a few dollars, one can also order from a publisher, in Washington State, a book on interrogating a kidnapped victim. It is legal, with full protection guaranteed by the *First Amendment.*

- What about "indecencies," "obscenities," and "offensive language?" Well, these cannot be defined thoroughly, but they are definitely a kind of *speech*, and therefore they are OK. And so, the level of elementary civility in relations among people in America has dropped below any imaginable limits. The f-word is a normal part of everyday speech, song lyrics, radio, TV, and movies. Just attempt to prohibit the public usage of this word, and the *First Amendment* right will be invoked in defense. On occasions, when "indecent" people are interviewed by "decent" radio programs, the interviewers substitute electronic "bleeps" for the f-words and their numerous derivatives. This is, without saying, blatant *censorship* and, in principle, could be the target of a lawsuit.

- Child pornography? No, no. Yet adult pornography is OK. Just look at the Internet. Hundreds of pages of free and subscription *adult* sites. But child pornography is absolutely unacceptable and uncivilized. It must be forbidden, and it is—in spite of the *Amendment*, as it is understood today. Recently, a seemingly unresolved controversy has arisen. It is about what can be called *virtual child pornography*, when an image of a naked child is created by a computer program without actually being an image of a concrete child, but is, rather, either a composite picture or an image created completely from scratch. How can this type of "child pornography" be interpreted in the light of the *First Amendment*? Only the image of a concrete person is interpreted as pornography, not any indecent image. In December 2001, our Supreme Court refused to ban virtual child pornography from the Internet.

- Against the background of unrestricted and sometimes vicious sex propaganda, in virtually all spheres of our society, our children and youngsters are under permanent assault. Just watch MTV or look at magazines addressed to adolescents, for example, *YM*, or *Seventeen*. Suppose we agree that, though poisonous, those magazines are inevitable. But recently, I saw a thirteen-year-old girl (I asked her how old she was) buying *Cosmopolitan* at an airport magazine stand. Just a few flashy items from the cover—"His Pleasure: There are Four, Yes, Four Levels of Male Bliss," "Naked Men. Well, Half-Naked. Feast

Your Eyes on Our Hunks And Trunks." "Loving Gestures that Secretly Irked Him," for example. Later, at the same airport, I saw an older girl (probably 17) reading the same magazine. All these publications are completely "covered" by the *First Amendment.* By allowing unrestricted access to such material, we willingly sacrifice moral health (perhaps, even the future) of our children and adolescents. We request a picture ID before selling a teenager a pack of cigarettes—but in no way may we prohibit or restrict selling children magazines published for adults, because it is authorized by the *First Amendment.* And it is OK.

• What about the *political correctness campaign* that haunts our university campuses and, in fact our media? Please, don't even mention it. Nobody dares challenge this ideology, although it blatantly violates the *First Amendment.*

• What about a special interest group that donates, as a part of an election campaign, a large sum of money (so-called "soft money") to a party or directly to a candidate to be elected in the hope that he or she will defend that group's interests in Congress? It is most probably OK that the group exercises its *First Amendment* rights protecting its intentions to achieve some, possibly tangible, benefits by promoting the propaganda of their ideas. If this is not a form of *corruption,* then what is a bribe? Is not a bribe—any bribe—always directed at promoting somebody's interests that can be coined as *ideas,* and (if not for the record), expressed in a persuasive *speech,* and therefore protected by the *First Amendment?* This is because in 1976 in the case *Buckley v. Valeo* the Supreme Court ruled that political contributions and campaign spending are equivalent to political speech. The consequences of this ruling for the moral climate of our politics have been devastating.

Senator McCain, who, for a long time, had been fighting in the Senate, against fierce resistance by both Republicans and Democrats, to legislate a law prohibiting soft money, said: "Sooner or later it's going to break. Americans are going to get fed and rebel. They're going to demand reform because it is corruption. It's worst I've ever seen....They're without shame. I'm talking about members of Congress, not the lobbyists, who are doing what they are paid to do. It's the system that makes good people do bad things because of the corrupting influence of money"[5].

Recently our Congress eventually passed, and President Bush signed into law the McCain-Feingold Bill, also known as *Bipartisan Campaign Reform Act* (BCRA), which objective was to eliminate soft money and thus to prevent the corruption of our legislators. However, since the ruling of the Supreme Court that *Buckley v. Valeo* is still valid, both the Left (AFL-CIO) and the Right (NRA) are already ready to fight tooth and nail this restriction of their "political speech" rights.

Just a few more words about the hate speech problem, and one more example of the most blatant abuse of the *First Amendment*. In both cases this abuse has had important social consequences. In fact, it has even (in the second example) completely changed the moral face of America.

Samuel Walker, in his book, *Hate Speech,* which I have already mentioned, suggests an explanation of why the United States has failed to protect its citizens from hate speech and its consequences. According to his theory, our judiciary has always been under the strong influence of powerful ideological interest groups, such as the American Civil Liberties Union—tending to defend and promote *unrestricted* human rights. "And there was virtually no political force powerful enough to counterbalance this pressure. The organizations defending the interests of Jews and African Americans, the two groups being the main targets of hate speech, were not willing to fight."

Walker suggests that the reason was purely political: "The major civil rights groups [such as the American Jewish Congress, the American Jewish Committee, and other Jewish interest groups, and the NAACP on the African-American side—GK] abandoned group libel legislation because they perceived it as a threat to their larger program of achieving equal rights" (p. 15). The whole situation had been possible because the majority of Americans were excluded from the debate in the decision-making process. Just a handful of people were instrumental in taking the decision: "To be sure, these people were not the mass of average Americans. The key actors were members of a policy-making elite: judges, lawyers, activists" (p.159). This has not happened in other democratic countries, not because they lacked the "American spirit of freedom" we are so proud of, but because the political interest groups there did not, and do not, have the power they have in America.

---

5   Quoted in E. Drew's *Citizen McCain*, p. 166.

My second example has to do with the so-called *litigation explosion* in America. While writing this essay I came across a book: Walter K. Olson, *The Litigation Explosion: What Happened When America Unleashed the Lawsuit*, 1991. The book reads like an adventure story. Here is the story.

Litigation Explosion. Until the mid-'60s, the widely accepted attitude of both the general public and the American Bar Association toward lawsuits was that they should be the last resort in solving legal problems. The American Bar Association's "moral code" in fact was as powerful in regulating the professional behavior of lawyers as the *Hippocratic Oath* of the medical profession. In its ethical canon number 28, it explicitly disapproved "stirring up litigation." The code also absolutely prohibited using two important tools of any commercial enterprise: general advertising and solicitation of legal services.

With the "will for money"—greed—gradually becoming the main objective of life, the ethical dams of the law profession began to collapse. This is how it happened: "By the 1970s the climate in the law schools had turned around on the subject of litigation, first to ostensible neutrality and then to admiring support. One oft-cited article on legal ethics struck a typical note when it assailed as 'distinctly medieval' the view that litigation is 'at best a necessary evil' and litigiousness is vice. Lawsuits increasingly came to be described, as litigious persons themselves describe them, an assertion of rights...The process culminated in 1977 with a five-to-four decision of the US Supreme Court officially endorsing the new idea that a lawsuit was no longer to be considered an evil" (p. 4).

The advertising dam was the first to crumble. That 1977 Supreme Court decision declared that the *First Amendment* protects advertising of lawyers' services as *commercial speech*. The impact was unbelievable: "Overnight, the most drastic sort of change came over America's legal profession. On June 26, 1977, in every state of the union, lawyer advertising was kept under close wraps if not banned altogether. On June 27, from Kiska to Key West, no combination of public discomfort and peer opposition could stop it. Because lawyers' newly discovered right to advertise was found to be lodged in the Constitution, it could not practically be revised (short of change of a heart of Court) no matter what lessons experience might turn out to hold" (p. 21).

However, if advertising to a million readers (or watchers) is all right, why not to *just one*? Why should not the solicitation of a lawyer's services to a *certain* person be allowed? Fair enough. And the 1978 Supreme Court decision that followed ruled that "solicitation with a primarily 'political or ideological' motive could not be banned" (p.24). Thus the last dam had disintegrated. The American Bar Association's resistance, no matter how strong it had been at the beginning, could not withstand the pressure of overflowing greed. The litigation industry had been born.

It is a fundamental elementary fact of economics that a business is doomed unless its technology is *state-of-the-art*. Litigation technologies are extremely sophisticated and are constantly improving. Among them: "ambulance chasing," when lawyers penetrate emergency rooms and wards, and intensive care units—even disguised as electricians or plumbers—in order to seduce a new client to litigation. Or scanning public hospital records for potential cases of malpractice suits, to say nothing of sophisticated psychological methods used to antagonize parties in divorce or property conflicts, thus expanding opportunities for litigation.

But the most ingenious and the most successful technology of the litigation industry is the so-called *contingency fee* device, *No Fee Unless Successful*. If the lawyer is successful, the fee is typically 30 percent of the client's winnings. The corruptive effect of this practice on American society simply cannot be overestimated.

And we are, again, in complete isolation from the civilized democratic world. "The tradition of the English common law, the French and German civil law, and the Roman law all agree that it is unethical for lawyers to accept contingency fees. In 1975 British judges strenuously opposed even a closely regulated version of the fee, in which a contingency suit could go forward so long as leading lawyers verified its reasonableness. They explained that lawyers would no longer make their cases 'with scrupulous fairness and integrity'" (*ibid.* p. 37).

Lawyers are probably the most hated profession in America. Numerous jokes are circulated and eagerly repeated again and again, about lawyers, their greed, ruthlessness, and the way they must be treated (ruthlessly). But how many people would throw a lawyer down the stairs (or in a less violent scenario—would hang up on him) who suggests suing someone for a large amount of money—and with no effort or responsibility on one's part?

Actually, as the *Harvard Medical Study* has discovered, only less than two percent of patients who could suspect "malpractice" in their treatment ever files suit. On the other hand, only a tiny minority among those who did sue for malpractice had solid grounds to do so.

Not only does the litigation industry in America corrupt both people and our social institutions, it costs *us, the people* billions of dollars. Widespread insurance fraud instigated by lawyers, and epidemics of malpractice suits against our health-care providers trickle down to the working Americans' bills.

The most disgusting—the most morally incredible—is the lawyers' assault on those who care for our health. So often a doctor or a nurse spends sleepless nights at a patient's bedside, neglecting their own families, and even their own health, only to be sued by irresponsible greedy lawyers—for it is the lawyers, not the alleged victims of the alleged malpractice who are the real litigators. No wonder medical doctors have to pay a good chunk of their income for malpractice insurance—the expense that then trickles down to increased medical insurance costs. And not only that, the whole strategy of *medical treatment* is now built on measures preventing a possible malpractice suit, such as unnecessary tests or second opinion consultations, rather than on the true medical necessity.

Of course, this flourishing business of robbing innocent people of their money, health and dignity would be impossible, were the power of money not so strong in our society today. Although it would be utopian and unrealistic to hope that every person who finds a wallet would always contact its owner or bring the wallet to a nearby police station, many Americans do so. However, if one day the police are removed from town streets, the town will be looted. That is what happened when the Supreme Court, by abusing the *First Amendment*, gave the green light to greed.

In no way do I imply that the whole law profession is criminal and corrupt. Democracy—any democracy—is based on law. Law is the basis of every developed civilization. What is tragic about our situation is that the abuse of the law—a *basic law*—has unleashed an avalanche of what in a humane, civilized sense can be called *unlawfulness,* to which a good portion of our society is victim.

A tragic consequence of this situation is the corruption of our young and talented, for the most able and talented of our youngsters aspire to the law profession, with the sole objective: getting rich, and quickly. Ask a ten-year-old what she or he would like to be. Most probably—if the child is smart enough—you will hear: "a lawyer *or* a doctor." Ironically, at this age—and possibly, even at the threshold of the university—the smarties and whiz kids do not know exactly which of these two options to take. Both are the best moneymaking professions today. Ironically enough, the latter is a prey of the predator former. Fortunately, we still have very many good and honest lawyers, and good, dedicated and selfless doctors. And yet, the situation is that of a town abandoned by the police.

By the way, as a part of the toppled Clinton healthcare reform (I discuss it below in this essay), some measures directed at curbing the *malpractice litigation* epidemic have been suggested. However, as a Russian saying puts it, "Having lost the head do not cry for the hair."

I am certain that a political reason having nothing to do with the interests of the majority of *us, the people* may be found behind any absurd interpretation of the *First Amendment*. It is interesting that the Left, the principal defendant of the unrestricted interpretation of the *First Amendment*, is silent when the *political correctness* is in question. And nobody has the guts to remind them that *political correctness* which blatantly violates freedom of speech, is a direct successor to the Communist and Nazi concept of *the one and only true* ideologies.

Abandoned Ninth Amendment. As one can see, the great *Amendment* can be easily turned into a farce by anyone who is irresponsible enough and morally corrupt enough, and who has political power. But why is it that the *First Amendment* is so vulnerable to abuse? What is wrong with it? At first glance, it seems that the basis for possible abuse lies in the fact that there are no restrictions on the rights protected by the *Amendment*. That is why any attempts to single out special cases, such as child pornography or hate propaganda, and exclude them from guaranteed rights seem to be *unconstitutional*.

I do not think that those who formulated the Amendment in 1791 were unaware of this vulnerability. But is it possible that they also thought that formulating restrictions would have opened a Pandora's box of abuses, which no one would be able to control? That including a sentence, such as "…so far as the above freedoms do not infringe on the rights and interests of other people" at the end of the *Amendment* would have created more problems than solutions to the problems at hand?

That is what I used to believe (and probably many people still think so), and this is probably true. But not many know (at least for me it has been a shocking revelation) that our Constitution *does contain* a clause which, in its spirit, is exactly what, as I believed, should have been included in the *First Amendment*, but deliberately had not been.

What I refer to is the *Ninth Amendment*, enacted together with the *First Amendment* in 1791. Here is its text:

> *"The enumeration in the Constitution of certain rights shall not be construed to deny or disparage others retained by the people."*

Is this not, in fact a paraphrase of my suggested modification: "…so far as they do not infringe on other's rights"? Why then don't we *ever hear* in situations such as the spewing of violence and indecencies on all wavelengths, the voice of our Supreme Court: "No, you are not protected by the *First Amendment*: your actions are violating the rights of our children and citizens at large to have a safe and dignified environment." Are the rights *enumerated*, i.e., explicitly mentioned in the *First Amendment* not qualifiable as *certain*? Or is the *Ninth Amendment* to be construed in the sense that only those rights that are also explicitly mentioned in the Constitution, must not be *denied or disparaged*?

Being virtually ignorant of the judiciary aspects of the American Constitution (as most of *us, the people* are), I have spent quite some time leafing through and reading from at least half a dozen books by experts in constitutional law (among them, P.Bobbit's, *Constitutional Interpretations*, 1995, and very informative *The Rights Retained by the People*, 1989—a collection of essays on the *Ninth Amendment*). And that is what I learned.

Authored by James Madison, over 200 years ago, the *Ninth Amendment* was neglected and ignored by both legal scholars and acting courts. In 1987, during the Supreme Court nomination hearing of Judge Robert Bork, the following dialogue took place (*Constitutional Interpretations*, p. 91):

> "*Senator Thornmond*: What do you believe the *Ninth Amendment* means?
>
> *Bork:* That is an extremely difficult question, Senator, because nobody has ever, to my knowledge, understood precisely what the *Ninth Amendment* did mean and what it was intended to do."

The Judiciary Committee was not satisfied with the answer. Senator DeConcini, a non-lawyer, insisted on more clarification; here is the response (p.105):

> "*Bork*: Senator, if anybody shows me historical evidence about what they meant, I would be delighted to [apply] it. I just do not know…I do not think you can use the *Ninth Amendment* unless you know something of what it means. For example, if you had an *Amendment* that says 'Congress shall make no' and then there is an ink blot and you cannot read the rest of it and that is the only copy you have, I do not think the Court can make up what might be under the ink blot…"

Judge Bork's nomination was rejected, and yet, the above opinion of a distinguished law scholar, on the *Ninth Amendment* as a judiciary "white spot" shocked me.

I also learnt that interest in the *Ninth Amendment* was revived after 1996 when the US Supreme Court struck down an anti-birth-control law in Connecticut. That decision was based on Supreme Court Justice Arthur Goldberg's opinion invoking the *Ninth Amendment*.

Since then, a host of scholars have been discussing the *Amendment*, but mostly in connection with the extent of individual liberties and unenumerated rights (such as the right to privacy). Scholars' main concern has been to guarantee the maximum possible extension of individual rights. Indeed, a conventional reading of the *Amendment* implies protection of unenumerated rights *in addition* to the rights already enumerated.

At the same time, an obvious interpretation of the *Amendment*—the possible *restriction* of enumerated rights in order to *protect* rights unenumerated—has been completely ignored. In most jurisprudential discussions of the *Ninth Amendment*, the focus has been to defend individual rights against the power of government. However, the *Amendment* may and should be also interpreted as *protecting* unenumerated individual rights from abuse by the freedom *guaranteed* by other, enumerated, individual rights, without any government involvement.

An obvious example: protecting the right to dignity (unenumerated) of an African-American from the racial slurs of a bigot (a fully enumerated right—free speech.). Most scholars agree that the broad language of the *Amendment* demonstrates that the founding fathers wanted it to be adaptable to the needs of a changing society. Is not it high time, are not the needs of our society today crying for a proper adaptation of the *Amendment*?

Of course it is a matter of *interpretation*—which rights are "certain" and which are not. It is also true that the Constitution does not contain as a *law* "the right of our children and citizens at large to have a safe and dignified environment." But then why is any presence of religion, such as the study of religion in public schools, and even mentioning the name of God in Pledge of Allegiance, interpreted as a violation of the *First Amendment*: "make no law respecting an establishment of religion"? Reading the Bible or meditating *is not* "making a law." Again, both in the case of religion and of freedom of speech, it is a matter of the *interpretation* of the *First Amendment*.

The interpretation of our Constitution is the sole responsibility of our Supreme Court. Why then cannot the *Ninth Amendment* be interpreted in such a way as to stop the abuse of the *First Amendment* and, in fact, protect the rights of citizens and our children, in the first place, to a life without the unrestricted propaganda of violence, indecency, and sex?

Of course, I do not have the answers to these burning and mind-boggling questions. Nor, probably, would millions of Americans. We implicitly believe that our Supreme Court *does a good job* in interpreting our Constitution. But the above examples of its ambivalence in interpreting the *First Amendment* and failure to call the *Ninth Amendment* to the defense of *us, the people*, simply show, in my view, a lack of integrity in our Supreme Court judges and the political or ideological *interest groups* they implicitly or explicitly support.

True, if properly interpreted, the *Ninth Amendment* would open a Pandora's box. If one believes that one's rights have been infringed upon by an action protected by the *First Amendment*, or some other *Amendment*, one could call on the *Ninth Amendment* in one's defense. Fierce clashes between those relying on the *Ninth* and *First Amendment*s (and definitely the *Second Amendment*—the right to bear arms) would bring about a litigation explosion even more powerful than the one that already haunts our society today.

This is where our courts—and the Supreme Court, in the first place—would be put to the test. They would have to decide, guided by the spirit of our great Constitution rather than by ideological or political interests, which rights *are to be protected* and which *must be sacrificed*. It would not be easy, and would require enormous effort and integrity from our judges. Then, gradually, we would begin to understand that *freedom*, first and foremost, is *responsibility*. I hope that the *Ninth Amendment* will eventually be resurrected to fulfill its important function today (a function perhaps not anticipated by the founding fathers)—to counter *abuse* with *responsibility*. We simply have no other option, for our Constitution *is* in danger.

Our Children's Rights

Here I want to say a few words about yet another example of our judicial sloppiness. I discussed elsewhere (see essay *Abandoned*) the fundamental problem that is partly the result of our crisis of meaning, and partly one of the powerful factors exacerbating this crisis. What I mean is a virtually complete abandonment by our society—in its many important functions—of our children, from the toddlers through puberty into their adulthood. One of the aspects of this societal neglect is the ambivalence of law as applied to our children and youths.

The imposition of a *curfew* for teenagers recently caused a storm in among our public. Libertarians claimed our children's *First Amendment* rights were been violated. In fact, the argument was whether the children should or should not have exactly the same rights as adults.

This argument, as a part of a public discussion, does not make much sense. In fact, if one agrees that an imposition of restrictions on children's behavior violates their constitutional rights, then one should agree that any restrictions imposed by parents also violate children's rights. And this creates a huge controversy. Then we cannot accept as permissible spanking, non-violent punishments, the so-called "grounding," or V-chips, for example. This seems to be absurd because then nobody, even parents, are able to control children's behavior.

Suppose the law superseding the parent's legal power is allowed to be *switched on* at a certain age. Above that age a youth is considered a *full-fledged adult*, and has the full protection of the Constitution. What is this age? Might it be the *driving license age*—16? It is presumed that a 16-year-old is responsible enough to be entrusted, at the wheel, with the lives of other people—both pedestrians and motorists. One may argue that 18 would be more appropriate. At this age, a youth is allowed to vote. He or she is mature enough to participate in the democratic election process. But then, why is the so-called *drinking age* 21 (in Massachusetts, and in a number of other states)? Is not the prohibition to sell liquor to a *mature adult*, who is already allowed to take political decisions, unconstitutional? The same argument applies to the recently passed gun-control law that prohibits selling firearms to individuals younger than 21. Does not an 18-years-old *full-fledged* and "law abiding" citizen have a full right to "bear arms" guaranteed by the *Second Amendment*? As a part of the (also recent) law prohibiting selling tobacco products to youths under 18, there is a clause allowing law-enforcement authorities to check identity papers of people up to the age 26. Is this not a blatant violation of the *Fourth Amendment* prohibiting "unreasonable" search? And, of course, R-rated movies may be watched only if one's photo-ID shows that one is 17 or older. Why 17? And on, and on, and on.

Ambivalence and inconsistency of American society toward our children and youths are enormous. The most harmful—both for the children and the society as a whole—is the ambivalence in educational and civility requirements. We allow children to chew gum and wear makeup in class, and we allow them to decide what to study and what not. As a *punishment* for misbehavior, we expel children from classes (is this not a *reward* for someone who hates to be at school?), and we allow teenagers to drop out of school (In some states, high school drop out rate reaches 10 percent, and nowhere is below 4), thus creating an army of societal outcasts and potential criminals.

If, for instance, *mandatory* high school education would become a law, then *dropping out* would be unconstitutional. Then those teenagers who drop out today would have to think twice. Either they study hard and graduate with a high school diploma (or its equivalency) or finish their education in a special boot-camp school. Such measures (against the background of the general rise of our children's educational level) may be the only way of curbing the juvenile crime and eradicating gangs. By the way, 40-50 years ago such schools did exist. Incorrigible troublemakers among the students, who had had problems with the police as well as the school authorities, were sent to a so-called "reform schools." Presumably, such schools have been eliminated as "unconstitutional," for they had violated children's right not to study and make trouble.

A few more words about the driving license age of 16. Very gloomy statistics show that the first year after receiving a license is the most dangerous. Thousands of teenagers are getting killed every year. The total number of casualties per million miles for 16-year-old drivers is more than 7 times the number of casualties for 30- to 59-year-old drivers. More and more voices are heard suggesting that receiving a driving license must be postponed for a year or two. It seems appropriate to have a unified "responsibility" age, and make it 18.

But why is it that the right to drive a dangerous vehicle has been given to children who are far from being mature and responsible? The answer is obvious. Teenagers must have means of reaching each other. In suburbia there is no public transportation. Children could use bicycles, and they do. But many parents prohibit this means of transportation because it is too dangerous. Bicycle paths are virtually unheard of in our towns and cities—in most towns even sidewalks are rare. Unfortunately, when we built our cities and towns we did not think about our children. And we still do not think about them.

And yet, even with the absence of bicycle roads and pavements, there is a way—not completely safe, but quite reasonable—to give our teenagers means of reaching each other. A one-seat motor scooter or moped (it is important that the second seat was prohibited) with the maximum speed of, say, 15-20 mph (that in no way could be increased) would make the car, as the only means of transportation, unnecessary. These mopeds would have to comply with all the traffic rules (with mandatory rules of staying in the rightmost lane and prohibiting passing other vehicles), at the same time, the right of our teenagers to be on the roads would have to be enforced by the new traffic rules and the police.

Such a reform would result in a significant decrease of teenage traffic casualties, and make teenagers much safer and even more mobile. But who will initiate such a reform? And will libertarians agree with such "violations" of teenagers' human rights as driving with any speed they desire, or riding with a friend sitting on one's lap?

The neglect of children is just another manifestation of our overall irresponsibility—one of the consequences of our wandering in existential darkness.

The Aborted Healthcare Reform

Here I want to touch on what was, perhaps, the ugliest demonstration of political irresponsibility in the ideological war between the Democrats the Republicans. The losers again are *we, the people.*

What I refer to is the Clintons' Healthcare Reform that has been toppled, nay, murdered, without even giving their authors and supporters an opportunity to explain the nation what it was about. Perhaps, some public relation errors were made by Hillary Rodham-Clinton or her aides—the people who undertook the enormous job of putting together the proposals for reform—but there was *no discussion* of it. Just stop a person walking on a street, leaving a car at a supermarket plaza, or playing with a child in a park, or walking a dog, and ask: "What was that healthcare reform proposed by Clinton about? What did you like or not like about it?" You would get something like this as an answer: "Sorry, I do not know much about it. But it would be bad because it would create some new government bureaucracies (I forget how many), and have us pay more in new taxes (I forget how much)."

In a discount bookstore I paid $1.99 for a copy of *Health Security: The President's Report to the American People. The Official Text* (Simon & Schuster, New York; no year of publication shown. Suggested retail price $7). I am afraid that most of the circulation has not been sold at all. The American people have not been given *the right to choose*. The baby has been aborted before it even had a chance to see the light.

Everybody knows how deep our healthcare crisis is. Forty million Americans (and among them ten million children) do not have health insurance, either because they cannot afford it, or because they have *preexisting conditions* and therefore have been refused coverage. Nor can most small businesses afford health insurance. Among those uninsured are people who do work but just cannot afford to pay the high premium. On the other hand, the existing system discourages people from leaving welfare. Beginning to work would mean losing Medicaid, with no chance to be covered by private insurance.

Almost 15 million of our children have not been immunized, partly because of their mothers' ignorance, but mostly because their families do not have health insurance. The children diseases that were thought to have been eradicated from America, but still existed only in poor third-world countries, are returning. And lice are often guests in our schools.

As I mentioned above, people do not know what the essence of the Clinton reform was. The frightened Clintonites gave up—they did not defend and, in fact, did not dare to defend their aborted baby. The accusations of promoting "big Government"—and what can be more *criminal* than a government controlled universal healthcare system?—are now considered even worse than accusations of being a *liberal*. Americans learn some details about the proposed healthcare reform—and always the negative ones—from Republicans. But *we, the people* have not been allowed—for nobody cared to explain the details to us—to compare the two systems—the existing and the new. We weren't allowed to compare the extent of healthcare bureaucracy that now exists (and it is enormous), with the ones to be created, to compare the cost we are paying now (please don't forget that the insurance companies *must* have profit, and a fat one, with multi-million dollar bonuses and salaries for their presidents and CEOs) with what we would have been paying if there were a new system, with the new government bureaucracies and the new taxes.

By the way, if a professor of social studies at a university were to ask students: "How do you think the decision regarding a problem of nationwide character and importance is to be reached in a developed democracy, a problem that will have direct and immediate impact on the lives of millions of people, both young and old, the majority of the nation's population?" The correct answer that the professor would expect is "by a national referendum." In just such a situation, Americans did not have any say.

We all buy this or that form of insurance: car insurance, home insurance, life insurance, for example. We pay a lot, and very often are pitilessly cheated. It is a normal way of life. We do not object. But when the government suggests its protection taking over from greedy insurance companies to become the provider of the most important insurance—*health insurance*—it is a no-no. Nobody in the government makes big bucks. Thank God it is still a nonprofit organization. If the government were allowed to spend our money for our healthcare, with a proper organization and control of bureaucracy, this, for most of Americans, and definitely for the middle class, would be less expensive than if we tried to buy the same services from the profit-oriented and greedy insurance companies.

And who are the victims of that murder?" *We, the people* are. Garry Wills, in his excellent book[6] writes (p.21): "The real victims [of anti-government culture] are the millions of poor or shelterless or medically indigent who have been told, over the years, that they must lack care or life support in the name of their very freedom. Better for them to starve than to be enslaved by 'big government.' This is the real cost of our anti-government values."

Half-a page before, Wills writes: "Are Americans less protected against threats to their health than other citizens of industrialized democracies? Say that is so—but are we to purchase health at the price of liberty? For that is what giving power to the government would mean, including power to provide medical care."

However, to millions of Americans who have silently consented to the crime, the most important factor was not relinquishing their "liberty," but rather unwillingness to let government "spend their money, rather than letting them to spend it themselves," or, translating from the language of the rhetoric, unwillingness to pay (by their tax dollars) for somebody else's healthcare.

---

[6]　Garry Wills. *A Necessary Evil: A History of American Distrust of Government.* Simon and Schuster, 1999.

Thus, the reform has been murdered in Congress by the cold and irresponsible majority, with the mandate of just 21 percent of eligible voters. And even that 21 percent had received no explanation of the decision that had been taken in their name. But the real mandate that the anti-reform law-makers carried was from one of the most powerful interest groups in America: *His Majesty the Insurance Business.* By the way (as I mentioned above), the *First Amendment,* as interpreted today, does guarantee the right of interest groups to interfere in the lives of millions of Americans via fat donations to politicians. The McCain-Feingold Bill is yet to win the litigations before the soft money bribery disappears in America. Something to think about.

Don't forget that, for the rest of the democratic world, universal healthcare is a reality. Sometimes, say, in Canada or Denmark, one has to wait for some time for surgery or a test requiring expensive equipment. This is not because of the flaws in the universal health systems—both Canada and Denmark simply cannot afford as many MRI machines and expensive operating rooms as we can. And that multimillion-dollar equipment, with which our hospitals and clinics are stuffed (and often over-stuffed), and of which America is so proud, has been paid for by *us, the people* through the high health insurance premiums that we pay or co-pay. Do those who scare us with endless waiting lines presume (and believe) that if America would implement the universal healthcare system most of our MRI machines would be scrapped and the operating rooms dismantled? It is nonsense, and yet people do buy this argument.

Even if one completely disregards the "idealistic" notion that, in a humane society, universal and affordable healthcare is supposed to be the right of every person, rather than a privilege dependent on one's ability to pay bills, one can easily see that without a form of universal healthcare, our society will eventually lose its title of *humane.*

Due to the progress in molecular biology and the revolution in our understanding of heredity and the mechanisms by which the genes operate, we are on the threshold of a new era in medicine. In one or two generations some genetically predisposed diseases like diabetes, Alzheimer's disease and, perhaps, some types of cancer, will be eradicated. But the development of new methods of genetic analysis that now are already instrumental in deciding on strategies for fighting the disease (or even avoiding it altogether), also opens a Pandora's box for practically unlimited abuse by insurance companies. This will result in the emergence of a category of people with *preexisting conditions,* who will have been rejected by our healthcare system. This group of people will be steadily growing larger with the further development in medical sciences and our understanding of the nature of disease. This is a gloomy, no-happy-end situation.

Our society is gradually aging. More and more elderly people become recipients of Social Security benefits, which puts our Social Security system in danger. Everybody knows about it, and the problem is discussed constantly in Congress. But there is another problem, perhaps more important for the elderly. It concerns a huge group of retirees, including those whose income is well above the minimum income guaranteed by our Social Security system. It is the problem of *long-term healthcare*, including the so-called *assisted living* and its ultimate form—*nursing homes*.

Nursing homes are incredibly expensive: $100-300 per day, depending on the state. Virtually nobody of that huge group of people can pay for them, even those who all their life worked hard and managed to accumulate significant savings. The elderly of this category will have to surrender almost all their assets in order to pay for their stay in a nursing home, some $70,000 a year (and who can afford this for a long time, even four-five years?), before they become eligible for Medicaid. I have leafed through half a dozen books in which instructions were given of how one can prevent the government from seizing one's assets and instead make it pay for one's nursing home from the Medicaid purse. However, the Medicaid coffers are not as full as they used to be.

What is the solution to this problem? Insurance companies offer a variety of long-term health care policies. None of them would completely cover one's stay in a nursing home (or even be sold at all if one has *preexisting conditions* undesirable to the insurers). All of the policies are expensive. Their documents are stuffed with fine print and details that only an experienced lawyer can understand.

The research undertaken by the Consumer Union[7] found that "only about 10 to 20 percent of the elderly can afford long-term-care insurance…A tax deduction that few are likely to use or benefit from is not a rational approach to the problem of long-term care. That leaves Medicaid…Medicaid pauperizes the families who must use it, and encourages the non-poor to shelter assets to qualify. Older Americans shouldn't have to become experts in techniques for divesting themselves of assets in order to plan for long-term care. Nor should they have to rely on welfare to pay for it. Rather than saddle the middle class with expensive insurance costs for policies that may be inadequate and unavailable to sick people, the public deserves a system like Medicare for long-term care." The conclusion of experts: "The US still needs a universal system for all medical care—including long-term care—funded by a broad-based tax, and supported by a sense of shared responsibility for and obligation to the elderly."

---

[7] *Consumer Report*, Oct., 1997.

Leaving alone the radical universal healthcare system, the problem of long-term care for the elderly could be solved almost literally with a few extra tax dollars from each taxpayer—young and old.

The Congressional Budget Office (www.cbo.gov) has estimated both the projected federal tax revenue and the total long-term care expenditures for the years most crucial for our Social Security system: 2000-2010. Upon just a brief examination of the figures one can see that in order for the long-term care be completely paid for from taxes, the tax revenue would have to be increased by just 6.9 percent in the year 1999, and 5.9 percent in the year 2010. For example, in the year 1999, a couple with two dependents and an adjusted gross income of $50,000 had to pay additional $500 in taxes to contribute to the complete support of their aging parents and grandparents, as well as all American elderly needing long-term care. This amount would scarcely cover a three-month premium on a private policy, covering, at best, only half the nursing home costs.

Although the cost of long-term care in the years 2020 and 2030 will substantially increase, the federal tax revenue will increase more steeply. However, even the most conservative estimates of tax revenue for the years 2020 and 2030 (the Congressional Budget Office gives the projections only up to the year 2010) shows that the tax revenue increase by respectively 5.2 percent and 5.9 percent would have completely covered the cost of nursing home and other assistance for all the retired baby-boomers.

Returning to the current situation with healthcare: So far I mentioned only the "ideological" arguments of the healthcare reform opponents. They, however, become irrelevant when the economic aspects of the current situation are looked into.

With the growing cost of treatment—high-tech diagnostic equipment, more sophisticated surgery procedures, research and development of thousands of new drugs—a hospital or a doctor association is virtually unable anymore to function as an independent, self-supporting and profitable private enterprise.

In order to cover the costs, the hospitals have to cut the workforce, resulting in tremendous overload on doctors, nurses, laboratory technicians, for example. The crisis situation with overworked and over-exhausted residents, as the most exploited working force in American hospitals, forced the *American Medical Association* to introduce a new regulation restricting the residents' work week to 80 hours. They used to work as much as 130 hours a week before. Eighty hours a week is equivalent to 13.5 hour per day six day week. This is more or less how much people worked in the "heydays" of unregulated 19th century capitalism in England and America.

Actually, in most cases, residents work shorter weeks but with longer shifts, without sleep. Of course, exhaustion and lack of sleep result in medical errors. The overwork of residents is not an exception in our healthcare system. Medical doctors—both in hospitals and private associations—in order to cover the growing operational costs and the sky-rocketing malpractice insurance premiums, and sustain reasonable salaries, have to work longer hours, perform more surgeries, and see more patients. This, in turn, results in low-quality healthcare, especially in preventive healthcare when an error in early diagnosis may become fatal.

It is possible that this crisis will become more severe if no measure is taken. In fact, the current health care crisis has exactly the same nature and origin as the anticipated crises of our Social Security system.

Unlike an ordinary business enterprise that becomes bankrupt and leaves business, healthcare cannot collapse. The only remedy that is seen today is the "socializing" of healthcare. Anathema as it may be to the conservatives, no other way out is at sight. The healthcare will survive only if the whole society agrees to pay for its sick (or elderly to that effect), rather than the sick themselves.

This dilemma, from the category of ideological argument—government vs. market—becomes a matter of economics itself, when free market capitalism can no longer support the healthcare system.

Recycling of garbage as a profitable business is virtually impossible. Because of that, many American towns do not recycle garbage, which severely damages our ecology, already fragile enough. The only way out—and this is exactly what has been done in all developed European countries—is *deprivatization* of the recycling industry. Besides, sewage systems in our cities and towns do not bring any profit, do they?

No money can prevent death when it comes. Death equalizes everybody by a universal action—destruction of the personal universe. Before God, all the dying are equal. For the beloved of the dying, it is always an irreparable loss, a tragedy that the brain refuses to comprehend, an event that often terminates the previous well-organized life, an ordeal that may never be overcome. The suffering of the rich is neither worse nor more important than that of the humble poor. That is why nobody has the right to refuse treatment to the sick. Perhaps this notion is too radical for our society today, but I hope many of my readers will agree with me, that it *is true*. It has definitely something to do with the notion of responsibility I mentioned above about being *one's brother's keeper*. I hope that with the rising educational standards of our society, more and more people will begin to understand that truth. The need for universal healthcare will be increasingly pressing with the aging of our society, and we must eventually develop a good and optimal universal healthcare system.

My Enemy—The Government

At this point I should say just a few words on how we view and treat our government. The word *government* in American psyche has almost inevitably a negative connotation. Many people actually believe that we can exist *without* a government, which main objective is *interfering in our lives*. Perhaps, they forget that that *sinful* institution was not invented by the liberals in the 20th century. It has existed for millennia, and for an obvious reason. There must be a central body that will both coordinate the functions of other institutions in society and enforce law and order. In modern democracies these functions are directed at guaranteeing certain rights of their citizens and creating a framework for normal functioning and stability of society as a whole.

> Even American presidents seem to be rather ashamed of the government. President Clinton, after his reelection in 1996, in discussing the necessity of introducing *national standards* in testing high school students, assured Americans that those will be *national* standards, not *government* ones. As if the government were not a national body, but rather something estranged from the nation and hostile to it.

As our Declaration of Independence puts it, among the *unalienable rights* of people are "life, liberty, and the pursuit of happiness." And further: "…to secure these rights, governments are instituted among men, deriving their powers from the consent of the governed." It was, in fact, a direct governmental duty, rather than the realization of some ideological principles, to establish a national healthcare system—as a matter of "securing" people's right to life. It is also a direct duty of the Supreme Court to interpret our Constitution in accordance with its spirit and the spirit of the Declaration of Independence, in order to "secure" the ability of citizens to "pursue happiness." The latter is impossible in the atmosphere of unrestricted violence in the media, virtually overt (and constitutionally supported) corruption and the millions of guns in the hands of irresponsible people.

However, the hatred of our own government is not something that has just recently appeared "from the cold." It is a long-standing American tradition. Garry Wills, in his book, *A Necessary Evil,* from which I quoted above, writes (p.16): "Hardly a modern controversy arises without instant recourse to founding fathers, and to a heavily distorted version of what they were up to when they drafted and ratified the Constitution....We are pious towards our history in order to be cynical towards our government. We keep summoning the founders to testify against what they founded. Our own liberty depends so heavily on distrust of government that the government itself, we are constantly told, was construed to instill that distrust."

This perverted view of government gives rise to a whole "culture." Garry Wills continues: "If government has the power to take away guns, all our liberties are gone. If the states, as lesser units of government, cede power to the central government, tyranny impends. The power to regulate businesses is a power to crush them. Increasing the size of government inevitably decreases freedom."

Against this background, it is, perhaps, only natural that typically Americans do not respect their government, to say the least. People, motivated by innumerable suspense and detective plots of our mass culture, do believe in all kinds of theories of the government's involvement in deliberate wrongdoing, cover-ups, and secret covert operations both at home and abroad.

Just a few examples: Millions of dollars have been made—and are still being made—by the authors of books "investigating" president Kennedy's assassination. All the theories, rejecting the findings of the Warren Commissions, imply some kind of conspiracy behind the murder. It is striking that, in the rage of the Cold War, right after the Cuban missile crisis, no conspiracy plots were attributed to the Soviets. Although it would have been quite natural, taking into account the general Communist mentality of the disregard of human life and the ruthless methods of the Soviet secret police and counterintelligence. Also, no plots were attributed to a Cuban or an anti-Cuban or an organized crime conspiracy, although these possibilities were quite real and could have been expected. Rather, a US government conspiracy was hinted at, Even now, 40 years later, theories still abound insisting on government cover-ups. According to a recent national survey, 51 percent of Americans believe it is "very likely" or "somewhat likely" that some federal authorities were "directly responsible for the assassination of President Kennedy."

A 50th anniversary of the Roswell "mystery" was celebrated in July 1997. According to widespread belief, in 1947 an alien spaceship crashed near Roswell, NM. "Witnesses" (who, by the way, changed their testimonies many times during this half of the century), supported by the loud crowd of believers (tireless journalists among them), insist on a major government cover-up. The cover-up has simply been taken for granted—in spite of numerous attempts by government officials and scientists to dissuade the believers. Roswell is just a tiny part of the whole *ET* hysteria. We do not know for certain if UFOs really exist, but it has been accepted without a shade of doubt that the government lies to the American people by deliberately concealing the important information about the UFOs.

As for the events of the less remote past, the mysterious Gulf War Syndrome—unexplained occasions of various sicknesses among the Gulf War veterans—is blamed on the government that had allegedly known the causes of sickness (use of nerve gas by the Iraqis or its accidental spills), but failed to prevent them and later covered up that failure. According to the above-mentioned survey, nearly half the Americans believe it is "very likely" that the government is "withholding what they know about nerve gas or germ warfare attacks on American troops during the Persian Gulf War"[8]..

According to general belief, the CIA is the most *amoral* organization in the world and is involved in disgusting cover-up operations abroad (and even at home), with its leaders blatantly lying to the American people.

It is almost *a self-evident truth* that our police are racist and corrupt. The O.J. Simpson "trial of the century" was won because the jury was convinced of the deliberate attempt by the police to implicate the alleged murderer. The word *cop* has an inevitably negative, contemptuous connotation. As a matter of fact, the word *policeman* is being used in our media far less frequently. It is taken for granted that the police do not do their job right, and therefore cannot defend us from growing crime. The anti-gun control lobby, apart from the "legal" justification of the necessity of proliferation of hand-guns,[9] as its main *practical* justification, claims that "law-abiding citizens" need guns to be able to defend themselves and their homes from crime perpetrators. This point of view actually implies that the police are unable to prevent crime and defend Americans. The difference between this concept and the self-justification of paramilitary militias in some of our states is only in degree, not in substance.

Are our government, our police, and our law-enforcement organizations so corrupt and rotten through and through, as many Americans believe? Definitely not. But the origin of this belief is easily traced to the anti-government rhetoric of the irresponsible political and special interest groups. However, it would be unfair

---

8 *Phyllis Schlafly Columns,* Jul. 30, 1997; downloaded from the Internet.

9 For a comprehensive discussion of all the aspects of the gun control problem (including the legal ramifications based on the Second Amendment) see: Franklin E. Zimring and Gordon Hawkins, *The Citizen's Guide to Gun Control.* Macmillan Publishing Company, New York, 1992.

to blame only our political Right for the extreme anti-government sentiments popular among the people. As I have already discussed, we do not know how the "innocent" anti-government rhetoric of our politicians is transformed in the minds of the mysterious "silent majority" (as Rush Limbaugh coins it)—the majority of which do not care to vote.

We may only guess. Fortunately, a part of that *silent majority* has become quite vocal during the recent decade. I mean the extremist "patriot" anti-government movement. The propaganda of its ideas and ideals is unrestricted thanks to the Internet, the most modern high-tech vehicle of enforcing free speech. "Fortunately," because, although some of these groups have paramilitary character and are paranoically conspiratorial, we at least know that they exist, and know what is to be expected from their activity.

We must not kid ourselves. What is to be expected is *violence*. The Oklahoma City bombing is just the beginning, not the culmination. The activity of "patriot movement" after that terrorist act has increased, not subsided. Those people were neither shocked nor disgusted. According to Timothy McVeigh, "We needed a body count to make our point." They got the "body count," but it is most unlikely that they have been satisfied. The bombing at the Atlanta Olympic site followed.

The effect of our conservative politicians' rhetoric, which I mentioned above, on this group of people, their ideology and actions is, most probably, absolutely insignificant. On the other hand, the emergence of these extreme anti-government and, in fact, pro-anarchy, ideologies could have been expected.

The majority of people who belong to or support these anti-government groups are the most tragic victims of our societal crisis. The degradation of our educational system has deprived these people not only of their ability to find *meaning* in their lives, that could make their lives intellectually and spiritually satisfying; it has deprived them of the ability to *sustain their families*. Unlike those who belong to the "underclass" and are chronically unable to find jobs because they do not have any marketable skills, these people work hard, very hard. But the level of education of the majority of these people simply makes it impossible for them to find jobs that could reliably support their families. These are farmers, on the brink of bankruptcy, or people doing jobs that do not pay, no matter how hard they work, with no hope of achieving any economic stability in the nearest future—not only for themselves but for their children, also already chronically undereducated. Often paying jobs even do not exist in their areas. Nobody is there to help them out.

In this situation, government, as a *scapegoat* is just what is needed. Once the villain has been found, all kinds of conspiracy theories—no matter how absurd (like the UN forces invading Texas)—seem convincing enough to explain the disastrous and doomsday situation. The whole ideology of these extremist groups seems so out of space and out of time—as if the D*ark Ages* have returned—that it is very difficult to counter it with any arguments based on reason or history. As usual, the easiest solution—law enforcement and severe punishments for terrorism—although necessary as a deterrent—are most probably *fruitless* as a *solution.* As have been so far fruitless all our multibillion-dollar attempts to stop proliferation of drugs or juvenile crime. Again we are treating symptoms of the illness rather than its cause.

Fortunately, the majority of Americans does not support these extremist groups. Yet, again, we do not know exactly what those almost a hundred million people who do not care to vote—presumably poorly educated and possibly far from affluence—think about our government and our social system as a whole.

But let me return to our conservative critics of government. A government can be bad or inefficient. Even if some of the functions are not being fulfilled by the government efficiently, it does not (in most cases) mean that those functions have to be abolished or taken away from the government. In a country like the United States, where the problem of education is, perhaps, the most acute and pressing today, one cannot (nay, has no right) to eliminate the *Department of Education.* Quite the opposite. If it is not efficient (and I do believe it is not) it must be made efficient by all means.

In no way am I defending the current governmental system. I worked for the government long enough to know too well what an irresponsible government bureaucracy can sometimes do. But when those who oppose *the government,* any government, as a matter of principle and ideology and claim that our government is "too big," they never explain what they mean. Is it the bureaucracy that is supposed to supervise the execution of the government programs that is too inflated? Or the number of government employees is too large? If the first claim is true (and I believe it is), then the *bureaucracy* has to be slashed, rather than the programs they are supervising. I am not saying there are no programs that should not be eliminated. But the wording of the attackers on the government is fundamentally wrong, if you wish, *morally* wrong, for it is directed at deliberately *misinforming* the people (who do not know or do not understand the details), and is eventually aimed at gaining some political scores, rather than being for the common good.

Do those who insist that the government is "too big" imply that the Environmental Protection Agency, or the world-famous for their scientific excellence *National Laboratories* and the *National Institutes of Health* have to be closed? In essay *Science and Society,* I mention the miserable image of scientific research in the American psyche. Do some of our legislators share the view of the ignorant that scientific research is unimportant for the future of this country? If they do not, why do they insist on closing the *Department of Energy*—a government body which, for decades, has been and is still instrumental in coordinating, supporting and funding both defense-oriented research and research directed at solving our energy problems, including the development of alternative energy sources?

The general irresponsibility of our politicians (on both sides of the aisle) is but an obvious sign of what Walter Lippman (*Essays in the Public Philosophy*, 1955) called "political Jacobinism"—a gradual shift from representative government to a populist democracy. This is extremely dangerous with the lowering (against the background of the general existential crises) of the educational level of our population and thus its ability to understand how a developed society and its institutions function.

The whole concept that the government *wastes* the taxpayers' money (if it does not directly abuse tax payers' trust) is fundamentally wrong, dishonest, and in many cases simply amoral. Just one example.

Proponents of budget cuts have always been brandishing the "gigantic" chunk of the government budget that is being spent on "entitlements": $993 billion (in 2002), i.e. 9.6 percent of the GNP. Over two-thirds of this amount, however, is paid to people in Social Security and healthcare benefits, for which they have been contributing money to the government coffers all their live. In Fiscal Year 2002 the working Americans paid $701 billion in social insurance taxes. As for the *welfare* entitlements, officially called "means-tested spending," in 2002 they comprised $287 billion, or just 2.8 percent of the GNP.[10] I believe that the urgent necessity of the welfare reform in late '90s was dictated not as much by our fiscal crisis and huge budget deficit, as by the welfare social consequences, such as perpetual poverty, destruction of family, growth of crime and illegitimacy, for example

When politicians, as a part of their election campaign, rhetorically ask: "Do you want to spend your money yourself or would rather have the government spend it for you?" this question insinuates what is an ugly lie and imparts misinformation to people whose votes they want to win. Not only for the homeless and the unemployed, but also for the millions of the American middle class, the government is a sort of *blanket insurance policy*. Most of our pension money and bank investments are insured by the government. Most of us do rely on the government benefits (Social Security) and the government healthcare (Medicare) after retirement.

As I have mentioned above, the problem of long-term health care cannot be solved unless the society takes on the responsibility for all its elderly, and this can

---

[10] These figures were taken from the Congressional Budget Office web page: www.cbo.gov.

be easily done by just an insignificant increase in taxes. For many poor families, their child's lunch at school is an important health and economic factor. The cost of education has sky-rocketed so high that soon almost nobody, but the very rich, will be able to send children to college, unless there is a government help.

And there is a serious problem of *spending our money ourselves.* Yes, it would be nice if *we, the people* were able to do that without the risk of being ruthlessly robbed by numerous societal gangsters, against whom the government is the only protection.

An interesting and rather curious illustration of the dilemma of who should spend our money: In 1980, in Ohio, a plan was developed of a high-speed train network that would connect 13 cities within the state, as well as Detroit, Michigan, and Pittsburgh, Pennsylvania. Part of the needed $8 billion was to come from a special *one-cent* state sales tax. Voters rejected this tax in 1982[11].

By the way, according to statistics, women (especially married women) are much less hostile toward the government than are men. They see in the government a last resort of economic support for their families in case of emergency. They also, more than men, support gun control—for they—without any ideology, are afraid for the lives of their children.

One can endlessly discuss the irresponsibility of our politicians, interest groups, or the media. Of course, our society can be turned into a battlefield between the abusers of our great Constitution and all kinds of courts, including the Supreme Court. The abuse of the Constitution can be made less blatant, provided the integrity of our courts is intact. Yet, it is not a solution. Stiffer penalties for dealing drugs and juvenile crime or domestic terrorism are not the solutions to our drug, juvenile delinquency problems and chronic unemployment of the undereducated. *Responsibility* is the solution.

Again, responsibility always means *voluntary* restrictions of one's freedoms. If, in response to President Clinton's plea to Hollywood, the latter started controlling the level of violence in their productions, that would have been be a definite *sacrifice* of their *First Amendment* rights (as interpreted today), but a thus far unprecedented act of *responsibility*. But this did not happen.

---

[11] *Scientific American*, Oct. 1997, p. 106.

If, instead of repeating Thomas Jefferson's calls for "spilling blood of patriots and tyrants," the ideologues and leaders of the *patriot* movement would insist on improving the quality of schools, would insist on serious government analysis of the economic situation in their states, and on organizing retraining facilities and efficient help to new businesses; if they explained to their *constituency* how awful, how devastating, how inhumane the American Civil War was—if they explained that civil wars, in general, never solve any problems, just make them worse, paying an exorbitant price for ideals, no matter how "bright," those ideals would be—again, an unprecedented act of *responsibility*.

And, returning to our *crisis*: If we find the means of restoring *meaning* to the lives of people—and a revolution in our educational system is, perhaps, the only way to begin moving toward that goal—the level of responsibility in our society would rise dramatically. Then we would begin to cherish responsibility as much as we cherish freedom today. Possibly, we may even decide, following Viktor Frankl's advice, to raise the *Statue of Responsibility* on the West Coast, overlooking the Golden Gate, as a second symbol of the new and great America.

CONCLUSION: THE FUTURE

"What man actually needs is not a tensionless state but rather the striving and struggling for a worthwhile goal, a freely chosen task."

—*Viktor Frankl, Man's Search For Meaning*

A civilization, like a mortal human being, has periods of good health, optimism, and success, but may also get sick, feel distressed and lost. We are lost now. In all our attempts—on various levels—we are trying to find solutions that would lead to a *tensionless state*. And as we fail to achieve them, we are instead, becoming increasingly ill. But we will be on our feet again only if we realize that "striving and struggling for a worthwhile goal" is what we need to be healthy and happy again. This sickness in our society (as well as in all the developed democratic societies on earth) is unique in that the virus of meaninglessness had never before been a *societal* virus, rather than a bug inflicting just isolated individuals or small groups. The question of the *meaning of life* has always been a burning question among the educated and affluent—but simply because they have had time, in fact, many of them have had actually nothing else to do, but to think about the matters existential.

But this question—this alarming anxiety—is something that has been implanted in our genes by God. It is the necessity, the urge to answer this question—and thus to find one's place in the world—which makes us really *great* and proud as God's children. We have already passed one of God's test: we have shown that, due to our unstoppable urge for knowledge, we can survive and build great cultures and great humane societies by working hard, sometimes falling deep, but rising high again.

We, in the developed societies, do not have to fight for existence anymore. Now comes the next test: We must show that life is not just making money, eating, sleeping, having sex, and having fun. I do believe we will also pass this test, and this time, with flying colors.

As if for a purpose, we have been made aware of our problems at the dawn of a new millennium. This way it is easier to count time. And, perhaps in the future,

267

a historian will write: "And there was evening, and there was morning: *day one* of the *new humankind*".

Meanwhile, having stepped into the new millennium, we are not quite ready to meet it, although both the high-tech technology and high-tech temptations are already here.

As I have stressed so often in all the essays of this book, our main problem, the most important and the most pressing one, is *education*. If we do not revolutionize our educational system now, we shall have to do it later anyway, but the price for the procrastination may be then much higher.

Perhaps I have been too aggressive in opposing the *Progressives* and their educational philosophy. The bitter truth, however, is that no matter how highly *trained* a person is, either in the concrete profession that he or she has chosen, or in the *politically correct* understanding of society, this is not a substitute for building a strong, mature personality. Only a strong, intensive general education can do that; the educational system that will challenge our children, force them to work hard and persistently from kindergarten on, and thus inspire them with the unstoppable urge for knowledge.

What will happen if we fail to fulfill this goal of revolutionizing our education? As I have already said in the *Preface*, even if we improve the quality of *training* in our schools and colleges, we may be able to sustain, possibly even for a long time, the high-tech development of our society, but we will not be able to significantly improve our social climate. Racial strife will continue to haunt our society. The drug culture will flourish and move into a new, and perhaps more devastating phase of high-tech drugs. And, as its companion, social inequity and crime will increase.

But if we do succeed, what will our future be? First of all, if we firmly decide on the kind of reform I have been advocating, this decision alone will have already significantly changed our society.

If we decide to launch the educational revolution, then we shall need hundreds of thousands, perhaps even millions of new teachers right away. Moreover, we will have to elevate the status of teacher—both socially and financially—to the level of *professor*. We will have to completely change our perception that the younger the child, the lower the professional level of the teacher should be. Then, we shall need, perhaps, millions of professors in toddler through kindergarten education with qualifications of not less than a master's degree.

If we are serious about giving our children a strong and broad education, we shall have to create a new *industry*, which may become the leading industry in our society—the industry of educating *and* training future teachers. We should also be prepared to accept that in order to sustain a high-quality education on all levels—through PhD programs—perhaps one professor per every 10 to 15 students (for the little ones, perhaps per every 5 students) would be needed. We will become a *society of teachers*.

Is this scenario possible? First of all, do we have enough *above-average* IQ people to be able to become good teachers? I am sure we have. If one makes a most conservative estimate from the distribution of the IQ curve (Herrnstein and Murray, *The Bell Curve*) one arrives at the figure of 40 to 50 percent of our population with a high enough IQ. In fact, we still do not know very much what the *cognitive ability* is, and how would a *below-average IQ* person respond to a systematic *high-quality education* (as I understand it) from the toddler age on.

And here is the second question: Will a society with an extremely high level of education be economically stable? Will there be enough jobs to accommodate millions of people with bachelor, master, and doctoral degrees? Nobody can tell you now—there simply have been no precedents in the history of Earth. Usually, a free economy has the tendency to adjust itself to societal needs. With the expansion of computer education and the proliferation of computers, a new multibillion-dollar branch of the economy—computer software—has emerged literally within just a few years. The new, born by the Internet, the so-called *dot com* industry is even younger.

Society's priorities will gradually shift to meet the growing demand for products having to do with all kinds of spiritual and intellectual needs. As a consequence, research-oriented industries will also proliferate. The standing of our society *vis-à-vis* the world problems will also change.

Isolationist tendencies that have already cost America dearly in the past (just recall the Pearl Harbor disaster), are still very strong in our society today. Every time America's involvement in mediating or putting down an international conflict is necessary, our administrations encounter strong resistance of a significant segment of politicians (both on the Left and the Right—the side always opposed to the administration, thus making the resistance blatantly political) backed by the support of a corresponding segment of the constituency. There are, unfortunately, too many examples of our "interference" in international crises that have happened to be either meaningless or counterproductive. This, however, does not mean that we should refrain from our inherent and unspoken obligations as the (at present) sole superpower. Our failure in those situations was mostly the results of the political obstacles that the presidents had to fight in order to implement those actions.

R. Kaplan, a distinguished journalist and author, wrote:[1] "Two or three decades hence conditions may be propitious for the emergence of a new international system—one with many influential actors in a regime of organically

---

[1] *The Atlantic Monthly*, July/August, 2003, p.69.

evolving interdependence. But until that time arrives, it is largely the task of the United States to maintain a modicum order and stability. We are an ephemeral imperial power, and if we are smart, we will recognize that basic fact. Because the consequence of attack by weapons of mass distraction are so catastrophic, the United States will periodically have no choice but to act pre-emptively on limited evidence, exposing our actions to challenge by journalists, to say nothing of millions of protesters who are increasingly able to coordinate their demonstrations worldwide."

These lines were written soon after the 2003 Iraqi war, against the background of the political and ideological anti-war, anti-American sentiments, mostly proliferated by the intellectual Left.

The concept of *world policeman* has a strong negative connotation, and yet, in the future, the United Nations will eventually agree to the logical idea that the world will need a permanent international police force that will act immediately and quickly, upon a direct order from the Security Council, at the first signs of an international conflict that violates the United Nations Charter and threatens the world's stability, much as a policeman in a city or a town reacts immediately to a crime.

I am proud that our presidents did find the strength and integrity to fight their shortsighted and populist-oriented political opponents in enforcing the role of America as the stabilizer to safeguard the world. It is especially important in the unprecedented situation of proliferation of world terrorism.

In the future, our more active involvement in the areas of potential conflict—our peaceful involvement—will be more and more instrumental in enhancing the political and economic stability of those areas.

The problems that are now becoming more and more pressing, and will definitely have risen to enormous proportions in the future, are the problems of the so-called *developing countries* (which were called Third World before the fall of Communism). Some doomsday scenarios[2] predict the eventual collapse of Western affluent democracies, unable to sustain and overcome the growing pressure on the part of the politically and economically unstable societies. Even a literal collapse is possible as a result of the immigration invasion,[3] which will be impossible to stop without killing millions of people.

---

[2] See, as an example, Jean Raspail's *The Camp of the Saints* (Scribner, New York, 1975). See also Matthew Connelly's and Paul Kennedy's article "The Rest Against the West" (*Atlantic Monthly*, Dec. 1994) for a very informative discussion of the problem.

[3] The immigration invasion has already begun in Europe. Millions of Muslims (the majority of them hostile to democracy) have settled in France, Germany, and other European countries, posing a serious (if not daring) political problem.

This danger is real. It is also natural in the sense that any valve eventually becomes not strong enough if the pressure is too high. We share the same earth, but the economic inequity is too great for any kind of stability in the future.

So far the reaction of Western democracies has been mostly to render economic aid. A good part of this aid too often does not reach the needy, being simply stolen away by corrupt governments, or used as an economic weapon in local military or political conflicts. But it is the *humanitarian* help that those countries (and societies) need much more, and need very badly, apart from direct economic aid. Thousands of medical personnel, agronomists, teachers, and engineers from all industrial nations are now working in Africa, India, and other remote parts of the world. But it is not enough.

With the rising educational level of our population, the understanding of the fact that the *wellbeing* of the world is also the guarantee of the wellbeing of our society will gradually become an accepted fact. The concept of the world's being *too small* is too important to be neglected or underestimated. Our involvement in humanitarian aid to the Third World is not only a matter of *moral obligations* or *responsibility*. The world being too small, fighting diseases in developing countries often means protecting the health of our own population. For example, if polio is eradicated worldwide we shall no longer have to vaccinate our children against polio.

In the future, a new and more efficient Peace Corps will be created in America. It may become an important part of American society socially, politically, and economically.

In essay *Science and Society*, I quoted a noted physicist: "I fear we may have seriously underestimated the consequences for our culture of a scientifically illiterate population....We ignore real dangers to our planet because we cannot understand the warnings."

When we learn to understand those warnings, we will see what enormous work must be done here, on the earth, in order for it to be livable for the generations to come. We shall then need an enormous cadre of all kinds of earth scientists: physicists, chemists, geologists, biologists, and meteorologists. And we will have them.

The educated society of the 21st century will be spending a significant part of its resources on scientific research and on space exploration, in particular. Perhaps, the 1040 Tax Form, apart from the box: "Do you want to make an additional donation to the *National Education Fund*?" will also have a box for donations to the *Project Mars Fund*. This is not science fiction. The interest among Americans in astronomy is enormous, and it is growing. Thousands of Americans already buy telescopes and other astronomical equipment, and amateur astronomers play more and more significant role in serious research.

But let me return to the earth. A society, where *Madonna* means only the Mother of Christ and nothing else, and where TV is not a proving ground of real-life violence anymore, is perhaps still far away. But if we start taking our first steps, just tiny first steps, we will see the results immediately. Begin reading to toddlers—every day—and go on till they begin reading themselves, and even beyond that and the *Bell Curve* may have shown the rise of IQ.

The impact of the movement *Kids Teaching Kids* on our society (which I discussed in this book) simply cannot be overestimated. It will make our educational system much more efficient and vibrant. Allow the children—make for most of them an internal necessity—to stay at school for another three or four hours doing something interesting and exciting, and juvenile crime and experimenting with drugs will drop significantly. Have a nearby university student play Chopin to tenth-graders and, perhaps, the number of condoms to be distributed in school will drop.

Just imagine your ten-year-old son returning from school at 8 PM with shining eyes: "Mommy, we were watching Jupiter in the telescope to night. It has sixteen moons! Oh, I want to be an astronomer, Mommy. No, I will not watch TV tonight, I have to finish this book." Or your fifteen-year-old daughter, being so late from school that you were already going to call her friends: "Mother, we were reading George Sterling tonight. He was a poet—an American. Listen, Mother: 'Thou art the star for which all evening waits…'"

Imagine that this happens not in just isolated families but is typical. With growing education and the return of meaning in our lives, we will gradually begin to understand that the *laissez-faire* capitalism, where money is the most reliable criterion of value; where, in fact, money often *is* the only value worth acquiring; and where our preoccupation with success, as measured in money, endanger our sense of right and wrong, is the source of many ills of our society.

We will gradually begin to understand that it is not worth having a thousand-dollar tax return, so that we can pay for our children's day care or private school education ourselves (with that money?). Rather we would entrust *society* to provide us with high-quality day care and education for our children—as other democracies have already been doing.

We will gradually become one big family. And we will also begin to understand that it is not that to bring up a child, is the duty of the *whole society*—one of its most important duties. Today, at this crossroads of our culture, it is *us, the people*—the parents and grandparents of our children—that are in charge of the future.

But is that possible? Is that possible at all, that the majority of our children may become happy and fulfilled, eagerly wanting to learn, and learn more, growing to be mature adults, able to love, wanting to make the world better, and transferring that treasure of their souls—*meaning*—to their children?

We *must* begin. And then…Here I want to share with you a funny story, which sounds like a parable, but is, in fact, an anecdote:[4]

The Hundredth Monkey

"The Japanese monkey, Maccaca Fuscata, has been observed in the wild for a period of over 30 years. In 1952, on the island of Koshima scientists were providing monkeys with sweet potatoes dropped in the sand. The monkeys liked the taste of the raw sweet potatoes but they found the dirt unpleasant. An 18-month-old female named Imo found she could solve the problem by washing the potatoes in a nearby stream. She taught this trick to her mother. Her playmates also learned this new way and they taught their mothers, too….

"Between 1952 and 1958, all young monkeys learned to wash the sandy potatoes to make them more palatable. Only the adults who imitated their children learned this social improvement. Other adults kept eating the dirty sweet potatoes. Then something startling took place. In the autumn of 1958, a certain number of Kosima monkey were washing sweet potatoes—the exact number is not known.

"Let us suppose that when the sun rose one morning there were 99 monkeys on Koshima Island who had learned to wash their sweet potatoes. Let us further suppose that later that morning, the hundredth monkey learned to wash potatoes. *Then it happened.* By that evening almost everyone in the tribe was washing sweet potatoes before eating them. The added energy of this hundredth monkey somehow created an ideological breakthrough.

"But notice: A most surprising thing observed by these scientists was that the habit of washing sweet potatoes then jumped over the sea—colonies of monkeys on other islands and the mainland troop of monkeys at Takasokiyama began washing their sweet potatoes. Thus when a certain critical number achieves an awareness, this new awareness may be communicated from mind to mind."

My book is finished. As I warned in the introduction, almost everything I have talked about was in *no-man's land*. Now the Left was furious, now the Right, and I expect to be under a massive crossfire.

---

[4]   Ken Keyers, Jr., *The Hundredth Monkey*, Vision Books, 1985, p.11.

I defend the government, and I believe that only a centralized effort, on the scale of the whole nation, can solve our educational problem. I also believe that a strong unified curriculum is a must. Hence the fire both from the Left and the Right.

The Left (first of all the *intellectual* Left) will accuse me of *elitism*. And I am glad, even proud of that, and I willingly accept this accusation. Yes, I am elitist: I want *this country to become elitist*. When the *Progressives* want the school programs to be as easy as possible, so that a child from an inner-city drug and crime infested neighborhood would still be able to grasp some knowledge (but unfortunately this does not happen), I want this child to be a proud human being, mature, with a developed personality and clear-cut *meaning* in his or her life. School must teach perseverance in learning, teach how to work hard in order to achieve the goal—knowledge. It is possible. Enthusiastic and courageous teachers in just such slum neighborhoods have already proved that this is possible. Our politicians just have to put their hearts to it.

Winston Churchill once said: "If one is not a liberal when he is twenty, he does not have heart; but when one is not a conservative when he is fifty, he does not have brains." I am almost seventy, and I did come through the above two stages. But in the world where in an unstoppable quest for pleasure and money, people are losing both hearts and brains, I'd rather stick to heart. And yet, one needs not only the heart, but also strong brains in order to clearly distinguish between *Good* and *Evil*. If one has the honest direction of pursuing *Good* and fighting *Evil*, one will (at least in our days) always be in no-man's land. For the *truth*, which always serves *Good* better than *Evil*, is where *reason* is, not where the political trenches meet and cross each other.

Well, one also needs a good portion of the *idealism* of a twenty-year-old to be in no-man's land under the fierce crossfire. But, as three decades ago, John Glenn, first American to orbit the Earth, said: "Ideals are the very stuff of survival." I believe I will survive the crossfire.

But this is not that important. If only my dreams of a better world for our children, for my beloved Rachel come true, then God's blessings will always be with you, America.

Greenville, DE, Dec. 1994—Peabody, MA, Dec. 2003.

0-595-31309-4

Lightning Source UK Ltd.
Milton Keynes UK
UKOW01f0236130117
291931UK00002B/453/P